THE

LIBERATION OF ITALY

1943-1947

By

LUIGI VILLARI, Jur.D.

C. C. NELSON PUBLISHING COMPANY
Appleton, Wisconsin
1959

To the Memory

of the

Victims of the Liberation

PREFATORY INTRODUCTION

In his distinguished volume, *Advance to Barbarism,* the English publicist, F. J. P. Veale, tells us how, after countless centuries of ruthless barbarism (total war), culminating in the butcheries and devastation of the religious wars following the Protestant Revolution, warfare gradually became "civilized" during the era of Louis XIV of France and so remained until the wars of the French Revolution and the Napoleonic era and the American Civil War (1861-1865). In Europe, in fact, warfare remained reasonably civilized down through the Franco-Prussian War of 1870-1871. Wars were fought between military forces, civilians were spared so far as possible when they did not get into battle areas, and defeated forces were treated decently, often generously, after the warfare had ceased. The menace of vindictive peace treaties was recognized by leading international lawyers. Beginning with the Civil War in the United States, this process was reversed. Hastening victory by regimenting or seizing civilian populations, destroying property, and ravishing the resources of the countries involved became the rule. Harsh peace treaties were made which held within themselves the seeds of inevitable future wars.

These traits of a reversion to total war were again manifested in the first World War, and the post-war Treaty of Versailles and related "settlements" made a second World War all but inevitable. The bloodshed and devastation reached an all-time peak in the saturation bombing of civilians, the savagery of guerrilla warfare behind the battle lines, and the systematic deportation and extermination of civilians by the Germans, Russians, Czechs, Poles and Yugoslavs in the second World War. The fury attained such extremes that no general peace treaty was possible after the War which would restrain to some extent the vindictiveness of the victorious powers in the period of so-called peace. The policies to be followed after victory were laid down by the leaders of the conquering nations in a series of wartime conferences when the bellicose emotions of the participants were at their height. It is only against this general historical background that one can truly understand the motivation and methods which dominated what is paradoxically, if not cynically, designated as the era of "Liberation."

According to the language of the dictionary and also in line with much historical experience, liberation means deliverance from beleaguerment, oppression, fear, suffering and the like, bringing in its wake freedom, popular rejoicing, public exhilaration, mass gratitude and ultimate contentment. According to the Oxford Dictionary, "liberation" signifies "releasing," that is, removing from a person, a city, or a nation, some burden to which he or it had previously been subjected, thereby enabling him or it to resume normal activities in full freedom. The Webster Dictionary defines "liberation" as "setting free" or "deliverance." In the light of what actually happened to or in the "liberated" countries after 1943, one might logically inquire whether it may not be necessary to revise our dictionaries and give new meaning to words which in the past have signified something quite different from what they came to imply after 1943.

Nevertheless, although the term liberation, as actually applied in practice from 1943 onward, may cause considerable semantic and lexicographical confusion to many, it will hardly do so to those who have some knowledge of the history of diplomacy and propaganda since the mid-1930's. Although the "liberating" process was carried out by the democracies as well as by Soviet Russia, and the democratic spokesmen used the term liberation freely, the novel and hypocritical verbiage and the bloody techniques by which liberation was executed during and after the second World War had already been "made in Russia" long before 1943. The Communists sold the democracies both the terminology and the liberating techniques on the heels of selling them the myth and hoax of "collective security" at Geneva and elsewhere.

As early as the mid-1930's, the Communists talked and wrote

a great deal about "liberating" China from both the Japanese and Chiang Kai-shek. In the autumn of 1939, they designated their coldblooded seizure of eastern Poland as the "liberation" of that area from the reactionary Polish régime. They stressed the hoax of liberation even more when they brutally seized the Baltic provinces and herded many thousands of the Baltic peoples into slave labor camps after having slaughtered a goodly number. They even had the gall to label their invasion of Finland as a "liberating" operation.

The pattern of the operational methods followed during the liberation process during and after the second World War was also forecast and provided by the Communists, starting with the execution of thousands in the notorious purge trials that began in the mid-1930's and the deportation of more thousands to Siberian slave labor camps. Stalin brought this approach to liberation down to date at Teheran in 1943 when he urged that German officers be summarily shot as soon as they were captured. This had been anticipated in actuality when he had thousands of Polish officers shot at the Katyn Forest massacre in the spring of 1940, or slightly earlier. To the Communists, "liberation" was a fusion of the liquidation and the gross deprivation of those elements which they thought incapable of being brought into a Communist order.

Since the Liberal and Labor groups who helped to push the democracies into war in 1939 and 1941 had been following the Communist line in regard to foreign affairs very faithfully for some years previously, it was not difficult for the Communists to sell the democracies their new diplomatic and political semantics. For the democracies to take over the Communist "liberation" verbiage was a natural and inevitable step after having been sold the War itself by the Communists.

Having accepted the new semantics relative to liberation, it was easy and logical for the democracies to adopt the same ethics and techniques that the Communists had been following for years in actually carrying out their liberation program. What made it doubly easy was the fact that in Germany, France and Italy the Communists laid out much of the program and carried on most of the activities connected with the more violent aspects of the liberation period. Indeed, the most bloody and brutal episodes of the liberation were mainly the work of Communists—the horrors of the expulsion of the Germans from their former homes and the attempt to starve those who were not dispossessed; the wholesale slaughter by the French *Résistance;* and the butcheries carried on by the Italian Communist partisans. There was a direct carry-over from the mock trials which led to the murder of tens of thousands of Russians during the great purges following 1935 to the mock trials at Nüremberg, Tokyo, and elsewhere. Even the Morgenthau Plan to starve Germans by the millions was conceived by Stalin and transmitted to Mr. Morgenthau by an American Communist or fellow-traveller.

When one has this realistic grasp of the historical background of the liberation during and after the second World War, he is not so much troubled by any semantic or lexicographical perplexity. What actually happened and what it was called were both inherent in the propaganda and politics of the preceding decade. In short, the semantic, ethical, and operational parentage of the liberation connected with the second World War must be sought in the pattern of the Communist purge trials of 1935-1938 and the Communist operations in Poland, the Baltic region, and Finland rather than in the noble, if hypocritical and soon forgotten, phrases of the Atlantic Charter of 1941.

Although the Communists provided the semantics and the main techniques of the liberation era, the Americans and the British were not without their potent contributions. Probably the main item furnished by the Americans was the idea that the war in Europe was a "crusade"—some sort of Holy War which could justify almost any type of behavior in its pursuit until victory was won. Now, crusades, in addition to being disastrous failures in the long run, have usually been notoriously bloody and destructive affairs, and that of 1941 to 1945 was no exception. It is difficult to check holy fervor when victory is in hand. We are told that the Crusaders of yore "waded knee deep in the blood of the Infidel" after the capture of Jerusalem

TABLE OF CONTENTS

Chapter I	Plotting the Overthrow of the Fascist Regime	1
Chapter II	July 24-25, 1943	10
Chapter III	The Armistice	17
Chapter IV	The Kingdom in the South	21
Chapter V	Co-belligerence	27
Chapter VI	Parties and Domestic Dissensions	48
Chapter VII	The Crisis of the Monarchy	64
Chapter VIII	The Moscow Declaration	68
Chapter IX	The Two Italian Armies	74
Chapter X	The Partisan Movement	77
Chapter XI	The Venezia Giulia	89
Chapter XII	Southern Italy in Servitude	92
Chapter XIII	The Situation in "Non-liberated" Italy	101
Chapter XIV	Russia Intervenes	104
Chapter XV	The Via Rasella Outrage	108
Chapter XVI	The Lord Lieutenancy	115
Chapter XVII	The Allies in Rome	122
Chapter XVIII	Military and Partisan Activities	135
Chapter XIX	Crisis in the Italian Cabinet	152
Chapter XX	The Venezia Giulia Again	161
Chapter XXI	The End of Hostilities	166
Chapter XXII	How the Communists Acquired Their Influence in Italy	176
Chapter XXIII	Treatment of Italian Prisoners of War	182
Chapter XXIV	Partisan Massacres After the End of Hostilities	193
Chapter XXV	Anti-Fascist Legislation	209
Chapter XXVI	Some Special Cases of Persecution	221
Chapter XXVII	The End of the Monarchy	231
Chapter XXVIII	The Peace Treaty	237
Chapter XXIX	Consequences and Conclusions	246
	Index	253

ILLUSTRATIONS

Following page 6:

DINO GRANDI

MARSHAL PIETRO BADOGLIO

Following page 38:

KING VICTOR IMMANUEL III

PREMIER BENITO MUSSOLINI

Following page 134:

KING HUMBERT II

COUNT CARLO SFORZA

BENEDETTO CROCE

GENERAL VITTORIO AMBROSIO

FIELD MARSHAL ALBERT KESSELRING

IVANOE BONOMI

PALMIRO TOGLIATTI

LUIGI LONGO

CARDINAL ILDEFONSO SCHUSTER

CLARETTA PETACCI

WALTER AUDISIO

GENERAL RAFAELE CADORNA

FERRUCCIO PARRI

DANTE GORRERI

COMMANDER JUNIO VALERIO BORGHESE

MARSHAL RODOLFO GRAZIANI

CHAPTER I

PLOTTING THE OVERTHROW OF THE FASCIST REGIME

THE operations conducted by the Western Powers against Italy in North and East Africa, and later in the country's metropolitan territory, down to the armistice of September, 1943, were of a purely military character and do not come within the scope of this book. It was only after the said armistice between Italy and the Allied Powers that the so-called "liberation" of Italy really began. It was preceded by the fall of the Fascist regime on July 25, 1943.

This event was not wholly unexpected. Opposition to Benito Mussolini's Government had always existed in some measure, but it was limited to small groups of persons of contrary tendencies. It was mainly the unfavorable course of the war which began to undermine the erstwhile solid position of the regime. For some weeks or months before July, 1943, a series of plots against Mussolini began to be hatched in different quarters, but, had the military operations proceeded as successfully for Italy as had been the case in the early period of the conflict, they would never have come to a head. They would have faded out, and we would have seen their authors becoming once more ardent supporters of the Duce, as many of them had been in the past.

A symptom of the first of these movements appears (February, 1943) in a note-book belonging to General Vittorio Ambrosio, afterwards Chief of the Staff (in substitution for General Count Ugo Cavallero), containing the words: "Visited Bonomi.[1] Badoglio's proposal. Abdication of the King. The Prince (Humbert, Heir to the Throne). Armistice. Cavallero."

It thus appears that a plot—one of several—against Mussolini was simmering in certain military quarters, and that it was directed even against the King for having supported Mussolini's

[1] Ivanoe Bonomi, Prime Minister in 1921-22.

1

regime. The other plotters, besides Ambrosio, were Generals Giuseppe Castellano and Pompeo Carboni, soldiers of no great distinction, but men of vast personal ambitions, extending beyond all restraints of patriotism.

At the time when the above notes were written, General Cavallero was still Chief of Staff of the Army, and the plotters realized that so long as he held that position they could not get rid of Mussolini. In the meanwhile, the three generals mentioned contacted Count Galeazzo Ciano, the Duce's son-in-law, a man of considerable intelligence and knowledge of international affairs, but of unlimited ambition, considering himself as the destined successor of Mussolini as head of the Government. He was also very much of a snob and delighted to move in aristocratic circles, where he often made imprudent revelations. He had long been known to be anti-German and pro-British, and he could not forgive Mussolini for having removed him from his post as Minister of Foreign Affairs. He regarded the position of Ambassador to the Holy See as a very inadequate consolation prize.

So keen were the plotters to oust Mussolini that they were willing to envisage the military defeat of their country if the success of their schemes could only be achieved through such a consummation.[2] Cavallero, however, had first to be removed, and the recent unsatisfactory course of the war induced Mussolini to dismiss him in February, 1943, and put Ambrosio, of whose intrigues he was totally unaware, in his place, although that general was notoriously opposed to the German alliance, and also, as a former Freemason, was an opponent of Fascism. This change in the high Command and certain other events soon aroused the suspicions of the German military authorities, who sent several officers to Rome to keep an eye on certain politicians and military leaders and on the proceedings of one or two military and political departments. According to the well-known Fascist journalist (later a member of Parliament), Ezio Maria Gray, on a certain day in March, 1943, the British General, Carton de Wiart, who had been taken prisoner in

[2] Giuseppe Castellano, Come firmai l'armistizio di Cassible (Milan, 1945), p. 34.

North Africa by the Italians, but had managed to escape, had been seen in Rome in the vicinity of Palazzo Vidoni, then the Italian GHQ.[3]

A fifth conspirator now appears on the scene, the most important of all, Field Marshal Pietro Badoglio, Marquis of the Sabotino and Duke of Addis Ababa. Born in 1871, he had followed a professional military career as an artillery officer, taken part in several colonial campaigns, and then become a member of the General Staff. In World War I, he had distinguished himself in the operations for the conquest of the Sabotino position, the key to Gorizia, was promoted to brigadier, then divisional general, and, finally, was appointed commander of the XXVII Army Corps. In that capacity, his leadership in the operations at Caporetto was much criticized because his corps was one of the two which collapsed before the Austro-German onslaught. Nevertheless, he was afterwards rehabilitated, appointed Assistant Chief of Staff under General Armando Diaz, and contributed to the preparation of the plans that led to the decisive victory of Vittorio Veneto (October-November, 1918).

After the first World War, he was assigned to important positions: he was made Chief of Staff in 1926, was created Field Marshal and Marquis of the Sabotino in 1929, and received the highest honor in the gift of the King, the Order of the Annunciation. In the Ethiopian War he was Commander-in-Chief, but his own activity was limited to the conduct of the operations in the northern sector, those in the south being under the command of the late Field Marshal Rodolfo Graziani, a much abler strategist. As a result of the Italian victory, Badoglio was created Duke of Addis Ababa and appointed Viceroy of Ethiopia; this position he held only for a month, but he succeeded in getting the vice-regal salary granted to him for life. He was also appointed President of the National Research Council (with an additional salary), and a large and handsome villa was given to him. His ambition, however, was not yet fully satisfied, and he was ever aspiring to yet further favors

[3] Article in *Giorni*, February 28, 1950.

and emoluments. In the existing conspiratorial situation he now saw possibilities for climbing still higher.

The difficulties of the War and the scarcity of war materiel from Germany, which had been repeatedly asked for and promised but was never forthcoming, made themselves felt ever more severely. Badoglio then told the well-known lawyer, Guido Cassinelli, on April 9, 1943, that he agreed with Ambrosio as to the necessity, should Germany continue to refuse Italy's requests, "that we should detach ourselves from her, with or without the Monarchy."[4] Here we have evidence of a twofold plot: (1) a breakaway from the German alliance and, consequently, a separate peace with the Western Powers, and (2) the possibility of abolishing the Monarchy, or at least of deposing King Victor Emmanuel III.

In addition to these various intrigues, Badoglio and Ambrosio frequently met with a sixth conspirator, but one of a different tendency, the Duke Pietro d'Acquarone, Minister of the Royal Household, who was quite ready to consider the elimination of Mussolini and of the German alliance, but not any action against the Monarchy or the person of the King, to whom he was (or professed to be) devoted. Indeed, the anti-Monarchist or anti-Victor Emmanuel move was not seriously considered until much later, except for Badoglio's hint in his above-mentioned remark to Guido Cassinelli.

About this time, Ciano raised with the King the question of a breakaway from the German alliance. His Majesty asked him if there were any special reasons or possibilities for such a move "without falling under the charge of treachery," a query which Ciano does not seem to have answered. None of the conspirators had considered this point, and, moreover, it is difficult to see how they could have thought of a compromise settlement with the Western Powers after the "unconditional surrender" decision made by Roosevelt and Churchill at Casablanca in January, 1943. It is true that, at first, this clause was not to have been applied to Italy, but President Roosevelt later decided that it must be enforced against all enemy nations.

[4] Guido Cassinelli, *Appunti sul 25 luglio, 1943* (Rome, 1944), p. 27.

The first definite suggestion for a change of international policy appears to have been made by the King himself on June 8, 1943, in a conversation with Colonel Alfonso Sorice, then Chef de Cabinet to the Minister of War (at that time Mussolini also held the War Ministry). The King hinted that a break-away from Germany might be really possible, but did not enter into any details.

The removal of Mussolini as head of the Government and the substitution of Badoglio was first envisaged on or about July 15, 1943, by a group of Generals (names not specified), meeting at Salsomaggiore. This conversation was reported to the then Secretary of the Fascist Party, Carlo Scorza, by the local Fascist secretary in Parma.[5] Scorza repeated the story to Mussolini who, however, does not seem to have believed it, for the King, in talking to Mussolini about that time, had said to him: "Go ahead; we are both in the same boat, and I shall be the last to let you down."[6]

On that same July 15th, Mussolini received several of the Fascist leaders, who openly criticized several of the measures taken by the Party, and also some of the Duce's own acts, but those men were not yet ready to detach their own responsi-bility from his.

The following day, the British Premier, Winston Churchill, and President Roosevelt issued a joint message to the Italian people stating that "the sole hope for Italy's survival lies in an honorable capitulation to the overwhelming power of the military forces of the United Nations." It is not quite clear how "an honorable capitulation" could be reconciled with "uncon-ditional surrender"; but both consistency and honor seemed to be out of fashion in those degenerate days.

About this same time, General Ambrosio spoke openly to Mussolini about the scarcity of war materiel, and advised him to inform Hitler that Italy could no longer continue to take part in the War unless more supplies were available. A meeting for this purpose between the Duce and the Führer was arranged

[5] Alfredo Cucco, *Non volevamo perdere* (Bologna, 1949), p. 94.
[6] Article by "Historicus" in *Risorgimento liberale*, January 27, 1948.

for July 19th at Feltre. It was also attended by the Italian
Under-Secretary for Foreign Affairs, Giuseppe Bastianini, the
German Foreign Minister, Joachim von Ribbentrop, the Italian
Ambassador in Berlin, Dino Alfieri, General Ambrosio, and
other political and military personages. Nothing definite was
settled at Feltre where Hitler was the chief and indeed almost
the only speaker, but, on returning to Rome, Mussolini told
the King that the Germans were still very strong and might
really help Italy if they chose to do so. He added, however, that
by the middle of September Italy would be detached from
Germany, a statement which shows that he was then evidently
contemplating such a move, but through a straightforward
and open agreement.

In a conversation with the journalist, Manlio Morgagni, head
of the Stefani telegraphic agency, Mussolini stated that "in a
few hours or a few days I shall be left alone to decide for everyone against everyone."[7] He was deeply concerned with the
situation and tormented by doubts and uncertainties. The
progress of the War filled him with dire forebodings, he was
indignant with the Germans for the inadequacy of their assistance and, above all, he was very apprehensive concerning the
future of his country, the one thing which for him stood above
every other consideration. He was even, as we have seen, prepared to detach Italy from Germany if that were in the nation's
interest, provided that it might be brought about in an honorable manner. In this matter, he differed profoundly from the
various plotters, who were not much concerned with the interests or honor of Italy, but only with the achievement of their
own ambitions.

It should not be forgotten that the fall of the regime, now
evidently approaching, was actually brought about less by the
plots and intrigues of factious generals and politicians, or even
by the unfavorable general military situation, than by the
bombing of Rome on July 19th. This event did not terrify the

---

[7] From information supplied by Morgagni to Augusto Turati, formerly Secretary
of the Fascist Party (recently deceased), and by the latter to Attilio Tamaro, who
reports it in his *Venti anni di storia* (Rome, 1953-54), Vol. III, p. 475.

Dino Grandi, Fascist Ambassador in London, Minister of Justice, President of the Chamber of Deputies, and a leading conspirator against Mussolini in 1943.

Marshal Pietro Badoglio, Italian military commander, a leading conspirator against Mussolini, 1943. He was Prime Minister in 1943.

were ready to see their country reduced to slavery, provided that they could get rid of Mussolini and the Fascist regime, to which many, if not most, of them owed their public position and influence. This was also the openly expressed attitude of Benedetto Croce, whose merits as a philosopher and a scholar cannot outweigh his dubious conduct as an Italian citizen.

Nor should we forget the incompetence, if not the treachery, of certain military and naval officers in the capital who were doing everything possible to sabotage Italy's war effort in North Africa and elsewhere, and who prevented the supplies, even when available, from reaching the fighting forces. The men at the front, the regimental officers, many of the generals, and the officers and crews of the warships and merchant ships did their duty admirably against heavy odds and with inadequate war materiel, the enemy being amply supplied with everything. But the conduct of the above-mentioned men at headquarters in Rome left much to be desired, to put the situation mildly.

CHAPTER II

JULY 24-25, 1943

THE Fascist Grand Council met on the late afternoon of July 24th, and sat throughout the night. Speeches were made by all those present and, although no exact record of the proceedings exists, we know what happened from the statements of various members of that body. The former Fascist Party Secretary, Roberto Farinacci, in submitting a resolution of his own, severely criticized the conduct of many of the generals, especially of Ambrosio. Dino Grandi then read his own resolution, which was as follows:

> The Grand Council, meeting in these fateful days, first addresses its thought to the heroic fighters of all arms who, by the side of the proud people of Sicily, in whom the single-minded faith of the Italian people shines forth, are living up to the noble traditions of strenuous gallantry and of indomitable spirit of sacrifice of our glorious armed forces. After examining the domestic and international situation and the political and military conduct of the war, the Council proclaims the sacred duty for all Italians to defend at all costs the unity, independence and freedom of the fatherland, fruits of the sacrifices and efforts of four generations from the Risorgimento to the present day, which are the life and the future of the Italian people; it asserts the necessity of the moral and material unity of all Italians in this grave and decisive hour for the fate of the Nation; it declares that for this purpose the immediate restoration of all State functions is necessary, attributing to the Crown, to the Grand Council, to the Government, to Parliament, to the Corporations, the duties and responsibilities laid down by our national and constitutional laws; it calls upon the Head of the Government to beg the King's Majesty, to whom the heart of the whole Nation faithfully and trustfully addresses itself, to take over, for the honor and salvation of the fatherland, with the actual command of the armed forces on land, at sea and in the air, in harmony with article 5 of the Constitution of the Kingdom, the supreme initiative of decision, which our institutions attribute to him, institutions which have always been throughout our national history the glorious heritage of the august Dynasty of Savoy.

The ex-Minister, Luigi Federzoni, who proved the best-informed of the speakers, while very critical of the Government, pointed out what would be the consequences of the coming vote. Bottai, Ciano and Bastianini were very bitter against the Mussolini Government, and supported the Grandi resolution.

After ten hours of stormy debate, a vote was taken—18 were in favor of the Grandi resolution, 7 against it, with 2 abstentions (Suardo and Farinacci). The Party Secretary, Scorza, who had voted for the resolution, afterwards withdrew his vote.

Mussolini brought the proceedings to an end with the words: "You have brought about a crisis of the regime. The meeting is now closed."

It should be borne in mind that the Grand Council was a body consisting of the members of the Government, some of the Under-Secretaries, and a certain number of ex-Ministers and other eminent personages not in office. Its powers were purely advisory, save on two counts: (1) the choice of Party candidates for election to Parliament; and (2) decisions to be taken should there be any uncertainty concerning the legitimate succession to the Crown on the decease of the Sovereign. On all other matters it was entitled only to express opinions as to what measures should or should not be taken, but the Government was not bound to follow its advice. Mussolini was thus, strictly speaking, not called upon to accept or carry out any proposal voted by the Council, nor, of course, to resign, should it, as it did, express an opinion unfavorable to his policies. He considered, however, that, in view of the lack of confidence felt in him by the majority of the Council, it was his duty to ask the King for an audience and to report on the proceedings to His Majesty.

The audience took place in the King's private residence, the Villa Savoia (not in the Quirinal Palace), at 5 p.m. on the 25th. Mussolini reported to the King what had taken place in the Council, whereupon His Majesty replied that, in view of the majority vote, he (Mussolini) was no longer Prime Minister and that the position would be conferred on Badoglio. The Duce, himself, afterwards stated that the King had added:

"In a few months you may be back in office";[1] which was to prove true, although not in the manner implied by the King.

On quitting the Royal residence, Mussolini was escorted not to his own car, but, as previously arranged, to a motor-ambulance, in which he was conveyed under arrest to the police barracks. He was detained there for some days, and thence removed, first to the island of Ponza, next to that of Maddalena off the Sardinian coast, and finally to Campo Imperatore, a mountainous holiday resort above Aquila in the Abruzzi. Thence, he was rescued a little later by a party of German parachutists under Major Otto Skorzeny, sent expressly for the purpose by Hitler, and conveyed first to Vienna, then to the German General Headquarters, whence he went to the Lake of Garda. At Gargnano near Salò, he set up a new Italian Fascist Government, afterwards known as the Italian Social Republic (RSI).[2] Mussolini declared that the King had forfeited his right to reign by his action on July 25th.

The arrest of Mussolini on the premises of the Royal domain has been the subject of endless controversy and innumerable publications, and the King's own conduct has been criticized in many quarters, although it is doubtful whether he himself had actually ordered the arrest of his Prime Minister. In this connection, the personality of Victor Emmanuel III deserves a few words.

He had been on the throne for over forty years, since July 29, 1900, when he succeeded his father King Humbert I, who had been murdered by an anarchist at Monza. Throughout his long reign he had scrupulously fulfilled his duties as a constitutional Monarch, as an Italian, and as a soldier. He was a man of considerable culture in many fields, widely read, speaking many languages, and as a numismatist he enjoyed a worldwide reputation.[3] Nominally Commander-in-Chief of the armed forces, during World War I, he had constantly remained at the

[1] Filippo Anfuso, *Roma-Berlino-Salò* (Milan, 1950), p. 338.
[2] It was also known as the Salò Government, Salò being the chief town in the district where most of the departments were scattered about.
[3] His monumental work, the *Corpus Nummorum Italicorum* (Rome, 1910), is universally regarded as a classic.

front, often in the most exposed positions, leading the same life as any other officer, only allowing himself the same furloughs, and keeping in close touch with the men in the front-line trenches. On the other hand, he never interfered in matters of command or strategy, and only once did he make a suggestion concerning a military appointment. That was on the occasion of selecting a new Chief of the Staff (who was actually the Commander-in-Chief) to succeed General Count Luigi Cadorna, who had been recalled after the debacle at Caporetto. The most obvious successor was the Duke of Aosta, the highly capable and gallant commander of the III Army. But for various reasons it was deemed inadvisable for a member of the Royal family to be invested with so responsible a position. Since none of the other Army Commanders was considered suitable, the choice had to fall on one of the Corps Commanders. It was then that the King himself suggested the name of General Armando Diaz, a man no doubt inferior to Cadorna in strategic abilities, but in closer touch with the troops of all ranks than his predecessor, very popular, and endowed with a well-balanced mind. As events were to show, no better choice could have been made.

The anti-Fascists had criticized the King for having accepted the Fascist regime; but in so doing he had acted in accordance with the most strictly constitutional canons and practice, for Fascism enjoyed the support of the immense majority of Parliament and of the nation, whatever one may think of the system. The King was, in fact, constitutionally bound to entrust the Government to Mussolini, for the Chamber of Deputies, elected *before* the Duce came into power, and the Senate whose members had been appointed by the King (for life) on nomination by successive Prime Ministers, had given their full confidence to the new Cabinet. It may be added that Mussolini's Government was of purely Italian origin, whereas the one that came into power after July 25, 1943, had no Parliamentary vote behind it, and those which succeeded after the armistice of September, 1943, were chosen by the Command of the Allied invading armies and held office only at their good pleasure.

Throughout the years of Fascist rule Mussolini had always shown the greatest deference for the King, conferring on the Monarchy an authority and prestige such as it had never enjoyed since the death of Cavour.

The King's conduct in the events of July, 1943, has been subject, as I said before, to criticism in many quarters, and not only among those who had remained faithful to Mussolini. But until his autobiography, now in possession of his son, the ex-King Humbert II, is published, it will not be possible to pass a definitive judgment on the matter. There is, however, reason to believe that either the policy which he followed had been imposed on him by force or by the threat of force, moral if not physical, or that his age, the weight of his responsibilities, and his declining health had induced him to undertake actions which he would probably not have taken in his earlier years. In any case, his conduct on the occasion in question does not appear in harmony with the whole previous course of his reign, and its result was to divide Italian public opinion into supporters and opponents of the Monarchy. The latter, in turn, were subdivided into followers of Mussolini, many of whom were Royalists at heart, even if they disapproved of the King's action at the time, and the extreme Leftists who were opposed, not only to the Monarchy, but to all patriotic and national policies. The purely ideological Republicans were, and still are, a mere handful, with no following worth mentioning.

On assuming power, Badoglio[4] issued a proclamation stating that "the War goes on," which gave some, but by no means full, satisfaction to the Germans, while Hitler was most indignant at the dismissal and arrest of his friend and ideological predecessor, Mussolini.

The new Premier formed a Cabinet consisting chiefly of officials. One of them, the ex-Prefect, Bruno Fornaciari, was a man of sterling qualities and endowed with an admirable fund of common sense. He had been appointed, much against his

[4]Badoglio, in his book *L'Italia nella seconda guerra mondiale* (Milan, 1946), p. 70, suggests that his appointment as Head of the Government by the King came as quite a surprise to him.

will, Minister of the Interior; but after a fortnight's tenure of office he resigned because he could not endure Badoglio's constant interference in the conduct of his own department.[5] The other Ministers were mostly colorless, many of them ex-Fascists who had developed a notable capacity for double-dealing.

The Fascist Party was now dissolved, its property confiscated, and all Fascist emblems removed from public buildings—virtually the only achievements of the new Government at that time. There was no attempt to apply democratic principles; indeed, Badoglio proved more dictatorial than his predecessor. The dismissal of many Fascist officials and their replacement by men of inferior qualities, both as regards intelligence and honesty, now commenced but on a much lesser scale than was to be the case later on.

The War dragged on ever more unsatisfactorily. The Allies landed in Sicily, occupied the island, and crossed over to the Calabrian coast. In many areas, Italian and German forces resisted valiantly. In others, the former showed signs of disintegration in consequence of the altered political situation, while in some cases, such as the fall of Pantelleria and of the Augusta base (which had occurred before July 15th) real treachery seems to have been present.[6] But everywhere it was the superiority of the Anglo-American war industry and materiel which proved decisive.

NOTE: The decision of the majority of the Grand Council in favor of the Grandi resolution was regarded by Mussolini and by many of the other leading Fascists as an act of treachery, leading to the fall of the regime and indirectly to the armistice and all the other disasters which befell Italy. Those who had voted for the resolution were afterwards proceeded against as traitors. The trial, before a special court at Verona, began on January 8, 1944, and the five of the accused who had been arrested—Ciano, Marinelli, De Bono, Gottardi and Pareschi—were condemned to death on the 10th and executed the following day, while others who had fled were condemned in absentia.

[5]Details communicated to me by Fornaciari himself.
[6]These and other facts of the same nature came out at the trial of Commander Trizziono; for statements contained in his book Navi e poltrone (Milan, 1952), he was condemned for libel in the first instance, but fully acquitted on appeal, the truth of his statements having been proved.

These proceedings, which were the subject of much discussion and criticism, I have dealt with in another book on the foreign policy of the Fascist era.

CHAPTER III

THE ARMISTICE

I HAVE dealt more fully with the negotiations for the armistice of September, 1943, in another book. It will suffice here to state that they had been going on for some weeks in Lisbon, in Sicily and elsewhere, and, on September 3rd the so-called "short armistice" had been signed at Cassibile in Sicily by General Giuseppe Castellano on behalf of the Italian Government, and by the American General, Walter Bedell Smith, on behalf of General Eisenhower, Supreme Commander of the Allied Armies in the Mediterranean. It was not published immediately, and the text is as follows:

The following armistice conditions are presented by General Dwight D. Eisenhower, comanding the Allied Armed Forces, acting on behalf of the Governments of the United States and Great Britain and in the interest of the United Nations, and are accepted by Field Marshal Badoglio, Head of the Italian Government.

1. Immediate cessation of all hostile activities on the part of the Italian Armed Forces.

2. Italy shall make every effort to refuse the Germans everything which may be employed against the United Nations.

3. All prisoners and internees of the United Nations shall be immediately handed over to the Allied Supreme Commander and no one of them shall be now or in any moment transferred to Germany.

4. Immediate transfer of the Italian fleet and of the Italian aeroplanes to such places as shall be set forth by the Allied Commander with the details for disarmament as shall be laid down by him.

5. The Italian mercantile marine may be requisitioned by the Allied Supreme Commander to provide for the requirements of his military and naval programme.

6. Immediate surrender of Corsica and of the whole Italian territory, both insular and continental, to be used as a base of operations and for other purposes, according to the decisions of the Allies.

7. Immediate guarantee for the free use on the part of the Allies of all air ports and sea ports in Italian territory, without considering the development of the evacuation of Italian territory on the part

of the German forces. These sea ports and air ports shall be protected by Italian Armed Forces until such duties shall have been taken over by the Allies.

8. Italian Armed Forces shall be immediately withdrawn from all participation in the War, to any area in which they may be at present employed.

9. Guarantee on the part of the Italian Government that if necessary, it will employ all its available forces to ensure the immediate and precise execution of all the conditions of the armistice.

10. The Supreme Commander of the Allied Forces reserves the right to take all such measures as he may deem necessary for the protection of the interests of the Allied Forces, for the prosecution of the war, and the Italian Government undertakes to carry out such measures of an administrative or other nature as may be demanded by the Supreme Commander, and in particular the Supreme Commander will set up an Allied Military Government in those parts of Italian territory where he may deem it necessary in the military interest of the Allied Nations.

11. The Supreme Commander of the Allied Forces shall be fully entitled to impose measures of disarmament, of demobilization and of demilitarization.

12. Further conditions of a political, military and financial nature, which Italy shall undertake to carry out, will be communicated subsequently.

The conditions of this armistice shall not be made public without the approval of the Allied Supreme Commander. The English text shall be considered the official one.

Three days after the signing of the armistice, on September 6th, one of the most ferocious air-bombings was launched on Frascati. The alleged object was to destroy the various German commands installed in or near that town, but only one of them was even slightly damaged, whereas some thousands of civilians were killed or maimed, most of them women, children and aged or sick persons, the able-bodied men being at the time either working in the fields or in Rome, and hundreds of private dwellings, several historic villas, and some churches, were wrecked.

On September 8th, Badoglio issued a proclamation stating that "the Italian Government, having recognized the impossibility of continuing the unequal struggle against overwhelming enemy power, with the object of sparing the nation any further

and graver disasters, has asked General Eisenhower, Supreme
Commander of the Allied Anglo-American Forces, for an armistice. The request has been granted. Consequently, all acts of
hostility against the Anglo-American Forces on the part of the
Italian Forces shall cease."

Stated in this form, the proclamation was definitely untruth-
ful. The armistice had not been requested, but imposed.

Eisenhower, himself, very rightly declared that the armistice
was "a crooked deal," and that it could only be published after
the end of the war.[1]

The armistice was followed by the surrender of the Italian
fleet, still a formidable fighting force, on the order of the Badoglio Government, while the Italian army rapidly disintegrated.

The Germans were, naturally, most indignant at what they
regarded as an act of black treachery by an ally, and immediately proceeded to take over all parts of the country not yet
occupied by the Western Powers, regarding Italy no longer as
an ally, but as a potential, if not an actual, enemy.

The King immediately decided to leave Rome, where German forces were concentrating, opposed only by a few Italian
units, and removed to Pescara on the Adriatic coast, whence,
in spite of the opposition of Prince Humbert, he sailed on a
destroyer for Brindisi; there a new Italian Government, still
under Badoglio, was set up.

With regard to the respective political status of the two parts
of Italy, it is interesting to remember that, a few days after the
signing of the armistice, Field Marshal Albrecht Kesselring,
Commander-in-Chief of the German forces in Italy, issued a
proclamation on September 11th, subjecting the whole of the
Italian territory under German occupation to German legislation. But, as soon as Mussolini's new Government was set up at
Gargnano in the North of Italy, that decree was officially declared by the German command to have then lapsed. (September 18th). This fact marks a main difference between the political conditions in the Italy of the RSI (Republica sociale itali-

---

[1] H. C. Butcher, *Three Years with Eisenhower* (New York, 1946), pp. 405-6.

ana) under Mussolini, and that of the Italy nominally under the Government of the King and of Badoglio, but actually under the authority of the Allied military command.

From this moment the "liberation" of Italy may be said to begin. But the armistice of September 3-8, 1943, was only the first phase of the Allied control of Italy and of the Italian people. As we shall see, something far worse was to follow.

CHAPTER IV

THE KINGDOM IN THE SOUTH

THE King's decision to quit Rome, together with the Government, leaving the capital without any recognized Italian authority, and placing himself in the hands of the Allied armed forces, was regarded in many quarters as an act of very doubtful political wisdom. He was inspired by various considerations, the first of which was that, independently of the possibility of being taken prisoner by the Germans, he would have been unable to exercise any authority, and his Government would have been equally impotent. But, as we shall see, even in the Southern provinces he was unable to reign, while his Government could not govern.

The Government set up in Brindisi consisted at first only of Badoglio himself and a couple of generals. Gradually, a few short-handed departments were set up, but they could do nothing, for all real authority was vested in the Allied occupation forces, who exercised direct rule in Sicily, which for the time being was virtually an Anglo-American colony, and indirect control over all the rest of the occupied territory.

What is particularly remarkable is that both the British and the Americans professed to believe that they had come to Italy to civilize the people and to confer democratic freedom on the country, and that many of them really believed it. As Winston Churchill himself said, they were there "to liberate her (Italy) from her conditions of servitude and degeneration," which Churchill had so highly praised in 1927 and later. Here we have the key to the whole attitude of the Anglo-Saxon invaders, who regarded themselves as invested with a divine mission to convert the Italians from being wicked Fascists into virtuous democrats. Moreover, the Anglo-Saxon invaders were inspired not only by a more or less genuine crusading spirit, but also, at

least in the case of the British, by a feeling of hatred and contempt for the Italians, which eventually came to be heartily
reciprocated, a hostile attitude hardly conducive to peaceful
international co-existence even in a later period.

The Allies attenuated their democratic professions, however
much they may have believed in them originally, by openly
stating that Sicily and Southern Italy were politically immature
and unfit for the freedom of the press, of which those areas
were wholly deprived as soon as they were conquered. An
acute British observer, George Glasgow, wrote that many
Englishmen repeated Kant's words or sentiments to the effect
that Italy could not be taken seriously as a nation of human
beings.[1]

As an example of Allied methods, it may be mentioned that
an obscure English pedagogue, G. R. Gayre, who had acted as
assistant anthropologist and "staff officer for education" at Oxford, and who knew nothing about Italy or the Italians, was
sent to Sicily to teach the islanders education and civilization.
He said that Italy must be made to "pay for Fascism and Mussolini's impertinence when he struck at us and London in 1940,
thinking that we were finished" (incidentally Italy never
"struck at London").[2] He wrote a lot of nonsense, in somewhat
doubtful grammar, about Italy and Sicily, and stated that the
Italians knew nothing of civilization and education except
where English and French influence had reached them. He
added that Garibaldi had been "a tragedy for Italy, for he gave
them the conception of a conquest by arms—and from that to
Mussolini and his fictitious Roman Empire was not too difficult
a road to travel."

Gayre went ahead with his task of reforming and, indeed, re-
constructing education in Sicily, and expounded various preposterous theories about Sicilian origins and characteristics. He
set to work to reorganize the University of Palermo, dismissed
one group of professors and appointed another lot in their
places, regardless of merit, raised the readership in Albanian to

---

[1] *Contemporary Review*, October, 1943.
[2] *Italy in Transition*, (London, 1946), pp. 13, 56, 172, 182.

a regular professorship, to please a friend of his own, casually suppressed existing chairs and created new ones, including one for psychology for the benefit of the almost non-existent Protestant community. To this very day several undistinguished university professors still hold chairs in which they were placed by the Allies.

At the same time, Gayre seemed to have bitterly disliked the Americans, and frequently criticized their actions and policy. He wrote, for instance, that in a certain town the American commander took over the police barracks and turned the building into a brothel, although it happened to be next door to a church, while he admitted and deplored the vast amount of drunkenness among both the American and the British soldiers,[3] and the widespread prevalence of venereal disease—one soldier in four being infected among the white troops, three in four among the negroes, in spite of the many prophylactic stations set up.[4]

While he severely criticized the measures employed by the Fascist authorities to stamp out the *Mafia* in Sicily, he admits that, after the Allied occupation, the *Mafiosi* were as active as they had been before the Fascist clean-up.[5] He tells us that there was an underground Fascist organization, "for ardent and deeply implicated Fascists were bound to go under-

[3]*Op. cit.*, p. 28.
[4]*Op. cit.*, p. 213.
[5]When the *Mafia* was stamped out under Mussolini all its leaders were either imprisoned or escaped abroad, mostly to the U. S. These escapees returned to Sicily with the U. S. forces, posing as political refugees, and secured the release of those who were still in prison in Italy.

The aid, direct and indirect, which the Allies gave to the revival of the *Mafia* has backfired on the Allied countries, notably the United States. One of the leading racketeers in New York City, "Lucky" Luciano, was freed from prison, ostensibly because of some aid he was supposed to have given the United States during the War, and was allowed to return to Italy. Here, it is alleged that he operates as the link between the Italian and American racketeers. The more powerful of the latter are thought to be members of the *Mafia*. They are especially active in the fields of labor violence, transportation, narcotics, bootlegging, and prostitution. They have also thoroughly "organized" the restaurant business in Chicago. The state police surprised a rather brazen "convention" of top *Mafia* and other racketeers at Apalachin in southern New York State in 1957.

A committee of the United States Senate under the chairmanship of Senator John L. McClellan, carried on an investigation of alleged *Mafia* leaders in 1958. It was difficult to extract direct evidence from the principals. Carefully coached by lawyers

ground."[6] He attached great importance to the Sicilian separatist movement, and says that the Sicilian Freemasons of the
Scottish rite were strongly in favor of it (does he think that
Scottish rite Freemasons had special sympathies with Scot-
land?) and that 60 percent of the Sicilians supported the movement. Although Gayre may have been an ass, it seems from this
and other statements of his that, at least at one moment, the
British authorities intended to detach Sicily from Italy, with a
view to making of the island a larger Malta or, at all events, a
British sphere of influence.[7]

It was such conceptions as these which inspired the policy of
the British authorities in occupied Italy, and to some extent that
of the Americans. Although the latter did not feel the same bitterness toward the Italians, they followed the British line because they suffered from an inferiority complex towards the
British, whom they regarded as more experienced than themselves in international affairs.

Nevertheless, many Allied officers and officials could not
help occasionally admitting that Italy's social legislation, food
regulations, health services and agricultural planning—all work
of the much decried Fascist regime—were excellent,[8] and one
British observer remarked that the railways of Sicily were far
superior to those of Wales. Some Britons and Americans ended
by expressing admiration for the domestic achievements of

notorious for their close association with racketeers, the men who were believed to
be the chief figures in the *Mafia* and other racketeering groups blandly refused to
answer the questions put to them by the committee, claiming immunity under the
Fifth Amendment to the Constitution of the United States which protects a person
from being compelled to testify against himself. Individuals who knew of the
racketeering, some of whom had suffered personally and directly from it, were
intimidated by ominous threats of reprisals if they testified against the racketeers.
Hence, few dared to come forward with any testimony.

But enough evidence was amassed amply to confirm the statement made by Senator McClellan early in the investigation: "The testimony we have heard can leave no
doubt that there has been a concerted effort by members of the American criminal
syndicate to achieve legitimacy through association with and control of labor unions
and business firms. The extent of this infiltration poses a serious threat to the very
economy of our country."

[6] Gayre, *op. cit.*, p. 58.

[7] When elections were held after the war, the Separatists secured only a handful
of votes, and then faded out altogether.

[8] *Neue Züriche Zeitung*, September 23, 1943.

Mussolini, although this was not, of course, the official view, according to which everything done by the Fascists was a sin against the Holy Ghost. On the other hand, most Allied officers had no use for anti-Fascist Italians, whom they regarded as cowards for having betrayed their own country and as cheats who did not want to pay their gambling losses, and generally despised them for having allowed themselves to be oppressed by Mussolini without resisting, if they had really disliked the past regime. Of course, many Italians who, after the armistice, posed as anti-Fascists, had previously been only too proud to wear the blackshirt, to applaud Mussolini enthusiastically, and to enjoy the fleshpots of the regime.

On their first arrival in Italian cities, the Allied forces were welcomed, for the occupation was regarded as signifying the end of the War and of air bombings. But this attitude soon gave way to disappointment and hatred when the people began to feel the ever-heavier burdens and ruthless impositions enforced by the invading forces. According to a writer in the London *Economist*, the Allies soon came to feel that they "could only count on a minority . . . who really saw this war in an ideological and not in a national light."[9]

Indeed, the first and immediate effects of the Allied occupation were the rapid rise in prices, the ever-increasing scarcity of foodstuffs and most other goods and services, including gas and electricity, and the many instances of brutality and looting by the Allied troops.

In Naples, which had been heavily bombed innumerable times, the people showed extraordinary calmness and courage under these trials. The Germans, while still in occupation of the city, applied severe measures to all who rebelled against their authority, recruited many men for work on the defenses, and wrought some damage to the port structures and to a few of the industrial plants, in anticipation of an early evacuation, thereby rendering themselves unpopular with a people who had not yet experienced the methods of the Allies. When they actually began to evacuate the city, a popular rising broke out against

[9] September 18, 1943.

the retreating forces, but its proportions have been grossly exaggerated by anti-Fascist writers. In the fighting, which lasted on and off for four days, only some fifty of the rebels were killed and very few Germans. By September 30th, the evacuation had been completed, and Naples was occupied by the Allies. The Neapolitans soon realized the difference between scourging with whips and the same process carried out with scorpions.

CHAPTER V

CO-BELLIGERENCE

THE armistice of September 3-8 had paralyzed Italy's war potential without completely destroying it. The Allies at once suggested that, if the part of Italy occupied by their forces and under the nominal authority of the King and of Badoglio's Government were to join them in the war against the Germans and Mussolini's new Italian Social Republic, the conditions of the Italian people would be greatly improved.

In fact, immediately after the signing of the armistice, President Roosevelt began to hint at the possibility of Italy's "cobelligerency" (an expression unknown to international law— or to the Oxford Dictionary), in his secret instructions to General Eisenhower and to Robert Murphy, United States civilian representative in Italy. He stated that, if Badoglio decided to declare war on Germany, his Government would be allowed to remain in power.[1]

The idea did not at first appeal to the British Government, which regarded itself as the predominant partner with regard to Italian affairs,[2] and seemed as usual, inspired by an unreasoning animosity against the Italian people, not shared, at least not to the same extent, by that of Washington.

The improvements in the conditions of Italy then suggested were as follows:

1. As soon as Italy declares war against Germany she will be recognized as a "co-belligerent."

2. Field Marshal Badoglio's Government will continue to remain in power.

3. The Allies will give full support to the authority of the King and of his Government, without prejudice to the right of

---

[1] Cordell Hull, *Memoirs* (New York, 1948), Vol. II, p. 1550.
[2] *Ibid.*, Vol. II, p. 1551.

the Italian people, once the Germans are driven from the whole country, to choose the form of Government which it may prefer.

4. As soon as possible, Badoglio shall form a new Government on a broad basis (i.e., comprising members of all the chief political parties, *including the Communists*).

5. Any possible modifications of the armistice terms and the restoration of Italy's territory will be proportionate to the efforts carried out by her in the war.

6 From time to time, instructions will be issued concerning political, economic and financial questions, as laid down under Article 12 of the armistice.

Badoglio himself admitted that few, if any, of the promises were fulfilled (except the maintenance in nominal power of the King and of his Government). It seems, indeed, that the Allies never had any intention of fulfilling them.

On September 29th, Badoglio proceeded to Malta, accompanied by Generals Ambrosio and Roatta, by Admiral De Courten, and by General Sandalli of the Air Force. They were received by General Eisenhower on the British warship *Nelson* with military honors. Badoglio there signed the fatal "long armistice," but protested against it because in it the words "unconditional surrender" were mentioned, thereby radically altering the whole character of the "short armistice" of September 3rd, the conditions of which had been carried out.[3] General Eisenhower, who, as we have seen, regarded the armistice in general as "a crooked deal," promised to get the "long armistice" modified; but he failed to do so, as both Roosevelt and Churchill were determined to get their pound of flesh and not to improve the conditions for Italy in any way.

Badoglio had been forced to sign the "long armistice" because, under Article 12 of the "short armistice," he had undertaken to accept all the additional military, political, economic and financial conditions which might be submitted to him, although in the earlier document there had been no mention of "unconditional surrender."

After the signing of the "short armistice" Eisenhower had

[3] See text in appendix to this chapter.

written to Badoglio that the document was based on the situation obtaining before hostilities had ceased, that subsequent developments had already altered Italy's status, and that many of the armistice conditions would not be carried out. The contents of this letter are very different from the definition of Italy as merely a "vanquished nation" in the words of the British Foreign Office.

Aboard the *Nelson* on the 29th, Eisenhower went on to state that Italy must declare war against Germany, to which Badoglio replied that the King insisted that a Government on a broad basis should first be formed, and that this could only be achieved after His Majesty's return to Rome. In the meanwhile, he offered Eisenhower the Italian "Nembo" division as a first contribution to the operations against Germany, adding, with more optimism than accuracy, that eight or ten more divisions were available.

Here, however, the British General, Harold Alexander (afterwards Field Marshal Earl Alexander of Tunis) intervened, saying that the plan of campaign in Italy had been minutely prepared, and that Italian cooperation could not be considered.[4]

Badoglio then stated that in 1918 the Italians had delivered a decisive blow at the Germans (which was true), and that "this time too we shall deliver a decisive blow against the Germans" (which was obviously impossible).

After these discussions, refreshments were served and Badoglio drank "to the victory of the Allies," a toast which he might well have spared himself.

We have here obvious signs both of disagreement between the British and the American points of view on Italy and of a conflict in Badoglio's mind between his grovelling subservience to the Allied invaders and an occasional *crise de conscience* for the appalling disaster of his country, to which he had so largely contributed.

[4] These conversations are reported in a publication issued by the Italian Ministry of Foreign Affairs entitled *Documenti relativi ai rapporti fra l'Italia e le Nazioni Unite*, pp. 103-107.

The Allies had chosen that particular moment for presenting the humiliating "long armistice" to Badoglio, because they were determined to make him understand that, even with "co-belligerency," Italy should never forget that she had suffered defeat and must be made to pay for it through the nose.

The "long armistice," disastrous as it was for Italy, was a personal triumph for Badoglio, as it implied official Allied recognition of his Government. But, at the same time, it placed him completely under the orders of the Allied High Command, expressed in the form of the Allied Control Commission (ACC) and of the Allied Military Government (AMGM), without whose authority neither Badoglio nor any of his Ministers could move a finger.

The Allies at once ordered him to form a new Cabinet, with himself as Prime Minister, but comprising representatives of all the anti-Fascist groups, including, as we have seen, the Communists. Thus it came about that the Communists, under the aegis of foreign enemy armies, were able to lay the foundations of their future influence in Italy.

The formation of this Cabinet appeared to the Allies an urgent necessity at that moment, as a counterpart to the Government lately set up in Northern Italy under Mussolini. Even though the RSI was more or less dominated by the German forces in the country, it operated as an Italian Government and exercised full authority, through its own Italian officials, in all matters of a not strictly military nature. Badoglio's Government, by contrast, exercised no authority at all. In the area under its nominal control, Italian military collaboration came to be declared necessary in a general way, and even the British, in spite of Alexander's statement, ended by agreeing to it, although they were by no means keen about it. A British officer, Christopher Buckley by name, in speaking of the various armies to be brought into line in the Italian campaign,[5] writes that "somewhat in the distant future was looming the slightly

[5] The invading forces included, in addition to British and American troops, also French, Polish, Indian, Brazilian, Moroccan, Congolese, Hottentot, Malay and others.

disturbing prospect of Free Italians."[6] Alexander rejected the offer of the two Italian divisions then in Corsica (in addition to the "Nembo" division), and Badoglio's request that Italian prisoners of war should be utilized for Allied military operations was not even answered.

No Italian merchant ship, not even a fishing-smack, could sail without Allied permission, and the Government was compelled to issue any and all legislative or administrative measures regarded as necessary for the enforcement of the armistice conditions, and to obey any order of the ACC. Italian sovereignty was wholly in abeyance, and no Italian diplomatic representatives could be sent to any foreign country. No Italian citizen could go abroad or carry on trade with foreign countries without an Allied permit, which was very seldom granted, and full control was exercised over all commercial transactions by private citizens, and over banks, exchanges and industrial activities. Officials and judges had to carry on their duties under Allied control.

The Government was ordered to dismiss all Fascist officials (a process already begun) and to suppress all Fascist institutions. This involved depriving the administration of its best and most experienced officials, and in many cases replacing them with shady characters, nitwits, and illiterates. It also meant canceling legislation of all kinds, as many of the existing laws had been enacted under the Fascist regime, while "Fascist" institutions included hospitals, welfare organizations, charities, schools, maternity and infant homes, etc., down to the society for the prevention of cruelty to animals. It was found necessary to make certain exceptions, but in many cases useful institutions were closed down, to the serious detriment of the community— to be reopened several years later and presented as glamorous achievements of the new Italian Democracy.

There were in the air sinister warnings of the conditions to be imposed on Italy in the future Peace Treaty. The colonies

---

[6] This prospect was disliked, as it might involve better treatment for the Italian people.

were, in fact, excluded from the provisions of the armistice, full
protection was accorded to all Italians, who, during the War
and before the armistice, had committed flagrant acts of
treachery and espionage against their own country on behalf
of, and in the pay of, the enemy Powers (Art. 37), and it was
ordered that Mussolini and his chief supporters were, if captured, to be handed over to the Allies (Art. 29).

Pressure to induce Italy to declare war against Germany was
continuous, even if only few Italian troops were wanted. For
some time, the King refused to take this action, and we do not
know the grounds of his hesitation. But, as Badoglio, on announcing his request for an armistice in September, had definitely stated that Italy could no longer continue to wage war
at all, it seemed, to say the least, inconsistent suddenly to discover both the necessity and the possibility for embarking on a
new war against a power which, until a few weeks previously,
had been an ally.

Between October 1st and 7th, Badoglio had twice met the
delegates of the United States and Great Britain, General Maxwell Taylor and General Frank Mason MacFarlane, who again
insisted, especially the latter, that Italy must declare war on
Germany. The King hesitated for some time longer, but, finally,
on October 8th, Taylor informed Eisenhower that Badoglio
had received His Majesty's consent and that war would be declared on the 11th. Possibly the object of this decision was to
protect such Italian soldiers as might be fighting against their
old Allies from the risk of being treated as *francs tireurs,* if captured by the Germans.

On the 11th, Badoglio wired to the Italian Ambassador in
Madrid, the Marquis Paolucci de' Calboli (formerly Mussolini's
Chef de Cabinet and an ardent Fascist, who had gone over to
the other side), instructing him to inform his German colleague
that, in view of "the persistent acts of hostility committed by
the Germans against the Italians," Italy considered herself at
war with the Reich as from 3 p.m. (Greenwich time) on October 11th. It was indeed a most peculiar way of declaring war,

and can only be explained by Badoglio's ignorance of the elements of diplomatic procedure.[7]

The British, United States, French (that of DeGaulle) and Russian Governments now officially informed Badoglio that they recognized Italy as a "co-belligerent" in the war against Germany, which, as we have seen, meant exactly nothing at all. On that occasion, they made two declarations which deserve to be recorded.

With the first they demanded the "democracity"[8] of the Italian Government, and duly took note of Badoglio's undertaking to submit to the will of the Italian people through a general election to be held as soon as the Germans were driven out of the whole of Italy and the Italians were free to choose the political regime that they preferred.

In this connection, a speech delivered on November 14, 1942, before the "Mazzini" Society of New York, consisting of a handful of anti-Fascist Italians, by the Assistant Secretary of State, Adolph A. Berle, Jr., is worth quoting:

> There can be no compromise with the cult of Fascism, nor with any of the men who have carried it on . . . There can be no compromise between free men and slave-masters. Until the Fascist domination of Italy is ended, and while Italians, however blindly, follow Fascist leaders, there can be no valid dealing save by force alone. Nevertheless, we in America insist on hoping that the day will come when we can once more welcome into the brotherhood of civilization a free and friendly Italian nation, giving again to the world the finest of her shining culture and her splendid traditions . . . that Italy must be saved, for who can imagine a world without her? . . .
>
> This is little to ask. It asks that the people of Italy shall not condemn themselves and their children to further slaughter . . . that they shall submit only to those restraints which must bind a free people if freedom is to remain in the world. In the truest sense, the Italian nation is offered a freedom beyond the wildest Fascist dreams: freedom of religion, freedom of thought, freedom from want and freedom from fear . . . She is asked to accept those obligations which

[7] It should be borne in mind that Italy, being occupied by foreign armies and totally devoid of sovereignty, could not declare war at all. She was an object and not a subject of international law, and could not be regarded as being at war with Germany.

[8] A word not in the Oxford Dictionary nor in Webster. New editions of both are desirable.

make those freedoms equally possible for her neighbors . . . The destiny of the Italian people rests in their hands.

To those true patriots who undertake the liberation of Italy we say: You do not act alone. The armies of America and the United Nations are close at hand, and behind them the full strength of the most powerful nations in the world.[9]

While there is a large component of cant, not unmixed with pure humbug, in the egregious Mr. Berle's oration—to say nothing about the conspicuous absence in the parts of Italy occupied by the Allies of freedom of thought, and freedom from want and from fear—his statement is interesting as confirming the worst error in the conduct of the Allies towards Italy, viz., their determination to impose on the Italian people a form of government which might theoretically be admirable but took no account of the wishes and necessities of the Italians themselves. By "democracity," they merely meant the suppression of Fascism, not because the Italian people repudiated it, but because they—the Allies—disliked it and regarded it as responsible for Italy's intervention in the War "on the wrong side." Even if they were right on this point, they were not entitled, if they really believed in democracy (or "democracity"), to impose one regime on, or exclude any other from, Italy. It was a matter for the Italians alone to decide whether they wanted a Liberal, a Republican, a Monarchical, a Socialist, a Communist, a Clerical or a Fascist Government. The Allies could fight against Italy under a Fascist or any other regime, but they had no right to decide what regime was best for her and to force it down her throat. This latter attitude, as I said in Chapter IV, was to be their dominant attitude towards Italy throughout the war and for some years thereafter.

It was the same error as that committed by revolutionary and Napoleonic France in trying to impose by force on her neighbors governments similar to her own, and as that of the victorious Coalition Powers in restoring by force the Bourbon Monarchies and the Austrian regime on France and other countries, and trying to prevent by force the rise of national Liberalism

[9] V. Louise and Hajo Holborn, *War and Peace Aims of the United States* (World Peace Foundation, Boston, 1943).

among the peoples of Europe after 1815. In Cordell Hull's *Memoirs* we find him also perpetually insisting on the necessity of imposing a "democratic Government" on Italy, quite regardless of what the Italian people might or might not want. All this was contrary to the main and sound principle of minding one's own business in the domestic affairs of other nations, as laid down by the "Fathers" of the American Republic. The result has been that the various Cabinets in power in Italy during and since the War have all been tainted by their foreign origins. Until 1947, the successive Governments were imposed on Italy by foreign armies.[10]

The second declaration made by the Allies when Italy became a "co-belligerent" stated that "co-belligerence" in no way altered the armistice conditions, but these might be adjusted according to the measure of Italy's military contribution to the Allied cause. Here we find blended together the somewhat more reasonable attitude of the Americans with the vindictiveness of the British, but, it cannot be too often repeated, it was nearly always the British who prevailed in the end.

At the same time, Italy's contribution to Allied war aims, small as it was, found itself constantly handicapped by Allied suspicions. Badoglio replied to the second declaration with a request that Italy be placed in a position to play her part in the military operations, within the limits of her possibilities, and stated in a proclamation to the Italian people on October 13th that they must fight on the side of their "friends" in the United Nations. But all the Allied talk about co-belligerence really amounted to very little. Even when, a year later, in October, 1944, Roosevelt declared his readiness to resume diplomatic relations with Italy, the British Government retorted that the British nation would regard it as beneath the King's dignity to address a letter to a foreign State still legally at war with him.[11]

The Allies, in fact, in their kindness of heart, merely "allowed" Italy as a favor to go to war against Germany, although

[10] Not to mention the fact that they comprised men such as De Gasperi, who had been first an Austrian and then a Vatican citizen, Togliatti, a Russian citizen, and Nenni, a French citizen.

[11] Hull, *op. cit.*, Vol. II, p. 1567.

in reality it was something more than a permission, as they had actually imposed intervention on her. The British press repeatedly stated that Italy could hope for no improvement in the armistice conditions even through co-belligerence, and, although the United States Government hinted that she might obtain important help in the War,[12] it gave her no definite promises. This attitude was confirmed by the British Under-Secretary for Foreign Affairs, Viscount Cranborne, in his speech of October 13th, while another British Minister (Law) stated that Italian co-belligerence in no way altered the armistice conditions, although Italy had indeed begun to enjoy some of the fruits that "accrue to the evil-doer who turns King's evidence."[13]

Badoglio found no other way of consoling himself for this unsatisfactory state of things than by inveighing once more against Fascism. In a speech in October addressed to a group of officers at Agro San Giorgio Ionico, he defined the Fascist regime as a band of thieves and the ex-Ministry of Popular Culture as a brothel.[14] He added that the Germans had tried to seize Italy by the throat, that he had "asked for an armistice" which had been granted, that Italy was no longer a vanquished nation but a co-belligerent, that the working classes in Milan and Turin were fighting with arms in their hands against the Germans and the Fascists—which was a lie—and that the Italian IV Army was also fighting against them—an army which had completely disintegrated a month previously. He concluded by stating that Mussolini would never have the courage to return to Italy (whereas he was already back in the country and was to remain in it for the next eighteen months, until he was murdered in cowardly and brutal fashion by those friends of Badoglio and of the Allied Powers, the Communist partisans).

The "long armistice" may be regarded as the dress rehearsal of the Peace Treaty of 1947. It treated Italy simply as a defeated enemy without considering the "co-belligerence" then

---

[12] H. L. Stimson, *Prelude to Invasion* (Washington, 1944), p. 165.
[13] *The London Times,* Oct. 13, 1943. As a matter of fact, no Italian ever noticed these "fruits."
[14] Nino Bolla, *Dieci mesi del Governo Badoglio* (Rome, 1944), pp. 14 *et seq.*

being imposed on her as a prelude to the promise of more favorable treatment.

The first seven articles were of a purely military character, conceived solely with the object of bringing Italy's military operations against the Allies to an end, and call for no comment.

Article 19 placed Italian public services, ports, transport installations and communications, and refineries wholly at the service of the Allies.

Articles 23 and 24 deprived Italians of all possibilities for carrying on financial or business activities, save by permission of the Allied authorities.

Article 26 prevented any Italian from leaving Italian territory without Allied permission—which was nearly always refused.

Article 29 is a forecast of the Nuremberg trials, for it provided that Mussolini and his principal Fascist associates and all persons accused of having committed war crimes or "similar offences" should be surrendered to the Allies (what these "similar offences" might be was not stated, as no definition even of "war crimes" had been made; thus the Allies were entitled to secure and punish anyone they wished).

Article 30 was a flagrant interference in the internal affairs of Italy, inasmuch as it imposed the suppression of all Fascist institutions and the dismissal or internment of Fascist personnel and even the suppression of "Fascist ideologies and teaching," while Article 31 ordered the Italian Government to abrogate Fascist legislation, according to the directives of the Allied Supreme Commander (who probably knew nothing about such matters).

Article 32 imposed the liberation not only of prisoners of war, which was, of course, perfectly legitimate, but also of "all persons who have been placed under surveillance, detained or condemned in consequence of their relations with or sympathies for the United Nations," i.e., traitors to their own country on behalf of and in the pay of their country's enemies. This is a forecast of Article 16 of the Peace Treaty.

The armistice thus condemned the whole Italian people to

THE LIBERATION OF ITALY

had measures of this kind been imposed on an enemy nation,
unless we go back to the most barbarous ages. They are all the
more surprising when we consider that, even when Italy had
been forced by Allied orders to become a "co-belligerent," these
conditions were not in any way modified.

The whole document can only be regarded as characteristic
of the astounding moral decay of the so-called civilized nations.

NOTE: THE "LONG" ARMISTICE

Signed at Malta on September 29, 1943.
Additional Conditions of the Armistice with Italy

Whereas in consequence of the armistice of September 3, 1943, the
Governments of the United States and of Great Britain, acting in the
interests of all the United Nations on the one hand, and the Government
of Italy on the other, hostilities between Italy and the United Nations
have ceased, on the basis of certain conditions of a military character;

And whereas, in addition to these conditions, it had been laid down in
the said armistice that the Italian Government had undertaken to carry
out other conditions of a political, economic and financial character to
be further transmitted;

And whereas it is advisable that the conditions of a military nature
and those of a political, economic and financial nature to be subsequently
transmitted, without attenuating the validity of the conditions of the said
armistice of September 3, 1943, should be included in a subsequent
instrument;

The following, together with the conditions of the armistice of September 3, 1943, are the conditions on the basis of which the Governments
of the United States, of Great Britain and of the Soviet Union, acting
on behalf of the United Nations, are ready to suspend hostilities against
Italy, provided that their military operations against Germany and her
allies are not hindered and that Italy does not help those Powers in any
way and carries out the requests of these Governments.

These conditions have been presented by General Dwight D. Eisenhower, Supreme Commander of the Allied Forces, properly authorized
to that effect:

And they have been accepted unconditionally by Field Marshal Pietro
Badoglio, Head of the Italian Government, representing the Supreme
Command of the Italian forces on land, at sea and in the air, and properly
authorized to this effect by the Italian Government.

1. (A) The Italian forces on land, at sea and in the air wherever they find themselves, surrender.

(B) Italy's participation in the war in any area must cease immediately. There shall be no opposition to the landings, movements and other operations of the forces on land, at sea and in the air of the United Nations. In conformity with this the Italian Supreme Command will order the immediate cessation of hostilities of all kinds against the forces of the United Nations, and will issue orders to the Italian naval, military and air authorities in all war zones immediately to give the proper instructions to their subordinate commands.

(C) Further, the Italian Supreme Command will issue to the naval, military and air authorities and also to officials orders immediately to desist from destroying or damaging all real or personal property, whether public or private.

2. The Italian Supreme Command shall supply all information concerning the displacement and situation of all Italian armed forces on land, at sea and in the air, wherever they may be and of all the forces of Italy's allies who may be in Italy or in territories occupied by Italy.

3. The Italian Supreme Command shall take all necessary precautions for safeguarding the aerodromes, the port installations and all other plants against seizure or attack by any of Italy's allies. The Italian Supreme Command shall take all necessary measures to safeguard law and order and to make use of the available armed forces to ensure the prompt and precise execution of the present instrument and all its provisions. With the exception of the employment of Italian troops for the above purposes which may be sanctioned by the Supreme Command of the Allied Forces, all other Italian military, naval and air forces will re-enter and remain in their barracks, encampments or on board ship while awaiting the instructions of the United Nations with regard to their future status and their final destination. By way of exception, the naval personnel will be transferred to such naval barracks as the United Nations may indicate.

4. Italian military, naval and air forces, within the period which may be laid down by the United Nations will withdraw from all those territories outside Italy which will be notified to the Italian Government by the United Nations and will be transferred to those areas which will be notified by the United Nations. These movements of the military, naval and air forces will be carried out according to the instructions which will be issued by the United Nations, and in conformity with the orders imparted by them. In the same way, all Italian officials will quit the areas notified except those to whom permission to remain will be given by the United Nations. Those to whom permission to remain will be granted will act according to the instructions of the Supreme Commander of the Allied Forces.

5. No requisitions, appropriations or other coercive measures may be carried out by the Italian military, naval or air forces or by Italian officials with regard to persons or property in the areas specified under N. 4.

6. The demobilization of the Italian military, naval and air forces in excess of the number which will be notified will follow the prescriptions laid down by the Supreme Commander of the Allied Forces.

7. Italian warships of all categories, auxiliary and transport vessels will be concentrated, according to orders, in the ports which will be notified by the Supreme Commander of the Allied Forces, and all decisions in this matter will be taken by the Supreme Commander of the Allied Forces. (Note: If at the date of the Armistice the whole of the Italian war fleet will have been concentrated in the Allied ports, this article shall read as follows: "Italian warships of all categories, auxiliary and transport vessels will remain until further orders in the ports where they are at present concentrated and all decisions on the matter will be taken by the Supreme Commander of the Allied Forces.")

8. No Italian aeroplane of any kind shall take off from land, from water or from ships without the previous orders of the Supreme Commander of the Allied Forces.

9. Without prejudice to what has been laid down by articles 14, 15 and 28 (A) and (D) following, all merchant ships, fishing smacks and other vessels under any flag, and all aeroplanes and means of inland transport of any nationality in Italian territory occupied by Italy or in Italian territorial waters shall be prevented from leaving pending the ascertainment of their identity and position.

10. The Italian Supreme Commander shall supply all information concerning naval, military and air means, installations and defences, transports and means of communication constructed by Italy or her allies in Italian territory or in its vicinity, mine-fields and other obstacles to movements by land, sea and air and all other information which the United Nations may demand with reference to the use of Italian bases or operations, of the security or well-being of the military, naval and air forces of the United Nations. Italian forces and materiel will be placed at the disposal of the United Nations, whenever asked for, for the removal of the above obstructions.

11. The Italian Government shall at once supply lists indicating the quantities of all war materiel, mentioning the places where it is to be found. Unless the Supreme Commander of the Allied Forces decide to make use of it, war materiel shall be placed in magazines under the control which he will establish. The final destination of war materiel will be decided by the United Nations.

12. No destruction or damage, or, with the exception of what may be authorized or ordered by the United Nations, any removal of war ma-

teriel, radio, radio-localization, or meteorological station, railway, road or port plants or other installations or in a general way public or private services or property of any kind, wherever it may be found, shall take place, and the necessary upkeep and repairs will be the responsibility of the Italian authorities.

13. The manufacture, production and construction of war materiel, its importation, exportation, and transit are forbidden, save for such exceptions as may be laid down by the United Nations. The Italian Government will conform with those instructions which may be imparted by the United Nations for the manufacture, exportation and transit of war materiel.

14. (A) All Italian merchant ships, fishing smacks and other vessels, wherever they may be, as well as those built or completed during the period of validity of the present instrument will be placed by the proper Italian authorities at the disposal, in good repair and in good navigating conditions in those places and for those purposes and periods of time which the United Nations may prescribe. The crews will remain on board awaiting further instructions concerning their further employment or dismissal. Any existing option for the repurchase or restitution or re-acquisition of Italian ships or of ships formerly Italian which had been sold or otherwise transferred or chartered during the war will be immediately carried out, and the above-mentioned conditions will be applied to all the said ships and their crews.

(B) All Italian inland means of transport and all port installations shall remain at the disposal of the United Nations for the purposes which they will decide.

15. Merchant ships, fishing smacks and other vessels of the United Nations, wherever they may be, in the hands of the Italians (including for this purpose those of all countries having broken off diplomatic relations with Italy, independently of whether the deed of ownership has or has not been transferred in consequence of proceedings before the prize court) will be handed over to the United Nations and will be concentrated in those ports which will be decided by the United Nations, who will make such use of them as they may see fit. The Italian Government will take the necessary measures for the transfer of the deeds of ownership. All neutral merchant ships, fishing smacks and other vessels operated or controlled by Italians will be concentrated in similar fashion, awaiting arrangements for their final destination. All necessary repairs to such ships, if requested, will be carried out by the Italian Government at its own expense. The Italian Government will take all the necessary measures to ensure that the ships and their cargoes will not be damaged.

16. No radio set or appliances for long-distance communications or other means for inter-communications on land or afloat under Italian

control, whether they belong to Italy or to other nations not forming part of the United Nations, may effect transmissions until measures for the control of these instruments will have been issued by the Supreme Commander of the Allied Forces. The Italian authorities will act in conformity with the measures for the control and the censorship of the press and of other publications, of theatrical and cinema performances, of wireless transmissions and of all other means of intercommunication which the Supreme Commander of the Allied Forces may prescribe. The Supreme Commander of the Allied Forces may at his discretion take over wireless stations, cables or other means of communication.

17. The warships, auxiliary, transport and merchant and other vessels and aeroplanes in the service of the United Nations will have the right to make free use of Italian territorial waters and to fly over Italian territory.

18. The forces of the United Nations will occupy certain areas of Italian territory. The territories and areas in question will be notified from time to time by the United Nations, and all Italian military, naval and air forces will withdraw from those territories and areas according to the orders issued by the Supreme Commander of the Allied Forces. The provisions of this article will not prejudice those of art. 4 above. The Italian Supreme Commander will ensure for the Allies the use of and the immediate access to the aerodromes and naval ports in Italy under his control.

19. In the territories and areas mentioned in art. 18 all naval, military and air installations, all central electric power stations, refineries, public services, ports, installations for transport and communications, the means and materials and the plant and other depots which may be demanded by the United Nations will be placed at their disposal by the proper Italian authorities with the personnel necessary for their operation. The Italian Government will place at their disposal such other resources and services as the United Nations might demand.

20. Without prejudice to the provisions of the present instrument, the United Nations will exercise all the rights of an occupying Power in the territories and areas mentioned in art. 18, the administration of which will be provided for through the publication of proclamations, orders and regulations. The personnel of Italian administrative, judicial and public services will carry out their duties under the control of the Allied Commander-in-Chief unless otherwise provided for.

21. In addition to the rights concerning the Italian occupied territories described in articles from 18 to 20:

(A) The members of the military, naval and air forces and the officials of the United Nations will have the right to pass through or above Italian non-occupied territory and all necessary facilitations and assistance will be afforded to them in the exercise of their duties.

(B) The Italian authorities in non-occupied territory will place at the disposal of the United Nations all transport facilities which they may demand, including free transit for their materials and war supplies, and will carry out the instructions issued by the Supreme Allied Command concerning the use and the control of the airports, ports, navigation, systems and means of land transport system of communication, electric power stations and public services, refineries, materials and other supplies of petrol and electricity and the means for producing them, according to the specifications of the United Nations, together with the necessary facilities for repairs and construction.

22. The Italian Government and people shall abstain from all acts prejudicial to the interests of the United Nations and shall promptly and efficiently carry out the orders of the United Nations.

23. The Italian Government shall place at the disposal of the United Nations the Italian currency which the United Nations may demand. The Italian Government shall withdraw and redeem in Italian currency in the period of time and at the conditions which the United Nations may indicate all the currency available in Italian territory issued by the United Nations during military operations or occupation and will hand over to the United Nations the currency withdrawn without expense. The Italian Government will take such measures as may be required by the United Nations for the control of the banks and of business in Italian territory for the control of foreign exchanges of commercial and financial relations with foreign countries and for regulating trade and production and for carrying out all instructions issued by the United Nations concerning these and similar matters.

24. There shall be no financial, commercial or other relations of any kind or negotiations with or in favour of countries at war with one of the United Nations or with territories occupied by such countries or by any other foreign country, save the authorization of the Allied Commander-in-Chief or authorized officials.

25. (A) Relations with countries at war with any one of the United Nations or occupied by one of those countries shall be interrupted. Italian diplomatic, consular and other officials and the members of the Italian military, naval and air forces accredited or on mission to any one of such countries or in any other territory specified by the United Nations shall be recalled. The diplomatic and consular officials of such countries will be treated as may be decided by the United Nations.

(B) The United Nations reserve the right to demand the withdrawal of neutral diplomatic and consular officials from Italian occupied territory and to lay down and establish the regulations concerning the procedure relative to the means of communication between the Italian Government and its representatives in neutral countries and relative to communications sent to or destined for the representatives of neutral countries in Italian territory.

26. While awaiting further orders Italian subjects will be forbidden to leave Italian territory save with the authorization of the Supreme Commander of the Allied Forces, and in no case will they serve any country or in any territory to which art. 25 (A) refers, nor will they go to any place with the intention of undertaking work for any such country. Those who at the present time are serving or working in such guise shall be recalled according to the provisions of the Supreme Commander of the Allied Forces.

27. The personnel and the materials of the military, naval and air forces, and the merchant marine, the fishing smacks and other vessels, aeroplanes, vehicles and other means of transport of any country against which one of the United Nations is conducting hostilities or is occupied by such a country, are liable to attack and capture wherever they may be found within or over Italian territory or waters.

28. (A) Warships, auxiliary and transport vessels of any occupied country or territory, to which art. 27 refers, which are in Italian ports or waters or occupied by the Italians and aeroplanes and vehicles and means of transport of such countries within or over Italian territory or occupied by the Italians, will be prevented from departing, pending further instructions.

(B) The military, naval and air personnel and the civilian population of any such occupied countries or territories who are in Italian territory or occupied by the Italians, shall be prevented from departing, and they shall be interned pending further instructions.

(C) All property in Italian territory belonging to any occupied country or territory or to its nationals shall be placed under sequester and retained in custody, pending further instruction.

(D) The Italian Government shall obey any instructions issued by the Supreme Commander of the Allied Forces concerning the internment, custody or subsequent dispositions, utilization or employment of any of the above persons, vessels, aeroplanes, materials or property.

29. Benito Mussolini, his principal Fascist associates and all persons suspected of having committed war crimes or similar offences, whose names are found on the lists which will be communicated by the United Nations and who now or in future are in territories controlled by the Allied Military Command or by the Italian Government, shall be immediately arrested and and handed over to the Forces of the United Nations. All orders issued by the United Nations in this connexion shall be observed.

30. All Fascist organizations, including all branches of the Fascist Militia (M.V.S.N.), the secret police (O.V.R.R.A.) and the Fascist youth organizations, will be, if it has not been already done, disbanded,

in conformity with the provisions of the Supreme Commander of Allied Forces. The Italian Government will carry out all the directives which the United Nations may issue for the abolition of Fascist institutions, the dismissal and internment of Fascist personnel, the control of Fascist funds, the suppression of Fascist ideologies and teaching.

31. All Italian laws implying discrimination by race, colour, creed, or political opinions shall be, if this has not already been done, abrogated, and persons detained for such reasons shall be, according to the orders of the United Nations, liberated and released from all legal impediments to which they may have been subjected. The Italian Government will carry out all further directives which the Supreme Commander of the Allied Forces may issue for the abrogation of Fascist legislation and the elimination of all impediments or prohibitions deriving therefrom.

32. (A) All prisoners of war belonging to the forces of the United Nations or indicated by the latter and all subjects of the United Nations, including Abyssinian subjects, confined, interned or detained in any other manner in Italian territory or in territory occupied by the Italians, shall not be transferred and shall be immediately delivered to the representatives of the United Nations or otherwise treated as will be prescribed by the United Nations. Any transfer during the period between the presentation and the signing of the present instrument will be regarded as a violation of its conditions.

(B) Persons of any nationality who have been placed under surveillance, or detained or condemned (including those condemned *in absentia*) in consequence of their relations with or sympathies for the United Nations shall be released in conformity with the orders of the United Nations and freed from the legal impediments to which they may have been subjected.

(C) The Italian Government will take the measures which may be prescribed by the United Nations to protect the persons and the property of foreign citizens and the property of foreign States and citizens.

33. (A) The Italian Government will carry out the instructions which the United Nations may issue concerning the restitution, delivery, services or payments by way of reparations and payment of the expenses of occupation during the period of validity of the present instrument.

(B) The Italian Government will communicate to the Supreme Commander of the Allied Forces all information which may be prescribed concerning all assets both in Italian territory and outside it, belonging to the Italian State, the Bank of Italy or to any Italian State or semi-State institution or Fascist organizations or to persons resident in Italian territory, and will not provide for nor permit any such assets to be disposed of outside Italian territory save with the authorization of the United Nations.

34. The Italian Government will effect during the period of validity

of the present instrument such measures of disarmament and demilitarization as may be prescribed by the Supreme Command of the Allied Forces.

35. The Italian Government will supply all information and deliver all documents necessary for the United Nations. It is forbidden to destroy or conceal archives, minutes, projects or any other documents or information.

36. The Italian Government will enact and apply all measures, legislative or of other nature, which may be necessary for the carrying out of the present instrument. The Italian military and civil authorities will carry out all the instructions issued by the Supreme Commander of the Allied Forces.

37. A Control Commission, representing the United Nations, will be appointed, entrusted with the regulation and execution of the present instrument on the basis of the orders and general directives of the Supreme Commander of the Allied Forces.

38. (A) The expression "United Nations" in the present instrument comprises the Supreme Commander of the Allied Forces, the Control Commission and any other authority which the United Nations may appoint.

(B) The expression "Supreme Commander of the Allied Forces" in the present instrument comprises the Control Commission and those other Officers and representatives whom the Supreme Comander of the Allied Forces may appoint.

39. All reference to the Italian military naval and air forces in the present instrument is meant to include the Fascist Militia and any other military or para-military units, formations and corps which may be prescribed by the Supreme Commander of the Allied Forces.

40. The expression "war materiel" in the present instrument signifies all material in those lists and definitions which may from time to time be published by the Control Commission.

41. The expression "Italian territory" includes all Italian colonies and possessions, and within the meaning of the present instrument (but without prejudice to the question of sovereignty) shall be regarded as including Albania. It is, however, laid down that, except in cases and in the measures prescribed by the United Nations, the provisions of the present instrument shall not be applicable to nor regard the administration of any Italian colony or possession already occupied by the United Nations or the rights and powers possessed there or exercised by them.

42. The Italian Government will send a delegation to the Headquarters of the Control Commission to represent Italian interests and to transmit the orders of the Control Commission to the proper Italian authorities.

43. The present instrument will come into force at once. It will remain

in force until it is substituted by any other agreement or until the Treaty of Peace with Italy comes into force.

44. The present instrument may be denounced with immediate effect if Italian obligations under the present instrument are not fulfilled, or, otherwise, the United Nations may punish infringements of the instrument with measures suited to the circumstances, such, for instance, as the extension of the areas of military occupation, or air actions, or other punitive measures.

The present instrument is drafted in English and Italian, the English text being authentic, and in case of any dispute concerning its interpretation, the decision of the Control Commission will prevail.

Signed at Malta on September 29, 1943.

Field Marshal Pietro Badoglio
Head of the Italian Government

Dwight D. Eisenhower
General of the United States Army
Allied Commander in Chief

CHAPTER VI

PARTIES AND DOMESTIC DISSENSIONS

CONFLICTS now began to break out between Badoglio's Government and the various political parties. Several of these had recently cropped up, taking form mysteriously without any popular backing—they simply happened. Among the masses of the people, overwhelmed as they were by the ruin and devastation caused by the War, the unbearable economic conditions, and the food scarcity, there was a general apathy on all political matters, and few honest or patriotic citizens took any interest in party activities for the moment. In various places, the so-called Committees of National Liberation (CLN) were set up, formed casually, and consisted of second-rate politicians, radicals and Communists who claimed, no one knows why, to represent sections of political opinion. They were destined to prove a curse to Italian life for many years, and their factious influence unfortunately still survives.

One of the first consequences of the fall of the Fascist regime was the repatriation of several political exiles, who regarded themselves as victims of Fascism. They had been living abroad so long that they had quite forgotten what Italy was like; even the very landscape was a novelty for them. They had spent most of their time quarrelling with and intriguing against each other, forming "shadow" governments to be set up when the Fascists were ousted by foreign bayonets, usually doing no stroke of work but sponging on foreign Governments and organizations or on the few of their group who were bona fide anti-Fascists and possessed ample private resources. On returning to Italy they proved, like the Bourbons after 1815, to have learned nothing and forgotten everything.

Of these numerous parties the Liberals were the most traditionally respectable, but few of them had gone into exile and,

Such activities in connection with the occupation and liberation of Italy as went on during wartime, however brutal, can, when not in violation of the Geneva and Hague conventions and rules, be excused as something all too often associated with the passions and violence of warfare. But to continue the process, after hostilities had ceased, within the mental and emotional patterns of a lynching party in search of common criminals or worse, cannot be justified on the basis of international or domestic law, the relevant historical facts, or the ethics of civilized society. If the Allied forces did not, as a rule, directly participate in the illegalities and butcheries after the fighting was over, they often encouraged them and did little to check them. Stalin, of course, aided and abetted the violence against the Fascists, and his Italian partisan henchmen carried out most of the mass murders that followed the end of the War.

CHAPTER VII

THE CRISIS OF THE MONARCHY

I HAVE already mentioned the anti-Monarchist resolution of the underground CLN in Rome. Even in those parts of Italy where the Badoglio Government exercised its very limited authority, there was a good deal of opposition to it, and here and there rioting took place. But everywhere any single British soldier enjoyed more authority than the King himself, and one American GI counted for more than an Italian general.[1]

An attempt was now made to set up some sort of central administration. The late Minister Plenipotentiary, Renato Prunas (a career diplomat), had formed an embryo Ministry of Foreign Affairs at Brindisi with a handful of secretaries and clerks; the Councillor of State, Leopoldo Picardi, established one of Industry and Commerce, while the Duke Pietro d'Acquarone, ex-minister of the Royal Household, was appointed a member of the Cabinet.

In theory, freedom of the press existed but it was limited to a few weeklies and subject to severe censorship both by the Government and by an Anglo-American control office known as the Psychological War Department of SHAEF.

In certain districts, individuals, who in pre-Fascist days had been all-powerful and controlled local elections but had long since lost all authority, now raised their heads once more, hoping to regain their former positions and promote their own private interests. But in the confused situation of that time, even they failed to influence the course of events.

In the meanwhile, the stocks of foodstuffs diminished day by day, while prices soared ever higher owing to the unlimited requisitions of the Allied armies and to the masses of worthless

[1] Degli Espinosa, *op. cit.*, pp. 124 et seq.

paper currency manufactured by them and thrown upon the market, making life for the Italian people ever more intolerable.

The various parties continued their childish antics, which merely served still further to weaken the already enfeebled authority of the Government. Apart from the Communists, although it had lost all authority, there was the *Partito d'Azione*. Its members professed to believe that, once the King and Badoglio were eliminated as a hangover from Fascism, Italy would appear pure and unsullied before the Allies and be able to secure anything she wanted. They failed to realize that the Allies regarded all Italians as more or less responsible for Fascism and the War, because they had actually supported both, or, at all events, had not rebelled against the Fascist Government.

A gesture typical of the attitude of certain limited Italian circles was the action of Adolfo Omodeo, Rector of the University of Naples. After having received all possible benefits from the Fascist Government, he now kowtowed before the Allied invaders and, after they had occupied the city, he departed from the traditions of the University by conferring an honorary degree on General Mark Clark, commander of the enemy occupying forces. He went so far as to advise both the King and Prince Humbert to commit suicide.[2]

The Minister, Picardi, now also turned against the King, and informed Badoglio that none of the more representative men would join the new Cabinet about to be established until the King abdicated, Prince Humbert renounced his right to the succession, and a Regency was set up for the Prince's son, as Sforza had suggested. Nevertheless, when Humbert entered Naples soon afterwards, he received an enthusiastic popular welcome.

Sforza, as we have seen, had been permitted by the Allies to return to Italy after having solemnly promised Churchill that he would give his support to the King. But after proposing a Regency he ended by openly declaring himself an enemy of

[2]Nino Bolla, *op. cit.*, p. 40.

the Monarchy as an institution, and joined Benedetto Croce in his anti-Royalist campaign.

Croce enjoyed a world-wide reputation as a philosopher and a scholar, but was totally devoid of political ideas or of stable principles of any kind. While in the early days of Fascism he had voted for the regime, he had afterwards turned against it and, as we have seen, actually expressed the hope that his own country would be soundly defeated in the War so as to bring about the fall of Fascism. He now went to the point of attacking the King, and accused him of supporting the remnants of Fascism and of trying to carry on Fascist principles and methods in his own Government, which, of course, was quite untrue.

The weakest point of the Monarchy at that time was that it no longer represented Italian sovereignty and national independence. This was because there was no sovereignty or independence left in the parts of Italy occupied by the Allies, a fact which minimized the King's personal responsibility for anything then happening.

Mussolini and most of his supporters in the North were also anti-Royalist, but for quite different reasons. They charged the King with having brought about the coup d'état of July 25, 1943, the armistice of September 3-8, and the consequent betrayal of Italy's ally and the dissolution of the nation's armed forces. Mussolini, himself, felt that he had been personally betrayed by the King, whom he had served faithfully for over twenty years. It may be, as I have stated already, an open question whether the King had acted of his own free will but, in any case, it was a mistake on the Duce's part to set up a definitely Republican regime. A provisional Government would have been preferable, the final decision to be left to a popular vote after the end of hostilities.

By a fatality rather than by a deliberately wrongful decision, the King found himself placed in the hands of many groups then competing for power or for the shadow of power in Southern Italy and at a moment when the people, in the midst of disasters and hardships, had most need of a Monarch. Yet, at that very time, no Monarch could function.

The Allies themselves were uncertain as to what to do about the Monarchy. The Americans regarded the King as compromised by Mussolini's war policy and, while not wishing to bring about a radical change of regime for the moment, they encouraged anti-Royalist tendencies, whereas the British wished to maintain the Monarchy. In neither case was the advantage of a Monarchy or a Republic for Italy considered, but only the advantage of the one or the other to the Allied cause. Both Allied Governments were, in fact interfering in Italy's domestic policy exclusively for their own ends.

On October 21st, the King wrote a letter to General MacFarlane[3] setting forth his attitude in a democratic framework, just when Badoglio was proposing his abdication in favor of his grandson with himself (Badoglio) as Regent.[4] The King was unfavorably impressed by this proposal, and reminded the Field Marshal that, under the terms of the Constitution, only a member of the Royal Family could be appointed Regent.

Badoglio, after meeting Sforza, Croce and others in Naples, informed MacFarlane, on his return to Brindisi, that he would do his best to set up a representative government, and that, if he failed in this attempt, he would resign. His first move was to try to get Ivanoe Bonomi to join the government, but he was met with a refusal.[5]

[3] Attilio Tamaro, *Due anni di storia* (Rome, 1948-50), Vol. II, pp. 137-8.
[4] We have seen how he had already considered the possibility of the departure or abdication of the King.
[5] Ivanoe Bonomi, *Diario di un anno* (Milan, 1947), pp. 23-24; Degli Espinosa, *op. cit.*, pp. 16 et seq.

CHAPTER VIII

THE MOSCOW DECLARATION

A CONFERENCE of American, British and Russian representatives was held in Moscow, October 19-30, 1943, dealing among other matters, with Italian affairs. It was there once more confirmed that everything even remotely savoring of Fascism must be done away with, that all Fascists and pro-Fascists must be removed from the public service, and that all persons imprisoned under the Fascist regime must be released, fully amnestied and reinstated in their former posts. This involved the release of as many common criminals as purely political offenders, and, in any case, here we have a further example of a policy reminiscent of the Holy Alliance. The Italian people, it was decreed, were to be left free to choose their own form of government, provided that it was a democratic government, i.e., one agreeable to the Allied Powers.

But it was soon discovered that democracy meant one thing to the British delegate, Anthony Eden, and another to his U.S. colleague, Cordell Hull, while to Stalin and Molotov it meant nothing at all. It seemed strange, indeed, that Soviet Ministers should insist on introducing into Italy those very liberties which they denied "in toto" to their own subjects.[1] The new Cabinet which Badoglio was trying to form should, as I have said, have consisted exclusively of men who had always been anti-Fascists, but they proved somewhat difficult to find. The moment for its creation was to be decided by the Allied commanders, acting on the instructions of their respective Governments. One point insisted on by those Governments was that all Fascist leaders and generals denounced as "war criminals" or suspected of being such were to be ar-

[1] It was reminiscent of the policy of the Tsar Alexander I of Russia at the Congress of Vienna, where he insisted that France should be ruled by a Constitutional Monarchy, while he refused all liberties to his own subjects.

rested and tried by an as yet unspecified court and on unspecified charges. This demand was even applied, among others, to Generals Vittorio Ambrosio (one of the chief plotters of the July coup d'état), and Mario Roatta; both had been members of Badoglio's first provisional Government but were "wanted" by Tito—a demand which he might have extended to all the officers of the IV Army because it had fought in the Balkans, although Tito himself had been guilty of the most grisly atrocities not only against Italians and Germans, but against his own subjects.

It was further decided in Moscow that the Allied Control Commission in Italy (ACC) should include, in addition to American, British and Russian members, French, Greek and Yugoslavs on a footing of equality with the "senior partners." This body thus came to be a transformation of the Algiers Mediterranean Advisory Council, but endowed with more specific duties with regard to Italy, and it became, with the AMC, the real governing organization for that country. The addition of Yugoslav and Greek members showed that it was also intended to be an instrument for punishment and revenge.

The Russian Government was probably the inspirer of the Moscow Declaration; at that time it did not care so much about sharing in the domination of Italy, which it could always secure through the Italian Communists, as it did about intervening in Mediterranean affairs. At the meeting on October 22nd, in fact, Stalin demanded a part of the Italian fleet— a battleship, a cruiser, 8 destroyers and 4 submarines.[2] Roosevelt was perfectly willing to grant these requests, or indeed any others, which Stalin might make; but Cordell Hull made him consider the danger of Russia's appearance in the Mediterranean, and the scheme was dropped for the time being.[3] But the discussion showed that Italy's navy was merely regarded as war booty to be distributed among deserving—or undeserving—claimants.

[2] Mario Toscano's article "Guerra diplomatica" in the supplementary Volume II of the *Enciclopedia Italiana*.
[3] Several Italian warships were handed over to Russia after the war.

This Moscow international gathering had been preceded by
a Panslavist Congress (a name strangely reminiscent of
Tsarist Russia's program). Russia knew perfectly well what
she wanted and how to get it out of her Western Allies, and
was determined to lay her heavy paw on the Balkans. Great
Britain was then beginning to withdraw from that area, and
was lavish in her promises—and performance—to help Tito,
thus ceasing to lend any support to her ally, the King of Yugoslavia. She even allowed the Commander-in-Chief of the King's
army, General Mihailovich, to be seized and eventually executed by Tito's orders. Tito, the arch-enemy not only of Fascist Italy but of all Western civilization, was now invested with
the respectability of an ally of the great Christian and democratic powers. Through him, supported by those powers, the
Balkans were allowed to become Russia's exclusive sphere of
influence, with Tito as the Soviet's faithful henchman; from
the Balkans, Tito's Communist hordes were soon allowed to
reach the gates of Italy and to penetrate beyond them.

At Moscow, a decision was also taken to "liberate" Austria
and to raise her once more to independent status. Such a task
was to prove very difficult, as the country's extremely limited
resources made it practically impossible for it to become self-
supporting; it was for this reason that so many Austrians, perhaps even the majority of them, had seen in the *Anschluss* with
Germany the only possibility of economic survival.

Wiser men than the glamour-boy, Anthony Eden, would have
realized the danger of Russia's mass drive westward[4] and the
need for a new policy towards Italy as a bulwark of civilization
against the semi-Asiatic East—the "antemurale Christianitatis."
We find, instead, a hybrid coalition between Western capital-
ism and Russian Communism,[5] for which Italy was at first to
pay the costs, followed later by the rest of the Western world.

Mussolini and his supporters in Northern Italy fully realized

---

[4] Cordell Hull himself seems to have had no inkling of it.

[5] Some years later, we find the British Labor politician, Sir Stafford Cripps, declaring that the Communists were a greater danger to Europe than Hitler's armies
had been (statement made to an Associated Press correspondent, November 1, 1948).

the menace of the Moscow declaration, but in the South it was welcomed by the anti-Fascist groups, who saw in it only an instrument for an attack against the King and his Government and in favor of their own policies. The London *Times*, indeed (November 5, 1943), stated that the Moscow decisions concerning Italy were based on the program of the formerly exiled anti-Fascists, while the Communist paper *L'Unità* drew from them the conclusion that the Government of Italy should be entrusted to the various CLNs dominated by the Communists.

The Allied authorities were amused by the preposterous antics of the cheap politicians dominating the CLN, representing nobody but themselves, squabbling, shouting and bragging under the heels of the Allied soldiers' boots, even while they raved incoherently about the "unbearable" impositions of the occupying forces. The Allies themselves only wanted an absolutely subservient Italian Cabinet, and considered that, for the time being, the King and Badoglio best met this requirement. The Americans occasionally seemed inclined to take a different line, but usually ended up by giving way to the British. Only "the old fool," Sforza, fatuously thought that he could exploit one Ally against the other.[6]

On November 7th, the King himself went to Naples, and was warmly welcomed in that very Royalist city. Sforza had organized a hostile meeting at the University, and Croce had previously delivered a harangue to the same effect to the British journalist, Cecil Sprigge, and his American colleagues, Matthews and Lippmann.[7]

Badoglio was at last able to announce his new Cabinet on November 16th. It consisted of men belonging to different parties, but the only members of some capacity were the economist, Prof. Epicarmo Corbino, for the Departments of Industry, Commerce and Labor; and the Palermo business man, Guido Jung, for Finance. But Badoglio refused to invest his new colleagues with the rank of Minister, appointing them

[6]Hull, *op. cit.*, Vol. II, p. 1557.
[7]Benedetto Croce, *Quando l'Italia era tagliata in due* (Bari, 1948), p. 32; *Daily Telegraph*, November 11, 1943.

only as Under-Secretaries, as if the Cabinet formed on July 26th still existed.

The *Partito d'Azione* declared itself opposed to the new combination, but its hostility was of no consequence, as the Allies, who alone counted, for the moment decided to support it, although it was, of course, as unrepresentative and undemocratic a Government, devoid of all Parliamentary or national backing, as its predecessor had been. Mussolini's Government at Salò, although also without the support of Parliament, was far more substantial, owing to the fact that it comprised a number of very capable and thoroughly honest men.

Shortly before, on November 9th, the American General, Kenyon A. Joyce, President of the ACC, and the British diplomat, Harold Caccia (of Italian origin), presented to Badoglio a proposal for amending the naval clauses of the armistice. This stated that the Italian fleet was to be placed completely at the disposal of the Allies, and contained a protocol modifying some of the other clauses, but confirming the surrender and adding the words that it was accepted "without conditions" and "authorized by the Italian Government." Joyce warned Badoglio that, if he did not sign the naval amendment, he would not secure even the amending protocol. Badoglio replied that if the United Nations, whose original draft charter had been laid down at the Moscow conference, wished to make use of the fleet, the matter should be first discussed with the Italian Government. But his suggestion was turned down, and he was told that the Italian navy, like the army, was at the absolute disposal of the Allied Command.[8] Badoglio, of course, had to agree and, on his orders, Admiral De Courten signed the naval amendment under protest. Badoglio himself also sent a letter protesting against this imposition, but without obtaining the slightest result.[9]

The new Cabinet's first program (November 24th) dealt primarily with "epuration," thereby obeying the orders of the Allies, and particularly of Russia, with the utmost servility.

[8] Tamaro, *op. cit.*, Vol. II, appendix to Chap. XV.
[9] *Ibid.*, pp. 192-3.

Many categories of citizens were included in this list of proscribed persons to be dismissed from the public service and otherwise persecuted. All who had supported the Fascist regime were thus punished, except those who had "ratted" in good time. This program alluded to the Fascist regime as a period of "twenty years of arbitrary and illegal rule," a phrase indirectly condemning the King. But even this did not satisfy the extremists, and the Naples CLN stated that "it had disappointed the people"—the people who had expressed no opinion of any kind on the matter after the armistice and had no opportunity of so doing.

In Rome the underground CLN issued a number of empty proclamations. It often met in the dwelling of one Monsignor Barbieri, a prelate residing in the Lateran Palace and, on one occasion, it drafted a resolution demanding that an extraordinary Government be set up, invested with full constitutional authority, suggesting that there was full agreement between all the anti-Fascists both in occupied and in unoccupied Italy. Actually, there was nothing of the kind, and, except in Rome, there were almost no traces of the CLN in the unoccupied area, and only a few such committees existed even in the South. In any case, a Government of the kind suggested could not be created, as there was neither Parliament nor any other means of ascertaining what public opinion wanted, and in the South nothing could be done without Allied permission.

CHAPTER IX

THE TWO ITALIAN ARMIES

Two Italian armies were now in course of formation: one in the South, owing nominal allegiance to Badoglio's Government but actually under the control of the Allied commands and called upon to fight against the Germans and the Italian Fascists, and another in Northern and Central Italy in alliance with the Germans against the Western Powers. In both parts of Italy the necessity of relieving the fighting forces of the nation from the shame of the 1943 armistice and the capitulation, and of securing the liberation of Italy, not through foreign arms alone but with effective Italian participation, was keenly felt. In both cases, the foreign commands, Anglo-American and German, were not, unnaturally, skeptical. But, while Badoglio and his army commanders were mere subordinates of the Allies, the new army of the RSI, under Field Marshal Rodolfo Graziani, was a really Italian force, only strategically under German control.

The Allied command had been constantly urging the Italians to take part in the War, but refused to allow the formation of regular military units, or at all events would not agree to arm or equip them adequately. Badoglio had, first of all, to get rid of Ambrosio and Roatta, owing to the British and Yugoslav dislike of those generals, and to secure the services of such commanders as had offered some resistance to the Germans with the troops under their command during the events of September, 1943, or of those who had been taken prisoners by the British, such as Field Marshal Giovanni Messe, formerly commanding the Italian troops in Russia and in North Africa, a really competent soldier.

But conditions among the available troops in the South were deplorable; they were merely isolated groups, wandering about the country dirty, unshaven, in rags, half starved, having been left by their former commanders without orders of any kind. Many of them were working as laborers under the orders of American Negro N.C.O.'s, and the British treated them with openly expressed contempt.

Finally, in October, General Eisenhower authorized the formation of one division, the "Legnano," and of a motorized unit; but the British General, Alexander, continued to raise difficulties and held up the formation of other Italian units.

The atmosphere in both British and American circles underwent a change when a Fascist unit—a "Mussolini" battalion—first made its appearance on the Mondragone front on November 15th and fought very gallantly, inflicting serious losses on the Allied troops. This fact made the Anglo-American command realize that Italian troops should also make their appearance in the ranks of the Allies, and a mobilized unit under General Dagnino was sent forward. The possibility of getting Italians to fight against other Italians was regarded with great favor in certain Allied military and political circles, but it caused Mussolini and his followers the deepest distress.

There continued to be, however, conflicting tendencies in Allied quarters as to the employment of Italian forces. On the one hand, it was regarded as politically desirable, especially by the Americans, that they should be there but, on the other hand, the British were afraid of any measures which might lead the Italians to expect more generous treatment and even to be regarded as allies. Among the Italians themselves, the radical elements were conducting a pacifist propaganda against any participation in the war, and even in the small Italian units in the South desertions were numerous.

On November 20th, an Italian force, 5,500 strong, was ordered to the front under the United States II Corps and, on December 8th, it attacked the German positions on Monte Lungo, capturing them after an obstinate struggle. But it was left by the Americans with its flanks unsupported and, after suffering casualties amounting to 40 percent of the total group, it was forced to fall back. The American command said that these men had fought badly, which was quite untrue; General Mark Clark, in fact, sent them forward a second time; they again captured Monte Lungo and held it until, on December 21st, they were sent to a rest camp. Then, owing to political reasons, the men lapsed into a critical attitude and desertions again became numerous.

In the North, in spite of difficulties of many kinds and some obstruction on the part of certain German commanders, Mussolini's Government was able to create a small but efficient autonomous army under Field Marshal Graziani, who, as Minister of Defence, proved as able an organizer and administrator as he had proved a gallant field general. By agreement with the German OKW, four Italian divisions were sent to Germany for training, and proved highly satisfactory units. In these and in other units then created, officers and men were very properly forbidden to take any part in politics or to join any party—even the Fascist Party. The Minister of Defence and General Gambara were able to raise a large number of recruits and, in certain areas, such as Emilia, as many as 98 percent of the men called to the colors actually presented themselves at the recruiting stations.

Of course, the great majority of the forces fighting against the Allies in Italy were Germans under Field Marshal Albrecht Kesselring, but the Italian contingents went on increasing in numbers and efficiency and became a truly Italian fighting force. Nothing of the kind occurred in the provinces under Allied control, where there were, as we have seen, only small fragments scattered about here and there, and various labor units. Gabrio Lombardi, in his book, *Il corpo italiano di liberazione*,[1] does his best to present these troops in the most favorable light, but owing to the policy of the Allies and the incompetence of most of Badoglio's generals and organizers at the time, there was very little to show in the way of positive military results.

[1] (Rome, 1945).

CHAPTER X

THE PARTISAN MOVEMENT

THE one outward and aggressive expression of the activities of the CLN and of the various anti-Fascist parties was the Partisan Movement. Although it presented certain resemblances to the French *Maquis* or *Résistance* movement and to the activities of the Russian guerrillas behind the German lines in 1941-45, the Italian movement had peculiarities of its own. Although very largely a creation and creature of the Allied forces, it bore a striking resemblance to another Italian movement dating back to the time of the annexation of the South Italian provinces to the newly created Italian Kingdom in the early 'sixties of the nineteenth century.

At that time, although the great mass of public opinion in Naples and Sicily supported union with the Italian Kingdom under the Savoy dynasty, there were still a number of persons devoted, for traditional and other reasons, to the old Bourbon Kingdom. With the annexation of the Southern provinces, the old Neapolitan army was disbanded and its members sent back to their homes. But, immediately afterwards, they were called back to serve in the Italian army. A considerable number of the privates failed to answer the summons, for, having been disbanded, to some extent with ignominy, they did not wish to serve again, especially in an army and under officers alien to themselves. They thus became deserters, hiding in the woods and mountains. They were soon joined by other men of a different kind. With the change of government, a good many men imprisoned for political offences against the deposed Bourbon dynasty were released and many fell in line with the deserters. They were also joined by many common criminals who posed as political victims and had been let out of prison in the confusion due to the change of government, and by other shady characters not yet in prison, but liable to arrest and ready to commit crimes. A regular movement of deserters and others thus arose and came to form bands of armed brigands. To them were added some genuine supporters of the Bourbon regime, encouraged by a part of the clergy hostile to the new Italian Government, which it regarded as anti-clerical and irreligious because it had annexed a large part of the Papal States. A tone both legitimist and Catholic was thus conferred on the rebel bands. Finally, a number of foreigners devoted to legitimism and to the Church came to Italy on their own account or on behalf of foreign governments or organizations unfriendly to Italy, to serve under Bourbon leaders.

These various elements were soon welded into a large, organized rebel movement, which began by following a definite political line, but ended by becoming mere banditry. These gangs caused serious trouble to the Italian Government and were often guilty of acts of atrocious cruelty, so much so that some of the sincere Legitimists, native and foreign, ended by withdrawing from the movement. Severe and sometimes ruthless measures of repression were enacted by the Italian Government, but it took four years of bitter guerrilla fighting, with many casualties and not a few executions, to stamp out the rebellion, and complete success was possible only when the various foreign Governments, including that of the Papal States, formerly supporting the agitators, ended by withdrawing their assistance.

If we examine the character and operations of the Italian partisan movement during World War II we find a striking resemblance to that of 1861-65. In the first place, the bulk of the partisans were deserters from the Italian army which had disintegrated after the armistice and they had no wish to be recalled to fight on either side—neither under the RSI, which was creating a new army, nor under the Badoglio Government to serve the Allies against the Germans—and preferred to take to the woods and mountains. To these were added innumerable common criminals, released in one way or another in the chaotic state of the times, and not a few men to whom a life of adventure and plunder at the expense of the rest of the population appealed, together with a certain number of sincere anti-Fascists who thus hoped to contribute to the elimination of the Fascist regime, and various regular officers who, seeing in the RSI what seemed to them merely an anti-Royalist organization, joined the rebels. Finally the partisans, like their spiritual forebears of the 'sixties, readily secured foreign support, this time that of the Allied commands, which supplied them with unlimited arms, money and officers, discerning in the movement a means for sabotaging the German forces in North Italy from behind the lines. There was, however, in the partisan movement of 1943-1945 one all-important element which had no parallel in the banditry of 1861-65—international Communism. With this feature I shall deal later.

There is no serious account of the partisan movement yet available. Writers on the partisan side, mostly Communists or fellow-travellers, such as Luigi Longo or Riccardo Battaglia, have presented grossly exaggerated and preposterously glorified stories about it, wholly omitting its seamy side. The various Italian Cabinets, succeeding each other since the end of the War, have, owing to the electioneering strength and the excellent organization of the partisan movement, enacted a series of measures conferring extensive favors on the partisans and subjecting to criminal proceedings all who dare to give an accurate exposure of the facts. It is true that, in nearly all cases, when persons have been tried for offences of this kind they have been fully acquitted by the courts; but many writers capable of telling the truth about the movement prefer not to be involved in tiresome and expensive litigation.

The volume, *Un popolo alla macchia*, by Luigi Longo, himself one of the chief protagonists of the movement and now a member of the Chamber of Deputies, is so full of "suppressiones veri" and "suggestiones falsi" as to make of it a fairy tale, useless for the historian, although it does occasionally make some remarkable admissions.[1] Riccardo Battaglia's *Storia*

---

[1] Although the volume (Milan, 1947) appears under the name of Luigi Longo, it was actually written by the journalist Guglielmo Peirce, Longo himself being incapable of writing a book.

della resistenza italiana is little better. General Raffaele Cadorna, who played an important part in the movement on the
non-Communist side, has also produced a book, *La riscossa*,[2]
containing a good deal of information, but it chiefly concerns
his own disputes with other leaders and his attempt to get
himself appointed commander-in-chief of all the partisans. It,
too, contains much factious pamphleteering, and can in no way
be wholly relied upon as a source of historical information.

Ferruccio Parri, leader of the *Partito d'Azione*,[3] who played
an active part in the movement, has published several articles
about it.[4] He, too, is far from trustworthy, although like Longo
he does occasionally make some significant admissions. According to him, the movement arose by "spontaneous generation"
in September, 1943, but, as I have pointed out, it was chiefly
due to the existence of masses of disbanded soldiers and individuals eager for adventure and loot, of whom the Communist
leaders made good use. He claims that it was inspired by a
great political aim—that of carrying out "a war of liberation
and redemption arising from the people," but, while some individual partisans were no doubt so inspired, nearly all the
leaders and the majority of the rank and file were men with
very different aims.[5]

The aims and policy of Parri are well illustrated by an incident published in Guareschi's weekly paper *Candido* (April
17, 1955). At the end of November, 1943, a meeting took place
at Monchiero in Piedmont between Parri, Longo and an un-
named general then appointed by the Piedmontese CLN to
command the underground forces in that area. Parri told the
general that "a big noise must be made," to be produced as
follows: Fascists and German soldiers should be murdered, so
as to bring about retaliation against local inhabitants, and thus
intensify Italian hatred against the Germans and the Fascists;
bridges must be blown up, without troubling to ascertain

[2] Turin, 1952.
[3] After the war, Parri was for a short time Prime Minister—the worst Italy had
ever had; on his retirement he devoted himself to business activities.
[4] In *Mercurio*, December, 1945, and elsewhere.
[5] *Ibid.*

whether they were of importance for the communications of the occupying forces or not, but merely in order to provoke reprisals and make the population realize the dramatic character of the movement, even where no devastation had been produced by air bombings. These principles may be regarded as being in harmony, not with those actually held by Machiavelli, but with those commonly but wrongly attributed to that great thinker. They are certainly not in harmony with what is generally considered the conduct of civilized warfare.

Even Parri admits that "without Allied help partisan warfare would have been impossible." The Allies parachuted war materiel to them in large quantities and, as we shall see, ended by taking control of the movement as a whole. Parri also admits that "the partisans of the last hour" (those who joined up at the very last moment when hostilities were over and there were no more risks to be run) were a very bad lot, and that the movement was supported by a number of shady profiteers. He might have added that these undesirables were in the majority, even during the war.

The actual number of the partisans is very uncertain because they never had any central organization or register, and only a shadowy general command, which few of them recognized, and also because the Communist and other leaders always tried to exaggerate the dimensions of the movement.

Resistance did not begin immediately after the armistice, but only towards the end of 1943. Longo tells us that the birthplaces of the first groups were in the Castelli Romani and in parts of Umbria and the Abruzzi, and that one of the earliest formations was composed of Montenegrin prisoners who had escaped from the Colleferro and Spoleto P.O.W. camps and were then joined by some Italian partisans and a few regular officers. Other groups arose in various parts of Tuscany. One in Umbria consisted of about a hundred men of sundry nationalities—Greeks, Montenegrins, Croats, Slovenes, Albanians and Austrians, along with a handful of Italians, showing how the movement was at times to a large extent foreign. But few of these groups, in spite of Longo's magniloquence, carried out actions of a military character at that time, limiting themselves to a few murders and to a good deal of looting, besides some minor local operations.

The Royalist officers who had joined the movement found it very difficult to direct and command the partisans, who were suspicious of them and preferred to obey the orders of their own respective political parties, the various underground organizations, or the leaders chosen by themselves. Some of the latter tried to impose strict discipline on the partisan bands, not always successfully, and were often responsible for heavy losses in the ranks through their own incompetence and inexperience. General Operti, Q.M.G. of the Italian IV Army, then in Southern France, who had joined the movement, tried to give some unity at least to the bands operating in Piedmont, but only succeeded to a limited extent.[6]

Many of the partisan bands were composed primarily of Communists. Each of them was under a military commander, usually an amateur, and a political commissar, whose task was to keep the men operating consistently as Communists. These units took the name of "Garibaldi" battalions, brigades, or divisions—a strange misnomer, as the great Italian hero would have turned in his grave if he had found his name associated with gangs operating under orders from the foreign enemies of his own country.

Longo, with his experience in the Spanish Civil War and the radical "International Brigades," imposed a special character on the partisans and introduced into the units the typical Soviet institution of political commissars.[7] As he himself writes:

> They constituted one of the most disputed points in the military committees and the CLN. They were proposed and introduced by Communists and were at first opposed by all the others. They were not understood save in the manner described by Fascist lies and libels. The military officers saw in them an intolerable outrage to their own dignity and prestige; the politicians regarded them as a Communist innovation, designed to secure control of the military formations and to exploit them for party purposes; in the eyes of

[6]Cadorna, op. cit., p. 95.
[7]Longo, op. cit., passim.

the Conservatives, they were an exaggerated application of the political and popular principle in the military field which should remain purely military, i.e., exclusively in the hands of military men who alone could offer the desired guarantees of order, competence and discipline. We strove to the bitter end to support the institution of political commissars. Gradually, they were introduced into nearly all the formations, even if under other names such as that of representatives of the CLN or of civilian delegates, but always with the duties recommended by us.[8]

As a matter of fact, when commissars were introduced under the guise of CLN or civilian delegates into non-Communist units they acted like Trojan horses, operating with Muscovite methods. In any case, it was always Longo and the Communists who led the partisan movement and the CLN in general, neutralizing even the instructions of the Allied commands, and they usually acted under the orders imparted to them by the Russian MVD or of the Yugoslav OZNA.

Even though the Communists did not constitute an absolute majority in the partisan movement as a whole (they seem to have been about 48 per cent), it was always they who readily prevailed, because they were better organized than any of the others and had a definite policy of their own. The bands of a Socialist temper took the name of "Matteotti" units, those organized by the *Partito d'Azione* that of "Giustizia e Libertà," those of a Royalist and military character called themselves "Fiamme Verdi" (Green Flames). Although the Christian Democrats were very numerous in the country as a whole, their partisan bands were very few; some other bands professed themselves to be followers of Badoglio, and some belonged to the Rightist parties, but they amounted to very little. General Trabucchi, in his book, *I vinti hanno sempre torto*, states that the Communist and *Partito d'Azione* bands were of a definitely revolutionary character, and that their actions were in the last resort inspired by Moscow. Even when they received arms, parachuted by the Western Allies, they did not use all of them at the time, but buried considerable quantities for future use in a hoped-for Communist revolution.

[8] Adapted and abridged from Longo, *op. cit.*

There was often bitter rivalry between the different partisan groups and leaders. Many bands regarded particular districts as their own preserves, and resisted the interference of others by force of arms and with actual bloodshed. This state of things will remind American readers of Quantrill's band and other Civil War raiders who often degenerated into bandits, and of gang warfare among organized criminals and racketeers since 1920.

Many of the bands were devoid of all discipline, and got accustomed to the idea that, being well-armed and acting "on behalf of the Italian people for its liberation from Fascist tyranny," they were entitled to get all they wanted free, gratis and for nothing. According to General Trabucchi[9] and General Operti,[10] many of the bands consisted of common criminals or were dominated by them and indulged in every form of crime.

General Raffaele Cadorna, who played an important if not predominant part in the later events of the "liberation," deserves a few words. He was the son of Field Marshal Count Luigi Cadorna, the first Commander-in-Chief of the Italian Army in World War I, and descended from an old Piedmontese family of soldiers, traditionally devoted to the House of Savoy. He had followed a military career as a cavalry officer, without achieving any particular distinction, advancing by seniority. While professing dislike for officer-politicians (always a very small class in the Italian army before World War II) and great loyalty to the Monarchy, he admits that, even before July 25, 1943 (when he was in command of a division in the Royal army), he was already contacting some of the more active opponents not only of the Fascist regime, but of the Monarchy itself, such as Professor Concetto Marchesi,[11] one of the leaders of the underground Communist party, and the Republican, Dr. Cino Macrelli.[12] Later on, while still professing himself a Royalist, he did not hesitate to associate with various definitely anti-Monarchist politicians and to discuss with them the

[9] Op. cit., passim.
[10] Il tesoro della IV Armata (Turin, 1946) p. 144.
[11] Now a Communist Senator.
[12] La riscossa, passim.

advisability of getting rid of the King, and either placing the Prince of Naples on the throne under a Regency or even establishing a Republican regime. He seems to have studied the capacity of a "resistance" movement, quite independent of the Royal Army, to carry on guerrilla warfare behind the German and Italian Fascist lines, under the orders of the Allied Commands.

The latter saw some possible advantages in the partisan movement, which eventually became known as the "Corps of Volunteers of Liberty," and also recognized the authority, such as it was, of the CLN, then in contact with some of the partisan units.

Cadorna, living in Rome, while the city was still under German occupation, undertook to become the intermediary between the remnants of the regular army in the South and the underground parties and groups in the German-occupied areas. Through Colonel Giuseppe Cordero di Montezemolo, who possessed a wireless transmitting set, he could communicate with the Badoglio Government. Montezemolo was a gallant officer, a supporter of the Monarchy and an uncompromising anti-Fascist, but his actions in an area under German military occupation in wartime made him liable, if discovered, under the laws of any country in the world, to the severest penalties.

On October 16th, Montezemolo informed Cadorna that he had been asked by Badoglio to offer a seat in the Cabinet, then in process of formation, to Ivanoe Bonomi, and to find an officer to act as general commander of all the underground partisan units. Cadorna did not yet submit his own candidature for that position, although secretly aspiring to it, but he suggested Montezemolo himself as head of a military secretariat to coordinate the various disconnected units, outside and independent of political affiliations, promising to give him the support of his own authority. Cadorna, himself, again approached the politicians of the CLN, and his subsequent activities consisted chiefly of quarreling with the Communist leaders and political commissars. Bonomi and another ex-Minister, Count Alessandro Casati, innocently believed that the

underground forces, then about to be organized by Montezemolo, might be counted on to insure respect for law and order
in the transitional period between the evacuation of the Germans and the arrival of the Allies, a belief which future events
certainly did not justify.

Cadorna desired to secure a large number of regular officers
to command the partisan units. But, as he himself admits, he
found great difficulty in instilling in those officers a spirit of
"conspiratorial discipline." He tried to eliminate their old qualities of traditional military discipline and to convert them into
plotters collaborating with the Communists whom he professed,
probably honestly, to dislike. He had to take them into account,
owing to their organizing ability and ruthlessness, even when
those qualities were devoted to a policy going counter to the
interests of Italy and mainly conducted on behalf of a foreign
power. The most benevolent interpretation of his conduct
throughout this period is that, with his very limited political
insight, he failed to realize the utter subservience of most Communists to Russia.

Another difficulty hampering the activities of the partisans
was the lack of funds. Badoglio's Government had none to
spare, and Cadorna's appeal to an important Italian bank for a
loan, to be guaranteed by the said Government, was refused, as
the bank's directors had little confidence either in the movement or in its guarantor.

A puzzling point is the part played by some members of the
Italian clergy in the partisan movement, dominated as it was
by atheistic Communists. I have mentioned Monsignor Barbieri's action, and I may add that many monasteries offered
asylum to persons opposed to the German and Fascist authorities. This was done mainly from humanitarian motives, whatever may have been the personal sympathies of the abbots and
monks in those institutions, and the same hospitality was offered by them after the War to many Fascist personalities who
risked persecution at the hands of the Allies or the Italian anti-
Fascist authorities. But many ecclesiastics, some of them of
high rank, were definitely anti-Fascist, despite the great

favors conferred on the Church by Mussolini. It should be made clear that the Vatican itself never took any definite stand in this situation.

The Rome CLN was supposed to be the centre of the underground movements, but its authority never extended beyond the city limits, and its activities were mainly devoted to internal disputes and mutual jealousies,[13] while Cadorna continued to develop political contacts of various kinds. Early in November he met Manlio Brosio, an attorney of no particular distinction and a member of the Left wing of the Liberal Party,[14] who advocated the abdication of the King and the institution of a Regency, such as was suggested by Badoglio and Sforza, and expressed his belief in the possibility of an understanding with the *Partito d'Azione*. Montezemolo continued his Sisyphean task of extending the Rome underground front to the whole of unoccupied Italy, but without success.

In December, 1943, the Command of the fragmentary Italian army in the South issued a circular dividing unoccupied Italy into a number of military districts, each with its own military partisan units. The Command further decided to appoint General Quirino Armellini commander of the underground movement; his authority, however, proved short-lived, and was never recognized anywhere outside the capital.

Parri, who had now become head of the military department of the CLN, repaired to Switzerland to get in touch with Allen W. Dulles of the U. S. Legation in Bern, and with his British colleague, George B. MacCaffery, to prepare the plans for a general partisan campaign with hundreds of bands operating all over the territory of the RSI. But the Allied delegates, who seemed to have little confidence in the partisans, stated that what they wanted was merely a series of sabotage actions.[15]

In the meanwhile, the Allied armies were slowly advancing in the direction of Rome, meeting with vigorous resistance. At the end of October, the two main roads leading towards the

---

[13] Fulvia Ripa di Meana, *Roma clandestina*, (Turin, 1946), passim.
[14] Appointed Italian Ambassador in Washington in 1955.
[15] Parri in *Mercurio*, December, 1945.

capital were still strongly held by German and Italian units and, although General Montgomery promised his troops "Rome by Christmas," the autumn offensive failed with heavy losses. On the other hand, the Allied air bombings proved most successful and caused unlimited havoc in innumerable towns and villages of no military importance. Bombs were dropped anywhere and everywhere, and often parties of peasants and workmen on their way to or from their work were machinegunned from low altitudes. Large numbers of civilians of both sexes and all ages were killed or maimed in this manner.

CHAPTER XI

THE VENEZIA GIULIA

THE armistice had produced catastrophic confusion in the Northeastern provinces of Italy known as the Venezia Giulia, in Dalmatia, Croatia and Bosnia-Herzegovina, where the bulk of the Italian armed forces disintegrated. German forces then began to enter that area from the North, and took large numbers of the disbanded Italian soldiers prisoners and deported them to Germany. Two groups of Slavs had also been operating there—the Croatians of the newly-established Croatian State under Ante Pavelich, allied to the Axis powers, from the North; and Tito's Communist partisans, armed, financed and supplied by the Western Powers and by Russia, which had by now repudiated the Yugoslav Royalists, from the Southeast. Both of these two groups carried out wholesale slaughter of both captured prisoners and the civilian population.

By September 20th, Tito's bands were threatening the Italian city of Gorizia, which was defended by German and Italian forces, although a local CLN, largely composed of Communists, was ready to co-operate with Tito. Other of his units had penetrated into Istria and, before being driven out by the Germans and Italians, committed numerous atrocities on the population. Their method was to seize isolated Italian soldiers and civilians, bind their arms with wire, lead them to the edge of the *foibe* (natural pits) or the diggings of the bauxite mines, shoot them dead and throw them into these gullies. Many of them were tortured before being executed, while some were actually buried alive. Among them were some Italianized Slavs and a few German soldiers. We do not know the total number of the victims; according to some sources there were about 800 in all, but, according to others, this was the number of persons murdered in the town of Pisino alone. In one case, a woman was raped by fifteen Communists and tortured before being finally shot.

In one of the Quarnero islands, the local Titoist band was commanded by a man already condemned seventeen times for acts of violence. At Spalato, 105 persons were arrested, condemned to death and executed after a bogus trial; most of them were Italians, but they included four Croatian *Ustashi* (followers of the Croatian leader, Pavelich), and an Orthodox priest. In one place, a detachment of Italian soldiers came to an agreement with a band of Tito's partisans for the exchange of prisoners. The Italians released their prisoners and delivered them to the Yugoslav commander, but the latter, instead of releasing the Italians, sent the Italian commander a basket containing the eyes gouged out of the prisoners who had been murdered.

In Albania, too, the Communists had been helped by the Allies to seize power; they massacred all the Italians they could find, as well as thousands of non-Communist Albanians. Other Italian soldiers were killed by the Germans in the Ionian Islands.

In Bosnia and the Herzegovina, numerous Italian deserters formed themselves into an autonomous unit, allied with Tito's forces to fight against the Germans. But on November 29, 1943, a Yugoslav colonel ordered the disbanding of the unit and the incorporation of its members into a "Garibaldi" partisan Communist brigade, forming part of the IX Yugoslav Corps. Of these Italians, 3900 were thus incorporated, while others were disarmed and employed as forced laborers. The Italian commander, General Oxilia, had applied to the Badoglio Government for instructions, and was told to obey the orders of the Yugoslav Communist leaders. Badoglio thus hoped that those Italian soldiers might contribute to the Allied cause.

The various Italian groups who thus joined the Yugoslavs were then placed under the command of Communist political commissars, the chief of whom was an Italian renegade and deserter, Colonel Castagneri, an ex-centurion of the Fascist militia. Although he had in the end fought on the Yugoslav side against the Germans, he was later murdered by the Communists.

Many Italians, both officers and men, thought that after the armistice it was their duty to fight against the Germans on the side of the Western Powers. At first, they regarded Tito's Yugoslav bands as associated with the latter and believed that by lining up with Tito they were serving their own country and would be treated as allies. They did not realize that Tito, while taking advantage of all the Allied help he could get, was playing Russia's game to secure further support from Moscow, and aimed only at creating a Communist Yugoslavia of his own.[1] His persecution of non-Communists, which began at that time, has been going on ever since, intensified by his hatred of Italy and everything Italian. In this connection, he has made full use of the age-long rivalry between Italians and Slavs in the Adriatic countries.

[1] Fitzroy MacLean, in his book *Eastern Approaches* (London, 1949), writes that, while acting as British liaison officer with Tito's forces, he was summoned to London by Winston Churchill to report on the Balkan situation. On informing the Prime Minister that he believed that, if Tito proved victorious, he would set up a Communist Government in Yugoslavia, Churchill asked him if he intended to settle permanently in that country after the war. MacLean replied that such was not his intention, to which Churchill retorted: "Nor is it mine, so I do not care a damn what Government Tito sets up."

CHAPTER XII

SOUTHERN ITALY IN SERVITUDE

THE further the Allies advanced in Italy the larger was the area reduced to servitude, co-belligerence or no co-belligerence. On November 10, 1943, General Eisenhower informed the Badoglio Government that an Allied Control Commission for Italy (ACC), based on Article 37 of the "long" armistice, had been set up. While it was declared that some other provinces were to pass under Italian administration, this was to be exercised only under the supervision of the ACC or the Allied Military Government (AMG), the twin recently created Allied organizations. A third organ still operated to co-ordinate the policy of the United Nations in Italy—the Algiers Advisory Council, consisting of the British member, Harold Macmillan, the American, Robert Murphy, and the Russian, Vyshinsky, to whom the French diplomat, Massigli, was afterwards added. But, in Italy herself, the two ruling organs were the ACC and the AMG, dealing directly with the affairs of the country and with the Italian Ministers and officials. The British General, Maitland Wilson, who had succeeded Eisenhower as Commander of the Allied forces in the Mediterranean, again repeated (as per "long" armistice) that all Italy's economic resources were to be at the exclusive disposal of the Allies for any purposes they might wish.

The Allied Governments and their representatives in Italy continued to claim that they did not wish to interfere in the country's domestic policy (of a non-economic nature), but this was only "eye-wash," and the perpetual trotting out of the words "democracy" and "liberty" meant very little indeed. Even Senator Benedetto Croce, the worshipper of the Allies,[1] actually accused them (*horresco referens*) of resorting to Fas-

---

[1] *Per la vita della nuova Italia* (Naples, 1945), p. 24.

cist methods. The aim, particularly of the British Government, was, as the British publicist, George Glasgow, wrote, to ensure that Italy should always remain in the ranks of the have-not countries.[2] Another British writer stated that, if the War had been fought for democratic principles, "it would have been an infamous crusade and a negation of those principles," a destructive formula which subverted everything and destroyed all the best achievements of the past regime.[3]

Badoglio muddled along uncomfortably, without getting anywhere. He now took it into his head to create a new Ministry of Information,[4] and placed an obscure Socialist at its head, but this man's first statement to the press aroused such general hilarity that he was sent packing and the Ministry closed down.

In obedience to the dictates of the Moscow Conference, Badoglio enacted yet another decree (December 19, 1943) for the "defascistization" of the public services,[5] whereby all officials who had held authority under the past regime (himself excepted) were to be summarily dismissed. Bad as this measure appeared at the time, it was mild indeed compared with subsequent decrees of the same nature.

In the meanwhile, the members of the CLN never ceased abusing the King and the Government, while they continued to grovel before the Allied authorities. None of them adopted a dignified attitude or advocated greater autonomy for the country, but were ready to accept any humiliation. Nor did they cease wrangling among themselves, and their newspaper and pamphlet polemics reached an incredible degree of violence amid all the terrible sufferings and hardships of the people.

Of the various competing parties, the Christian Democrats had more supporters than any other, but it was the Communists, as usual, who secured the greatest influence, mainly because they were openly encouraged by the Allies.

[2] *Contemporary Review*, October, 1943.
[3] *The Nineteenth Century and After*, October, 1943.
[4] It was a revival of the Fascist Ministry of Popular Culture, suppressed after July 25, 1943, and now given a different name.
[5] See text in Tamaro, *op. cit.*, Vol. II, p. 338.

In the South, the Communists were in touch with those of
the North, and in a circular, reserved for the leaders only, they
made no attempt to conceal their real aspirations—the victory
of Russia and their own Italian dictatorship under Russian control. But, for the moment, cooperation with other parties was
advocated, together with expressions of national sentiment and
progressive democracy, so as to throw dust in the eyes of the
majority of decent citizens.[6]

The campaign against the King and Prince Humbert continued unabated, openly encouraged by Sforza and Croce.
Amidst the welter of grave problems overwhelming the country, these two men and a handful of others were so obsessed
by the single question of abolishing the Monarchy that they
ignored everything else, except the persecution of their political opponents. The economic crisis, reconstruction, and the
revival of national sovereignty, did not exist as problems for
them. The Western Allies, and even Russia, continued to support the Monarchy to some extent, so as to maintain the notion
of the responsibility of the whole nation for the War. Only Eden
once hinted in a speech in Parliament that the King and Badoglio might not always be left in power; he added, however,
that the question of the succession must be held over for the
time being, although the United States Government was not
too keen on leaving Victor Emmanuel on the throne.

A group of the South Italian CLN leaders now met in Bari
and decided to summon a congress of the whole organization
in Naples to decide on the chief questions of the day. The Allies,
at first, forbade the congress altogether for reasons of law and
order. The protests against this prohibition addressed to Roosevelt, Churchill and Stalin were probably not even seen by those
statesmen. Subsequently, however, permission was granted for
the congress to be held, but in some city not so near Rome as
Naples, and it was finally decided to hold it in Bari, in January,
1944.

The eminent Neapolitan jurist, former deputy and then Sena-

[6]Tamaro, *op. cit.*, pp. 319-320.

tor and ex-Under Secretary, Enrico De Nicola,[7] one of the few
competent political men then in Naples, succeeded in per-
suading Croce that the Monarchy should be maintained for
the present, although the King might be induced later to withdraw from public affairs and appoint Prince Humbert Royal
Lord Lieutenant of the Kingdom.

In addition to the various officially recognized parties, there
were still a great many Fascists, opposition to whom occasionally gave rise to riots, but there was no real Fascist movement.
Some former members of the party were arrested and prosecuted, and one of them, Salvatore Bramante, was tried for
sabotage and Fascist activities and condemned to death.

In Sicily, as we have seen, a movement of a separatist tendency arose, encouraged by the British authorities, with the
object of breaking up Italian unity and possibly of setting up
a British protectorate in the island.[8] Since the Allied invasion,
the authority of the Royal Government had been wholly eliminated there, and the egregious Gayre seems, as I said before,
to have acted in this connection on behalf of his Government.[9]

The ACC now ordered the Badoglio Government to remove
from Brindisi to Salerno, and on January 28, 1944, the CLN
congress was held at Bari, according to plan; but it merely
proved a talking shop of self-appointed politicians. The delegates were not to have been more than 90, but the ACC subsequently raised the figure to 120. Alberto Cianca, a repatriated
exile, and Tito Zaniboni, whose fame rested on his unsuccessful attempt to assassinate Mussolini in 1925, were chosen as
presidents. During the congress, the North Italian press published a letter that had been written by Zaniboni to Mussolini,
expressing his devout gratitude to the Duce for benefits accorded to himself and his family, and his hopes for the Duce's
success.[10]

At the Bari congress, Croce again openly admitted that he

[7] Raised to the Senate by the King on the proposal of Mussolini.
[8] Perhaps a reminiscence of the British occupation of Sicily during the Napoleonic wars.
[9] Op. cit., pp. 149-150.
[10] Giornale d'Italia of Rome, February, 1944.

had yearned for Italy's defeat because the War was a civil and not an international conflict, and he was then quite gushing in his praises of the Allies in their task of eliminating Fascism and all its works, apparently forgetting that one of the Allied Powers was Russia, who, wherever she established her domination, set up a tyranny far more ruthless than either Fascism or Nazism. He and Sforza again inveighed against the King and urged the abolition of the Monarchy, or at least the abdication of Victor Emmanuel III, which was demanded by other delegates. But, because the Allies had decided to keep him on the throne for the present, the demand was of no consequence. Sforza's speeches were so rabidly violent as to suggest that he was not in his right mind, while his statements on various subjects were, as usual, bristling with lies and nonsense. He afterwards addressed absurd messages to the United States Congress, the British House of Commons, General de Gaulle, Chiang Kai-shek, the Greek Government, and goodness knows whom else, and he "slobbered" over the Yugoslavs at the very moment when Tito was demanding the annexation of Trieste and Gorizia and burying murdered Italians in the "foibe" of Istria.

In the meanwhile, military operations were proceeding in a dilatory fashion and, after the occupation of Ortona on the Adriatic coast, the VIII Army front remained immobile, while the V Army in the Cassino area was continuously fighting without achieving any definite results. An operation of a different kind was undertaken on January 22, 1944, when an Allied force, consisting of one British and one American division and a Canadian unit under General Alexander, landed at Anzio to the south of Rome. The place of landing was unwisely chosen and the operation badly conducted, so that the hopes for a speedy occupation of Rome were disappointed: the German and Italian forces blocked the advance for the moment, while heavy losses were suffered on both sides.

The underground anti-Fascist elements in Rome were hoping that the Allies would soon reach the city, while the Allied command urged the partisans and the population generally to rise against the Germans. The CLN issued an appeal to that effect, but its members limited their activities to the usual internal rivalries, and the inhabitants did not move a finger. A few of the braver and really sincere anti-Fascist leaders, such as Montezemolo, De Grenet, De Carolis, and others, acted imprudently, and were arrested by the Germans.

If the Anzio landing achieved no immediate results, the air bombings continued to spread terror promiscuously. At Amelia in Umbria, a school was hit and 40 children were killed; at Rimini, Padua, Viterbo, Pistoia, Bologna, Pisa, Ferrara and other cities there were many civilian casualties, and priceless works of art were needlessly destroyed or seriously damaged. The railway lines and industrial plants were seldom hit, although much rolling stock was wrecked, together with hospitals, churches and private dwellings. On March 11th, the church of the Eremitani at Padua, with its beautiful Mantegna frescoes, was utterly destroyed, and in Rome the great Policlinico hospital and some private clinics were also hit.

Just before the Bari congress, President Roosevelt had cabled to the American representative on the Advisory Council for Italy on January 23rd that the Italian Cabinet must be reorganized on a democratic and liberal basis and remain in power until the complete "liberation" of the country had been achieved. He added that King Victor Emmanuel must be dethroned, but that the question of Monarchy itself should be decided later by the Italian people.[11]

Churchill was not pleased with these instructions, and insisted that the King should remain on the throne until some better arrangement could be made. For him, as indeed also for Roosevelt, the King and Badoglio were merely instruments to play upon, kept in power or removed according to the requirements of Allied policy at the moment; the wishes or interests of the Italian people were never considered, although Roosevelt did occasionally talk about them. The British Premier accused Sforza of having broken his promise about the Monarchy—he had known Sforza better than did Roosevelt, so

[11] Hull, *op. cit.*, Vol. II, p. 1552.

he should not have been surprised, and might well have described him as something worse than "the old fool."

On February 10th, the ACC issued a decree handing over various provinces, including the islands of Sicily and Sardinia, to the Italian administration, and Badoglio addressed grateful thanks to the Allies for this dispensation, stating that it was the first step towards the reestablishment of Italian unity and liberty, although it was actually nothing of the kind. General Eisenhower hastened to add, in fact, that the powers, rights and immunities of the United Nations, of the ACC, and of the Commander-in-Chief of the Allied forces in Italy, remained unaltered. On the removal of the seat of the Italian Government from Brindisi to Salerno, the King settled at Ravello. Badoglio then took over the Ministry of Foreign Affairs and promoted the Undersecretaries to the rank of Ministers.

An Italian executive "Giunta" was now set up with the task of regulating the general situation of the country through the various political parties, independently of, and sometimes in opposition to, the Government. This might appear an unnecessary super-structure but, as it had no more real authority than the Government itself, it did not very much matter what it did or said. On the question of a new Cabinet for Italy, Churchill stated in the House of Commons that the King and Badoglio had done much to bring Italy into the War on the side of the Allies, but that a new Government would be formed after the occupation of Rome.[12] At the end of January, Badoglio again asked Roosevelt that Italy be recognized as a regular ally, but the President replied (February 21st) that he could not grant this request "until the Italian Government came also to include the articulate political groups of anti-Fascist liberal sentiments" (i.e., including the Communists). Two days later, the United States Government instructed its representatives on the Council for Civil Affairs of the General Staff to lend moral support to the above-mentioned "Giunta," for Washington regarded it as something vaguely democratic, without knowing exactly what

[12] Hull, *op. cit.*, p. 1554.

it was, and without consulting the British Government on the matter.[13]

A certain number of Italian prisoners of war were now repatriated from overseas countries and concentrated in camps in Apulia; but, to the consternation both of the Allied and Italian authorities, they at once proceeded to sing Fascist songs.[14] General Reisoli told the Allied officers that he had collaborated with them only in obedience to the orders of the King, and that otherwise he would have considered it his duty to remain on the side of the Germans. The British received this statement very respectfully.

Fighting of a desultory nature went on all through February, with no special results except the destruction of several towns and villages in the Pontine area and also of the extensive land reclamation works carried out before the War. Because these constituted a Fascist achievement, their destruction was in harmony with a general anti-Fascist policy. Further south, the town of Cassino was wrecked, but the Germans still held out among its ruins. On February 15th, a general bombardment of the historic abbey of Montecassino (high above the town) was begun, under the pretext that important German forces were concentrated in it. As a matter of fact, there were no Germans in it at the time, and the Allied command knew this, but the magnificent building was reduced to a heap of rubble.[15] The junction between the Allied forces on the Anzio front and those near Cassino was not yet effected.

Some partisan bands operated here and there in the Monti Lepini and in the Sabina, their activities being limited to the murder of some German and Italian stragglers and the sprinkling of nails along the roads. East of Cassino, a band of common criminals, who had escaped from the Sulmona penitentiary, posed as partisans and took to plundering the local inhabitants.

Among the political and economic activities of the ACC were the prohibition of any rise in wages, despite the heavy

[13] Tamaro, *op. cit.*, Vol. II, p. 140, note.

[14] Reisoli, *Fuoko su Adolfo, fuoko su Benito* (Naples, 1948), p. 117.

[15] This was the third destruction of the Abbey—the first by the Saracens, the second by an earthquake.

price inflation, the holding up of all improvements in the chaotic state of communications, and the strict limitation of food supplies for the civilian population. The various parties continued their dog-fights amid the indifference of the mass of the people. The Allied authorities allowed the Leftist parties to hold a public meeting in Naples, but it was attended by only some 4,000 persons out of a total population of close to a million. Violent speeches against the King and the Government were delivered, and the general tone of the meeting was definitely Communist. We have here still another example of the Allied policy of supporting the Communists, which was to reach its climax after the end of hostilities.

CHAPTER XIII

THE SITUATION IN "NON-LIBERATED" ITALY

Mussolini had hoped that, with the enactment of the law of February 12, 1944, providing for the socialization of many industries, he would secure the unanimous support of the working masses for his Government. A part of them did, indeed, give it their adherence, others continued to remain more or less attached to extremist tendencies, while the majority waited on events without listening to Communist propaganda.

Early in March, the Communist members of the Rome CLN tried to stage a general strike throughout the territory of the RSI, but the Socialists, who at that time were about to come to an agreement with Mussolini, largely through the influence of the journalist Carlo Silvestri,[1] refused to take part in it. A strike of sorts did, indeed, break out, and the underground Red press claimed that the strikers were a million in all, obviously an exaggeration. According to the RSI Government services, the total number was only a little over 200,000, probably somewhat less than the true figure. In Piedmont, the main railway lines operated regularly, and only a few local lines were held up by partisan action. The strikes in the industrial plants were very few, and had come to an end by March 8th. Throughout the strike, Mussolini had refused to countenance the drastic measures of repression demanded by Hitler.

It may be remembered that at this time strikes were going on in England, in the dockyards, the coal mines and elsewhere on a larger scale than those in Italy.

Strife between groups of Fascists and anti-Fascists was occurring sporadically in various parts of the RSI, causing deep distress to the Duce, who had always hoped for unity and

[1] A Socialist journalist, but a personal friend of Mussolini.

101

cooperation throughout the country in view of the grave international and military situation. The underground GAP (partisan action groups) had murdered various Fascists, among others Eugenio Facchini, Commissioner of the Bologna Fascist Federation, a disabled war veteran and a man of sterling honesty and high character. The Fascist Party Secretary, Alessandro Pavolini, at once proceeded to Bologna to carry out measures of reprisal, and had ten men arrested and tried before the special tribunal for complicity in the crime. The accused were condemned to death, and while Mussolini heard of the matter in time to pardon one of them, the others were executed, a serious and unnecessary mistake.

The partisan movement was beginning to show some activity in Central Italy by the end of 1944, but nothing of importance occurred, and the local population was not involved or subjected to reprisals by the Germans.[2] Greater rigor was shown when the movement spread further north. In the Val Brembana, the Val Masino, the Valle di Pellico and the neighborhood of Intra, severe reprisal measures were carried out by the Germans, and 100 rebels were executed. Similar events took place in Tuscany.

It should be borne in mind that, under the Hague Conventions on the laws of war, an occupying army in time of war is entitled to execute *francs tireurs* (i.e. partisans) unless they are organized in regular units under recognized commands and wear uniforms or other visible distinguishing signs and emblems. Few of the partisans in Italy met these requirements, especially in the early period of the movement.

In spite of these acts of violence, Mussolini was convinced that the time had arrived for a new attempt at pacification, and he instructed the Prefect of Turin to meet the above-mentioned General Operti for this purpose. The negotiations lasted some time, but no results were obtained and Operti withdrew from the partisan movement.[3] But 57 partisan leaders recently captured by the Fascist authorities accepted Mussolini's amnesty

[2] Cadorna, *op. cit.*, p. 94.
[3] From Operti's unpublished memorandum.

and, while some of them abandoned the movement and retired to their homes, others actually entered the service of the RSI.

What caused Mussolini the deepest distress was the risk that there should be fighting between Italian regular armed forces on the two opposed sides, but as a matter of fact such encounters rarely took place. On the other hand, he derived intense satisfaction from all reports of acts of bravery performed by Italian soldiers, such as those of the "Barbarigo" battalion on the Anzio front, of the "Nembo" division in Corsica, of a Bersaglieri battalion operating against Slav partisans on the Carso, and of the Black-Shirt legion against Tito's forces in Croatia. One day, a communiqué issued by Badoglio's Government reported the brilliant action of another Bersaglieri battalion fighting against German forces in the South, and the Under-Secretary for Foreign Affairs, Count Serafino Mazzolini, heard the Duce expressing his deep satisfaction at the news. "But they are Badoglio's troops," exclaimed Mazzolini. "They are Italians and they are fighting bravely," replied Mussolini, "and that is what counts above all!"[4] That Italian soldiers should fight and fight bravely was in Mussolini's opinion essential in order to redeem the Italian army from the ignominy of the armistice, on whichever side they might be fighting.

[4]From a statement made by Count Mazzolini's Chef de Cabinet, Alberto Mellini, and reported by him to Tamaro.

CHAPTER XIV

RUSSIA INTERVENES

O<small>N</small> March 3, 1944, Roosevelt announced that a part of the Italian fleet was to be handed over to Russia, a decision which produced a deplorable impression all over Italy, except of course among the Communists. Even Badoglio, showing for once a modicum of dignity, threatened to resign. Later it was agreed that, while Russia was entitled to a share of the Italian fleet, she would, for the present, receive instead a corresponding tonnage of Allied shipping, to be returned when the Italian ships were handed over to her later on. In this way, Russia was to be strengthened in the one field of armaments in which she was weakest, so that she might be a greater future menace to civilization on the sea as well as on land and in the air. This was regarded by the Western Governments as one more step towards the total destruction of Nazism and Fascism, and as a guarantee of general peace for all.

On March 13th, the Russian Government suddenly took a step which surprised the Western Powers and aroused their strong disapproval. It, in fact, announced that, at the request of the Government of Italy, it had agreed to an exchange of diplomatic representatives between the two countries. This was done without informing the Western Allies.

Bogomolov, Vyshinsky's successor on the Allied Advisory Council, had on March 4th informed Badoglio that, if he would put in a request for an exchange of representatives, it would be granted; on the 7th, the Italian request was, in fact, sent in, and on the 11th it was granted. Thus, while the initiative was undoubtedly Russian, it was made to appear as if Badoglio had taken the first step—a typically Russian *modus operandi*.

Russia's object was not, of course, to bring the war with Italy to an end, but to impress Italy with the Russian moderation and generosity as compared with other belligerents, and to let her see that it was easier to come to an understanding with Moscow than with London or Washington. Italy was thus offered the possibility of emerging from the iron cage of the armistice, but the Government, while pleased at the idea of diplomatic exchanges, failed to take advantage of the possibilities offered and merely thanked the Russian Government, while remaining ever more closely associated with the Western Powers. This rebuff Stalin did not forget.

Both Great Britain and the United States were much annoyed at Russia's unexpected move, and General MacFarlane at once protested that Italy had no right to conclude agreements with any Power save by permission of the Allied High Command, and that all matters of the kind should pass through the sieve of the ACC. A *Reuters* message flatly stated that if Italy was a "co-belligerent" against Germany, she was also an enemy of the Western Powers, i.e., she was both a friend and an enemy at the same time, a somewhat illogical statement.[1] Cordell Hull placed Italy on exactly the same footing as Germany, and threatened her with foreign control for an indefinite period if she misbehaved. He then sent instructions to the American Ambassador in Moscow, Averell Harriman, to the effect that all questions concerning Italy must be submitted to the Allied military authorities in that country and that no separate negotiations could be allowed.[2] In the end, however, the United States and Great Britain accepted Russia's action, as they always did, and eventually, as we shall see, they themselves established diplomatic relations with Italy.

While the Western Governments professed to be terribly shocked at Russia's initiative, they made a move which contributed more than anything else to the expansion of Russian influence in Italy. It was, in fact, an American ship which landed Russia's confidential agent and Muscovite lord lieutenant, Palmiro Togliatti, in Naples. He was the bearer of the Kremlin's

[1] In World War II, logic, like international law, justice and generosity, seems to have gone out of fashion.
[2] Hull, *op. cit.*, Vol. II, pp. 1556-7.

106   THE LIBERATION OF ITALY

orders to the Italian Communist party to support Badoglio's Government, but to get some Communist members into it.

Togliatti, a corpulent, bespectacled, Piedmontese quasi-intellectual, had as a young man joined the Socialist party in Turin (the Communists were then nonexistent). But, soon after the outbreak of World War I, he resigned from it and joined Mussolini's secessionist Socialist movement in favor of Italian intervention in the war against the Central Powers. After the War, he got himself reinstated in the old Socialist Party and, when the new Communist Party was founded at Leghorn, in 1921, he at once joined it and became its leader. On its outlawry, in 1925, he migrated to France and organized some of the Italian emigrants in that country for revolutionary action in Italy, at a time when the Soviet Government had begun to adopt a more conciliatory attitude towards the West.

He then proceeded to Russia as the delegate of the Italian Communists at the Moscow Congress of the Third International where Stalin was opposing Trotsky's policy. Togliatti, hitherto a devoted follower of the latter, now declared his fealty to Stalin, returned to Paris and proceeded to get rid of some of the Italian Communists opposed to his own policy by sending them to Italy on bogus secret missions, thereby enabling the Italian police to get hold of them. In 1927, he assumed Russian citizenship and settled in Russia, where he secured an appointment on the board of the Third International. He went to Spain during the Civil War, not to take part in any fighting but to direct administrative activities. After the collapse of the Spanish Reds, he returned to Russia, where he remained until he was brought back to Italy under American and British auspices, to take over the leadership of the resuscitated Italian Communist Party.

Russia now intended to take the lead in Italy's domestic affairs, and made a first step by adding one more performer to that somewhat shoddy contraption, the CLN, in the person of Togliatti. For the moment, his line was to profess himself an advocate of Italian national unity, while keeping himself ever subordinate to the instructions and interests of Russia. His immediate program was to produce order, whereas the Western Allies tolerated and even encouraged disorder. He did not "blabber" outworn democratic commonplaces, but spoke a new language—that of Stalin, who declared that he wished Italy to have her place in the community of nations provided she toed the Communist line.[3]

[3] See Togliatti's first speech in Tamaro, *op. cit.*, Vol. II, pp. 503-5.

CHAPTER XV

THE VIA RASELLA OUTRAGE

THE situation in Rome in the early months of 1944 was a peculiar one. Although nominally under the RSI Government, Italian officials, unlike their colleagues further North, only exercised limited authority, and the city was ruled for the most part by the German command, represented since 1943 by General Stahel, an intelligent officer, but a rigid disciplinarian and no friend of the Fascists. At the end of October of that year, he was succeeded by General Mältzer, a mixture of good nature, buffoonery and ferocity, and very often intoxicated, assisted by Kappler and Dollmann, intelligent men but of doubtful character. Field Marshal Albrecht Kesselring, the honest and highly capable Commander-in-Chief of the German forces in Italy, exercised his authority in Rome only indirectly.

The food situation, never good at any time in Rome, was constantly getting worse, as the Allied bombing raids interrupted communications by rail and road; even the supplies collected by the Papal Assistance Committee only reached the city irregularly and with difficulty. The water supply, electricity, gas and coal were always in danger of being cut off from time to time, and the cost of living increased, although at a lower rate than in occupied Italy.

On February 3, 1944, the Rome police entered the San Paolo College and arrested 63 persons—anti-Fascists, Royalist officers and Jews—who had taken refuge within its walls, some of them, including a general, sacrilegiously attired as monks. The Jews were being hunted by the German rather than by the Italian authorities, who, in spite of the racial laws of 1938, tended to disregard them and even to help those in distress. But the police were trying to get hold of certain politically dangerous persons hiding in the building. The Vatican protested against this action, as the College enjoyed extraterritorial privileges under the Lateran Pacts of 1929, and on this point it was in the right; but the Italian Government was also in the right, for the immunity should not have been exploited for purposes other than those for which it had been established. Among the persons arrested in the college there were none for whom Christian charity and the right of asylum might have been invoked. The Italian authorities called attention to the fact that, while the Vatican protested concerning this incident, it had never done so with regard to the large number of priests, friars and nuns killed or maimed and the vast number of churches and convents wrecked by Allied air bombings.[1] Finally, after an exchange of sharply worded notes, the matter was tacitly dropped, both sides realizing that they had been in the wrong.

In addition to the deplorable food situation, the population of Rome was in a state of constant alarm and apprehensiveness owing to the frequent arrests carried out by the German authorities, the roping-in of men for labor on the defense works, and the occasional curfew ordinances. The members of the underground revolutionary groups went on ceaselessly talking and plotting, but without inflicting any serious damage on the German or Italian authorities. There were occasional acts of mild sabotage, a few murders, and the throwing of a bomb at a small Fascist parade, which killed or injured several passers-by who had taken no part in the ceremony. Underground plotting became a fashionable pastime in certain circles, and the plotters liked to compare themselves with the Italian conspirators of the *Risorgimento* period, but the comparison was hardly apt, as the latter were working for a really national cause and not on behalf of invading foreign armies.

General Armellini, who, as I said before, had been appointed by the Italian command in the South as head of the underground forces, then limited to a few groups of partisans in Rome and the Latian hill districts, was bitterly opposed by the Communists in the CLN. They finally induced Badoglio to

---

[1] Down to the end of September, 1943, the number of monks, nuns and priests killed was, according to the data of the Holy Office, 1347, while the damage done to church property was estimated at two billion lire.

cancel his appointment, substituting General Bencivenga in his place as "head of the civil and military command in Rome." Bencivenga was an honest man, with a good military record in World War I, but filled with great personal ambition. He ended by detaching himself altogether from the CLN, whose internal dissensions went on increasing.

Several of the anti-Fascists arrested by the Germans were interned in the German police prison in Via Tasso, under the sinister Kappler, and often brutally treated, even if some of the stories about what went on in that place were exaggerated. Among the men arrested were General Simone Simoni, Colonel Giovanni Frignani (who had arrested Mussolini on July 25), Colonel Giuseppe Cordero di Montezemolo and the diplomat De Grenet.

In Via Romagna, an irregular and unauthorized Italian police organization set up a prison similar to that in Via Tasso, under a man named Koch, and the prisoners were not less brutally treated there than in the German prison. There were still other irregular police bodies on the rampage, but occasionally the German regular police forces raided their premises and disbanded their members. It is a significant fact that the partisans and other anti-Fascist plotters never committed, or even attempted to commit, acts of violence against Mältzer, Kappler, Koch, or any of the leading German or Italian Fascist personalities, but usually chose quite insignificant and inoffensive individuals as their victims.

Countess Fulvia Ripa di Meana, a relative of Colonel Montezemolo, tried to secure the release of the latter and of some other persons detained in Via Tasso. In the case of Montezemolo nothing could be done, but several others were released by means of forged documents, while some prominent men, such as the Socialist leader, Pietro Nenni,[2] and the Social Democrat,

---

[2] Pietro Nenni, a funny little man with an egg-shaped head, afterwards the leader of the Socialist Party, closely allied to and practically absorbed by the Communist Party, had been one of the founders of the Bologna Fascist group in 1919, and is said to have turned against Fascism when Mussolini was chosen as its leader instead of himself. While an exile in Paris and in the Spanish Civil War, he engaged in unexplained business affairs. For a short time he was Minister of Foreign Affairs and flooded that Department with Socialist and Communist incompetents.

Giuseppe Saragat (both of them afterwards Cabinet Ministers) succeeded in evading arrest.

The Rome Fascist Federation had intended to celebrate the anniversary of the foundation of the Fascist movement (March 23rd) by a public parade, but the German authorities, very wisely, under the circumstances of the time, forbade it. The mass of the inhabitants of Rome had indeed adapted themselves to the situation, uncomfortable and unsatisfactory as it was, and the Allies were beginning to be anxious about this apathy, which did not help them to speed up their plans. They felt it necessary to do something to stir up greater hatred against the Germans and their Fascist allies. In this connection the Allied aims closely coincided with those of the Italian Communists, although the ultimate aims of the two groups differed very considerably. The Communists now thought that the time was ripe for a sensational *coup*, even if it involved disastrous consequences for innocent people. These then were the twin origins of what is known as the Via Rasella outrage, with its grim sequel at the Fosse Ardeatine.

Two members of the "military committee" of the Rome CLN, Pertini and Bauer, had intended to take advantage of the Fascist anniversary celebration staged for March 23rd for an action of their own, but, when the German authorities, as I have said, forbade the ceremony, they decided to seek another occasion for an outrage calculated to create a deep impression on all concerned. There was a small unit of the German traffic police, consisting of South Tirolese from the Alto Adige, physically unfit for front-line military duties, and these men were selected as victims. They usually returned from their duties to their quarters every afternoon in a motor truck, passing along Via Rasella, a narrow street in the centre of Rome near Via del Tritone.

The decision to commit an outrage was definitely contrary to the orders of General Armellini, still nominally in command of the underground groups (his dismissal being scheduled for March 22); but the plotters paid little attention to the orders of men supposed to be their superiors, or to the German posters announcing rigorous reprisals for all acts of violence. The circumstances of the affair were as follows:

A student named Romano Bentivegna, disguised as a crossing sweeper, and one Alfio Marchini, had filled a rubbish cart with explosives and placed it in Via Rasella. When the truck conveying the traffic policemen arrived on the scene, another conspirator, Franco Calamandrei, gave the prescribed signal and Bentivegna lighted the fuse, after which all the plotters took to their heels in good time. Soon afterwards a terrific explosion followed, killing 32 of the policemen and several passers-by, including a child, and wounding many other persons. The underground press described the episode as "an act of magnificent and heroic patriotism."

The Germans were, naturally, furious, and Hitler, as soon as he heard of the foul deed, ordered that fifty hostages be executed for every German soldier killed, while Himmler demanded that all the inhabitants of the quarters of Rome most infected with Communism—San Lorenzo, Testaccio and Trastevere—should be deported. But Field Marshal Kesselring declared that such a vast transfer of people along the roads leading out of Rome would attract concentrated machine-gun fire by the Allied air force and cause the deaths of thousands of persons, while the feeding and housing of the survivors would represent an almost insoluble problem. It would also involve the withdrawal of two German divisions from the Anzio and Cassino fronts, which could ill be spared. General von Mackensen and his chief of staff, Colonel Hauser, were of the same opinion, as were also Dollmann (then chief interpreter) and other German officers and officials in the city, and the deportation plan was dropped.

The number of hostages to be executed was reduced to ten for every policeman killed, or 320 in all, later raised to 330 as one of the men wounded in the explosion died soon afterwards. This proportion of reprisals, terrible indeed, was no higher than that applied by other belligerents; the British shot many hundreds of Sicilian peasants and destroyed whole villages in the island where a few parachutists had been killed in consequence of the indignation aroused by the wholesale slaughter of the inhabitants of the district by air bombings. In other instances, even higher proportions of hostages were executed by both sides in various theatres of the war. The Hague Convention recognized the legitimacy of the execution of hostages, without specifying or limiting the actual proportions of such actions.

Kappler had ordered that the men to be executed by way of reprisal should be chosen among such prisoners as were already under sentence of death; others liable to the same penalty were added. Because, even so, the requisite number was not reached, the Rome Chief of Police, Caruso, was contacted and ordered to hand over a few more men accused of common crimes, and also some Jews, so as to reach the figure of 335 hostages. On March 24th, they were conveyed to a spot along the Ardea road where there were some natural caves known as the Fosse Ardeatine, shot by a German firing squad and buried in the caves. Among those executed were General Simoni, Colonel Montezemolo, De Grenet, Lordi, Martelli Fenulli, Professor Pilo Albertelli, Colonel Friggani, head of the military organization of the *Partito d'Azione,* the priest Don Pappagallo, Aldo Finzi, formerly one of Mussolini's secretaries, to mention only a few names. All of them met their fate bravely.

The authors of the Via Rasella outrage might well have saved the lives of the 335 hostages if they had had the courage to give themselves up, as the heroic carabiniere, Salvo D'Acquisto, had done at Torre di Palidoro north of Rome, falsely accusing himself of an outrage against German soldiers, in order to save the lives of the innocent villagers. But the Via Rasella terrorists took good care to save their own skins by flight, leaving the hostages to their cruel fate. It was only after all danger was past that they reappeared on the scene to pose as patriotic heroes, to be decorated with medals for valor, and receive other rewards as well.

The episode is commemorated every year on March 23rd, and tablets have been placed on the houses of the men executed. The reprisals were certainly cruel and ruthless, but the action of the terrorists was infinitely more criminal, both with regard

to the German victims and to those of the Fosse Ardeatine, for
the plotters were directly and personally responsible for all
the tragic consequences. According to Carlo Silvestri, the outrage did contribute to some extent to the result desired by those
who had inspired it.[3] If it in no way weakened the German position, the responsibility of the Italian authorities and especially
that of the Chief of Police Caruso was involved and a further
breach was effected between the RSI Government and a large
section of public opinion in Rome. This is exactly what the
Allies wanted, and if it cost the lives of 33 Germans and 335
Italians, no matter. The end justifies the means.

Other episodes of the same kind, although on a smaller and
less sensational scale, occurred in various parts of Italy. While
Mussolini did all he could to prevent reprisals, whether carried
out by the Germans or by the local Italian authorities, his intervention was often unsuccessful, owing to the chaotic situation, the inadequate means of communication, and the existence
of many different police forces under conflicting authorities, or
sometimes recognizing no authority at all—"he don't obey no
orders unless they is his own."

[3] *Mussolini, Graziani e gli antifascisti* (Milan, 1949), pp. 107 et seq.

CHAPTER XVI

THE LORD LIEUTENANCY

O^N April 3, 1944, Badoglio addressed yet another request to Roosevelt that Italy be regarded as an ally, declaring that a new Government, comprising representatives of all the anti-Fascist groups, such as the President himself had demanded, was about to be formed. He added that the United States would thus secure for itself a predominant position in Italy and in the Mediterranean, to the exclusion of Russia, and that Great Britain would be induced to adopt a more constructive and less uncompromising policy.

Hull answered on April 9th that Italy was free to choose whatever Government she preferred, but that every trace of Fascism must be wholly obliterated, and that the chief obstacle to the formation of a really free Government was the King. Hull, accordingly, instructed Robert Murphy to tell His Majesty that he must abdicate.[1]

On the 10th, in fact, Murphy, together with Harold Macmillan and General MacFarlane, asked to be received by the King on the pretext of presenting to him the new High Commissioner for Italy, Sir Noël Charles.[2] On being received, Murphy instead brusquely intimated to His Majesty that he must abdicate the next day.

Victor Emmanuel rejected this ultimatum and only agreed to resign his royal authority in favor of his son Prince Humbert when the Allies occupied Rome. Murphy finally accepted this compromise solution (April 12th), but he used very discourteous language during the interview. The King stated that he was ready to issue a proclamation renouncing his powers, (without actually abdicating), but that he did so only under the compulsion of the Governments of the United States and

[1] Hull, *op cit.*, Vol. II, p. 1558.
[2] Formerly Councillor to the British Embassy in Rome.

of Great Britain. He then concluded: "Now I must ask you gentlemen to withdraw, as your presence has annoyed me sufficiently."[3]

The whole episode was literally a diplomatic "hold-up" of the aged and ailing King, whose situation, after a reign of 44 years, often glorious ones, in which he had lost one war after winning five, was indeed worthy of a Greek tragedy. Whatever errors he had committed, his conduct in this tragic situation was at least full of dignity.

The ACC issued a communiqué stating that its representatives had merely made a suggestion to the King, but this was, to put it mildly, a "terminological inexactitude." Even Badoglio commented: "It was a suggestion, but one presented with a pistol pointed at the King's head."[4] On the 12th, the King's proclamation was issued concerning the institution of the Royal Lord Lieutenancy, which was to come into operation after the Allies had reached Rome.[5]

The King, in speaking with some intimates of the discourteous manner in which he had been treated by the representatives of the victorious Powers, contrasted this with the extreme courtesy shown by Charles V towards Francis I after the Battle of Pavia in 1525. A report of this remark happened to reach the United States Command, and caused much surprise and some confusion, for nobody in either the Information services or the Department of Psychological Warfare seemed to have heard of the battle to which Victor Emmanuel was alluding. One of the persons present exclaimed in astonishment: "But what on earth did the King mean in talking about a battle at Pavia? That city is much too far behind the front lines for any battle to have taken place in its vicinity." The gentleman thus puzzled was a prominent American communications (telegraph, telephone and radio) executive. Although he had been for nearly thirty years in the American Naval Reserve service, he had seen little or no active battle duty at sea or elsewhere. But,

[3] Degli Espinosa, op. cit., p. 333.
[4] Badoglio, op. cit., p. 194.
[5] Text in Tamaro, op. cit., Vol. II, pp. 560-1.

by 1944, he had somehow managed to attain the rank of rear admiral, and was wearing an admiral's uniform on the occasion mentioned. He was vested with virtual proconsular powers in Italy as High Commissioner of the Allied Control Commission. His name was Ellery Wheeler Stone.

After a sequence of further disputes between the different parties, both within and without the CLN, the new Cabinet was formed on April 21st. Badoglio remained Prime Minister and also kept the Ministry of Foreign Affairs in his own hands, while the civilian members of the previous Cabinet had to re-sign. The Liberal Professor, Arangio-Ruiz, became Minister of Agriculture, the banker, Quintieri, Minister of Finance, Professor Omodeo (of the *Partito d'Azione*) of Education, the journalist, Alberto Tarchiani (of the same party), of Public Works, the Christian Democrat, Albini, of the Interior, while the Communists, Togliatti and Gullo, Count Sforza and Croce became Ministers without portfolio. It was the first time that, in Italy or in any other country, two Communists sat in the same Cabinet side by side with a multi-millionaire banker. The Allies themselves had insisted, as we have seen, that all the Italian parties (except the Fascists, who still were supported by a very large sector of public opinion) be included in the new Government, although this insistence seemed superfluous because the Allies could impose whatever measures or decisions they pleased, whoever happened to be in office at the time.

Sforza and Croce, who had repeatedly covered the King with vulgar abuse, now swore fealty to his Government, no doubt with their tongues in their cheeks. The new combination was, indeed, like its predecessor, a shadow Government, under the orders of the invaders and devoid of all authority. Although it called itself a "War Cabinet," it was only allowed an army of 14,000 men, nearly all of them employed in non-fighting services.

The day before the King's proclamation, the British Government informed that of the United States that it repudiated any idea of an alliance with Italy, and that it intended to request Russia not to suggest the least modification of Italy's

international status. The intention, in fact, was to wait until
the whole of Italy was occupied by the Allies, and then to impose still harsher conditions on her. Badoglio's letter to Roosevelt (April 24th)[6] on the disastrous conditions of the country
had no effect, and Hull, indeed, cabled to Murphy on the 29th
reaffirming that there was no idea of conferring on Italy the
status of an ally.[7]

Sforza, although not yet Minister of Foreign Affairs, took it
upon himself to issue a program for Italy's foreign policy, which
was based on a sniveling and servile attitude, but stated that
the Italians were proud of fighting against the Germans (which
they were not allowed to do).

The Government's general program (April 27th) stated that
a constituent Assembly would be summoned at an early date,
but their chief activity for the moment was, as usual, to be a
continuation of the policy of persecuting the Fascists, which
could be done without interference on the part of the Allies;
indeed, with their encouragement and cooperation. Sforza was
now appointed High Commissioner for sanctions against Fascism, a task in which he reveled, with the fanatical Mario
Berlinguer as his chief lieutenant. A drastic new decree was
enacted for "defascistization" on May 26th[8] which even the
most anti-Fascist Liberals criticized. Togliatti, of course, gave
it his blessing, stating that Fascism should be regarded as "a
crime against the Italian people." The Allies, whose officers
and officials took part in these proceedings, perhaps, did not
then realize that they were merely playing the game of the
Russians and of Communism in general.

Another large batch of Fascist or pro-Fascist civil servants,
diplomats, professors and teachers were dismissed, many of
them imprisoned, and not a few condemned to death for acts
which were not offenses when committed—a foretaste of the
measures enacted on July 27, 1944, and of the Nuremberg
abomination.

[6] *Ibid.*, pp. 569-70.
[7] Hull, *op. cit.*, Vol. II, p. 1559.
[8] Text in Tamaro, *op. cit.*, Vol. II, pp. 579-581.

In Northern Italy, further measures against the partisans and other political plotters were decreed by the RSI. On April 5th, the members of the "military" command of the Turin CLN had been arrested, tried and condemned by a Fascist Court, and eight of them executed. They were undoubtedly guilty of plotting against the State, but their execution was a political error, and it would have been well to have pardoned them or granted amnesty, as had been done in other cases of the same kind. On that same day, Turin was heavily bombed, and while no military establishments were hit nor was any of the judges of the Fascist Court killed, about a thousand civilians perished.

A few days later, the priest, Don Giuseppe Morosini, who had confessed to having committed acts of espionage on behalf of the Allies and supplied arms to the partisans, was executed by the German authorities. He had been arrested in the previous January, but the Germans had delayed his execution for several months, awaiting the intervention of the Vatican on his behalf, but no such intervention had materialized.

One of the worst criminal acts committed at that time was the murder in Florence, on April 15th, of the eminent Italian philosopher and scholar, Professor Giovanni Gentile. This deed had been suggested to the Florence partisans (the G.A.P.) by the London and Bari radio services. They resented the support given Mussolini's Government by so distinguished a scholar and by a man of such high moral character, that support having conferred upon it considerable added prestige. Hence, his "liquidation" was regarded by the partisan organization and by the Allied Governments as a necessity. Gentile was murdered on his return home from a visit to the Prefecture where he had been to plead the cause of some anti-Fascist professors who had recently been arrested.[9]

[9] The murder of Professor Gentile was first suggested by the London radio through the Bari radio in Italy, which was under British control. Instructions to that effect were sent to the Florence G.A.P. The message was picked up by the authorities of the Florence Prefecture, and the Prefect warned Professor Gentile of his danger. The latter replied that he was helpless to prevent violence. The facts have been set forth several times in the press, and I received detailed personal information in discussions with Professor Gentile's son, Benedetto. The incident takes on special interest at the present time in the light of the horror expressed by the British over the fact that the Cairo radio has suggested the assassination of King Hussein of Jordan.

Great satisfaction was expressed over the Bari radio for this foul deed, but even the *Partito d'Azione* felt obliged to register a protest and to regret the dastardly act. Immediately after the murder, Gentile's sons hastened to the Italian and German authorities in Florence, urgently requesting that no reprisals be carried out, as they were sure that their father would not have wished it. In fact, no reprisals did take place.

Partisan violence increased in some of the Northern provinces, and in that of Rieti fourteen soldiers were murdered, in consequence of which deed the Germans carried out a series of reprisal actions, and some hundreds of partisans were captured and many executed. Both the Germans and the partisans showed themselves ruthless towards their captives, and Mussolini, himself, after a number of Italian soldiers and civilians had been murdered by the partisans in circumstances of unusual cruelty, occasionally ordered severe measures. But whenever such men as the Ministers, Piero Pisenti or Piero Parini, or the journalist, Carlo Silvestri, intervened on behalf of captured partisans, the Duce immediately suspended the infliction of the death penalty. While he was usually severe against the Communists, whom he regarded as the enemies of Italy, acting on behalf of, and in the pay of, the Soviet Government, especially those operating in the Venezia Giulia and serving under the orders of Tito, he was indulgent towards non-Communist rebels. Ferruccio Parri, one of the chief organizers of the partisan movement, was arrested more than once, but always released soon afterwards on Mussolini's orders, as he actually believed Parri to be an honest man. Parri responded to this magnanimity by uncompromising hatred against the Duce, a form of behavior compatible with his character.

With a view to crushing the partisan movement, Mussolini issued a decree on April 25th, imposing the death penalty on all partisans found with arms in their hands and on those who voluntarily aided and abetted them, but it was also provided that those who surrendered before May 25th would be freely pardoned and not subjected to any discrimination. The Bari and London radio services started a violent propaganda campaign against this measure, urging the partisans not to accept the proffered amnesty. But by the date mentioned many thousands of partisans had submitted to the Italian authorities.

The great mass of the inhabitants of the territory of the RSI continued to attend to their own business and remained quiet and peaceful, in spite of the ever-intensified air raids and the constant interruptions of communications. Food conditions, although difficult, were better than in occupied Italy, the public services operated more or less regularly, industries carried on, the cost of living never reached the peak it did in the South, and the public finances were, unlike those of Badoglio's Government, quite normal, with an Italian and not a German currency.

CHAPTER XVII

THE ALLIES IN ROME

THE situation in Rome was becoming daily more difficult, with the excessive overcrowding due to the large numbers of refugees flocking in from bombed-out towns and villages. They hoped that the presence of the Vatican would save the city from further raids.

Much bitterness had been aroused against the Germans by the Fosse Ardeatine executions. This had been the purpose of the authors of the Via Rasella outrage and of those who had inspired them. But many Romans rightly attributed the responsibility for the tragedy to the terrorists themselves, and the commemoration of the victims of the German reprisals was attended by very few persons. Some other isolated outrages took place; in one case, because the murderers of a few German soldiers had taken refuge in the Quadraro quarter on the outskirts of the city, German forces surrounded the district and deported a number of the men found there to Germany.

The advance of the Allied forces from the South continued slowly and with heavy losses. The hardest fighting was entrusted to the Poles under General Wladyslaw Anders and to General Alphonse Juin's Moroccans. The Poles proved the most humane of all the Allied forces in their treatment of the local inhabitants, whereas the Moroccans were the most savage. At Esperia, although there had been no resistance, those swarthy heroes distinguished themselves by raping every woman between the ages twelve and sixty in the small town, with the approval of their gallant general (and future Field Marshal), who looked on, enjoying the spectacle. In the Frosinone province similar exploits occurred.[1]

[1] The Socialist leader, Nenni, reported these facts in the *Avanti!* for July 4 and 6, 1944. See also Gorresio's *Un anno di libertà* (Rome, 1945), p. 11.

Field Marshal Kesselring had ordered all German forces withdrawn from Rome, so that it might be declared an "open city," free from all further danger of air bombings. But, although the Vatican took up the question with the Allies, they rejected the proposal. In the meanwhile, the junction between the forces on the Anzio beachhead and those advancing from the Cassino area was at last effected, and it was obvious that Rome could not be held by the Germans much longer.

By the end of May, the actual evacuation of the city by the German forces began. A deplorable incident occurred at La Storta, a few miles north of Rome, where General Dodi, the Socialist leader, Bruno Buozzi, and a dozen other prisoners, who had been released from the Via Tasso jail and were leaving the city, were met by a party of German policemen and shot for no known reason.

Fighting still continued around Rome, and Italian units, together with German troops, played an active part in the rearguard actions on the Anzio front and elsewhere. A detachment of 930 men of the "Folgore" division held out to the last at Decima on June 3rd, and all its men were killed or wounded except about fifty. Of Badoglio's forces a few men took part with the Allies in the operations round Picinisco (May 27 and 28), but encountered only slight enemy resistance.

On the eve of the Allied occupation, General Alexander had ordered the partisans within the city to rise against the Germans, but they failed to move and the Germans were allowed to withdraw undisturbed. As soon as the last German soldiers had evacuated Rome, the Allies entered it on June 4, 1944, encountering no opposition.

When the first Anglo-American units arrived they were welcomed by a part of the population as "liberators." A number of partisans, who had never attempted to revolt against the Germans, suddenly appeared on the scene fully armed and strutted about, making a noise like heroes, but devoting themselves chiefly to looting private dwellings, well knowing that they were free to do so under the auspices and following the example of the new occupying forces.

The fall of the capital was a painful blow throughout unoccupied Italy, and among a large part of the people of the
occupied provinces as well. Mussolini himself was heartbroken,
although he still believed in the possibility of a final victory
for the Axis Powers.

On the 5th, the King issued a proclamation whereby the decree of April 12th appointing Prince Humbert as Royal Lord
Lieutenant of the Kingdom came into force. He had applied
for permission to issue it from Rome, but Hull cabled to the
new United States Ambassador in Italy and to Robert Murphy
that in no case should the King be allowed to return to his
capital.[2]

The next task was the formation of a new Cabinet, and the
CLN regarded itself as alone invested with representative
authority. General MacFarlane had forced Badoglio to resign,
and on June 7th he informed the Premier-designate, Ivanoe
Bonomi, that Italy could only have the Government which the
Allies imposed on her (democracy and liberty again). A meet-
ing of Italian politicians was held at the Grand Hotel in Rome,
under the chairmanship of MacFarlane, at the end of which
Prince Humbert entrusted Bonomi with the formation of the
Cabinet, which was to be created within two hours. The men
chosen were Giovanni Gronchi, Tupini, Marquis Casati, Romita,
Silienti, De Ruggiero, Soleri, Gullo, Cerabona, Admiral De
Courten, and some others without portfolios: Croce, Sforza,
Cianca, De Gasperi, Togliatti, Ruini and Saragat. The Ministers
belonged to six different parties, and the Government was con-
sequently known as the "Hexarchy."

MacFarlane had vetoed Sforza's appointment as Minister of
Foreign Affairs, that position being entrusted to the new Prime
Minister, Bonomi, and decreed that there was to be no Minister
of the Colonies, thereby already implying that Italy was to be
deprived of all her colonial possessions, a prohibition accepted
by the feeble Bonomi without a word of protest.

In assuming office at the hands of Prince Humbert, Bonomi
agreed that all power emanated from the CLN, on which, as

[2]Hull, *op. cit.*, Vol. II, p. 1563.

a matter of fact, none had ever been conferred; the Christian
Democratic party had still the largest number of supporters in
the country, but in the CLN it was always the Communists
who dominated. In publishing the biographies of the new
Ministers, the press took care not to mention the fact that Marquis Casati had been a member of Mussolini's Government even
after the Matteotti affair, that Bonomi himself had been a can-
didate for Parliament on the same ticket as the Fascist Party
Secretary, Roberto Farinacci, that Giovanni Gronchi had been
an Under-Secretary in the Fascist era, and that De Gasperi (the
future Prime Minister from 1946 to 1953) had expressed his
approval of the vote of the 107 deputies of the *Partito Popolare*
(which gave birth to the Christian Democratic Party) in favor
of the Fascist regime. Gronchi became President of the Italian
Republic in April, 1955.

MacFarlane subjected the new Ministers to every form of
humiliation, ordered them to return to Salerno and announce
the formation of the Cabinet from that city, and canceled from
the communiqué the passage about its imminent return to
Rome. The Ministers accepted every injunction in the most
servile manner, thereby forfeiting any shred of self-respect
which they might still have possessed. They continued to be
treated with contempt by the Allies, a forecast of Italy's final
degradation under the Peace Treaty in 1947.

Churchill did not have much respect for the new Cabinet,
and on June 10th he cabled to Roosevelt protesting against
replacing Badoglio's team by "this group of aged and hungry
politicians." Roosevelt, however, replied that it was the best
solution possible.[3]

With regard to the oath of allegiance to the Crown, it was
agreed that Bonomi should take it in the usual manner, while
the other Ministers should limit themselves to a promise made
to the Premier personally (this in order not to offend the Republican principles of Sforza).

The CLN was certainly not respected by public opinion,
which regarded it as a mere clique of politicians, like those of

[3] Hull, *op. cit.*, Vol. II, p. 1564.

pre-Fascist times. It was commonly said that the letters CLN stood for "Come loro noi" ("We are just like the others," i.e., the Fascists). The situation of the country demanded the collaboration of truly competent statesmen capable of dealing with the appalling problems of the time, whereas most of the Ministers were very second-rate figures, whose only policy was to shriek against Fascism.

The Government, but not the King himself, now returned to Rome under the escort of Allied tanks. There was, of course, no real democracy, but only the six-party oligarchy. Three of the groups of the Hexarchy—the Communists, the Socialists and the Christian Democrats—restored trade union unity under the Italian General Confederation of Labor (C.G.I.L.), which, being predominantly Communists, enjoyed the favor of the Allied authorities. There was a single labor exchange installed in each province, thus restoring class warfare, the abolition of which had been one of the most important and beneficial achievements of the Fascist regime, with its labor courts to settle labor disputes on the basis of law and equity without resort to strikes or lockouts. The other parties tried to set up their own trade unions, but failed.

On June 25th, the Cabinet issued a decree setting forth the provisional organization of the Government and declaring that a Constituent Assembly would be summoned at an early date. The Christian Democrats and the Liberals regarded this decision as a mistake, and even the Leftists were afraid of the people whose opinions they professed to voice; they would, indeed, have preferred a Convention of a purely Jacobin type. On one point alone was there full agreement: the granting of full powers to the Government to continue and intensify the persecution of Fascists, regardless of the most elementary principles of law and equity. This was, indeed, the new Government's only real activity, as it had been that of its predecessors. Reconstruction and an efficient provision of supplies were matters too difficult to handle, and did not even interest the Ministers themselves.

The Monarchy, in spite of its reduced prestige, still remained the only national institution, although it was but feebly supported in some quarters, and bitterly opposed in others, both in the North and in the South. The Communists at that time were less hostile to it than the *Partito d'Azione,* because they hoped to manipulate it for their own purposes. The fact that Prince Humbert was only Lord Lieutenant and not King weakened the position of the Monarchy, in general, while leaving the King himself formally responsible for the errors and iniquities committed by the Government.

The uncompromisingly anti-Fascist attitude of the Christian Democrats savored somewhat of ingratitude if they considered themselves really good Catholics, as the Church had received great benefits from the Fascist regime. Their policy can only be accounted for by their factious spirit, which seemed to be far stronger than their religious devotion. De Gasperi, in setting forth his own program as head of that party, expressed cordial friendship for the Communists, who would certainly have cut his throat if they had come into power, advocated the redistribution of property and the limitation of the powers of the State, together with a great deal of eye-wash about religion. On the question of Monarchy or Republic he kept discreetly vague, waiting to see on which side the cat would jump.

While all the six groups of the Hexarchy talked glibly about liberty, democracy, Socialism and Catholicism, there was never a word about Italy, as anyone mentioning such a thing risked being branded as a wicked reactionary or a bloodthirsty Nationalist, and unfriendly to the invading armies. It seemed, indeed, as though none of the party leaders took any interest whatever in the conditions of their country or its people. In addition to the six parties, a score of other groups cropped up, rich in programs, but devoid of ideas and able leaders.

In Rome, as everywhere else, the joy of "liberation" very soon turned to gall and wormwood. The Allies had promised an abundance of everything, but rarely delivered anything. The food situation, bad as it had been before, became steadily worse; only coffee and gasoline were available in abundance, owing to the business activities of British and American sol-

diers, ever ready to sell anything to those who could afford to
pay. The water supply was suspended in the summer of 1944,
electricity and gas were almost wholly lacking, and the street
car and motor bus services broke down completely. There were
occasional riots on account of these deficiencies, quickly re-
pressed by the military police, who did not hesitate to apply
drastic methods undreamed of in the past.

The bread ration was 150 grammes a day per person (in a
country where bread is an all-important article of consump-
tion), olive oil 10 grammes, canned meat 13.3 grammes, soap
(when there was any) 3 grammes. On June 17th, the AMG
fixed the following rations for every five days: olive oil ½
decilitre, sugar 45 grammes, dried vegetables 60 grammes,
canned meat 70 grammes. This was the plan, in theory, but in
practice these commodities were often totally lacking or obtainable only in much smaller quantities. Soup kitchens were
opened by the American authorities, and by the Vatican, which
served plates of soup to about 325,000 persons in Rome who
had nothing else to eat.

The black market, which had existed more or less throughout
the War, now flourished like a green bay tree, and provided
supplies for those who could afford to pay very high prices.
While milk and sugar for children and the sick were almost
unobtainable, there were plenty of cakes and sweetmeats and
other luxuries in the pastry cook shops and bars. These abuses
could not be stopped because the places in question were much
frequented by Allied soldiers and their tarts. The Allies provided much-resented spectacles of gluttonous overfeeding
amidst the wretchedness and starvation of the Italian people.
They also encouraged corruption in all forms, and numbers of
miserably poor children eked out a precarious existence by
selling obscene publications to Tommies and GI's, white or
colored, or by acting as pimps.

The amount of drunkenness among the Allied soldiers, also
mentioned by the egregious Gayre, scandalized even a population as much given to wine drinking as the Italians. Peaceful

citizens were liable to be beaten up by Allied soldiers, many of whom would jump into cabs or taxis after kicking out the persons already in them. On one occasion, a group of soldiers bludgeoned an Italian to within an inch of his life because he had refused to supply them with the address of a brothel. It was no uncommon sight to see soldiers relieving nature inside the doors of palaces in the Corso Umberto. Women were frequently beaten or otherwise maltreated in the streets for refusing their favors to soldiers, while the presence of the Allied forces attracted prostitutes from all parts of the country to Rome, and many otherwise honest women sold themselves for the sake of food or cigarettes. Occasionally, young Romans reacted by shaving the heads of girls who had been seen in the company of Allied soldiers. A large hotel in the Via Veneto was turned into a casino-brothel.[4] Allied soldiers often practiced banditry, many streets became veritable jungles infested with uniformed gangsters; every night citizens came home without clothes or shoes, and not a few were picked up on the sidewalks with their heads bashed in.[5]

Looting was general, often practiced by men who should have known better. To quote one instance in Naples, an American officer, on visiting the home of a Neapolitan lady of noble family, calmly carried off her collection of valuable miniatures as "souvenirs." In Rome, an old lady of American birth (a Daughter of the American Revolution) and the widow of a Roman prince, had her collection of antique watches carried off in the same way.

Wholesale corruption was rife in American camps and barracks, and to a somewhat more limited extent in those of the British. Quantities of stores were withdrawn from the military magazines and canteens by Allied officers, N.C.O.'s and soldiers, and sold in the black market openly in the streets, and companies were actually formed for carrying on these activities. On at least one occasion, a large steamer laden with

[4] Repaci, *Taccuino politico* (Milan, 1947), pp. 55 et seq.; Candamo, "Roma sotto inchiesta," in *Cosmopolita*, N. 4, 1944.
[5] Bacini, *Roma prima e dopo* (Rome, 1945), p. 144.

supplies of all kinds vanished mysteriously after the cargo had been sold at a large profit.[6]

In many cases, Italian industrial plants were dismantled and their equipment removed. In the Sila (Calabria) great tracts of forest were cut down and whole mountainsides denuded of vegetation by the Allies, who afterwards accused the Italians of having no respect for trees.

Nor was anything omitted to humiliate the Italians. The aged Duchess of Aosta had refused to receive British generals at her villa at Capodimonte on the outskirts of Naples, regarding them as representatives of a Government which had treated her son, the heroic defender of Italian East Africa, so harshly while, as a prisoner of war, he lay dying in a Kenya hospital. The retort to this motherly gesture was that the Capodimonte park was turned into a bivouac for colored troops. At the same time, the magnificent Royal Palace in Naples was turned into a combination of a club and a brothel for the troops, and when finally evacuated was found reduced to the conditions of a huge pigsty.

The general economic situation was made ever worse by the vast quantities of paper currency, not covered by any reserve, thrown on the market, thereby serving to inflate prices still further.

In Rome, nearly all the theatres, cinemas and hotels were requisitioned for the Allied forces. MAAFI stores and officers' messes occupied clubs, academies and the embassies of Axis Powers.

The harshness and, above all, the incompetence of the Allied authorities aroused ever-increasing bitterness and indignation in all classes, except among the few who made a good thing out of the occupation. Charles Poletti, a prominent New York lawyer-politician, who had somehow got the rank of colonel without having seen any war service, was appointed Governor of Rome, and for a long time his authority in the city was practically unlimited. He made and unmade laws, set up innumerable offices, boards, institutions of all kinds, at his own sweet

[6]The same things happened in France.

will, without the foggiest notion of administrative practice, sometimes merely to provide lush jobs for his friends. His presumption was only equalled by his incompetence, and every Wednesday he lectured the Romans over the wireless in bastard Italian instructing them as to how to become civilized and telling them to wash more—when there was neither soap nor water available.[7]

Requisition and illegal occupation of private dwellings were carried out both by Allied officers and soldiers and by Italian partisans or other men of shady antecedents. A friend of mine, an official of the Ministry of Foreign Affairs in the RSI Government, on returning to Rome after the end of the war, found that his flat had been turned into a brothel, and it took him several years to get the inmates ousted. Another friend, also a civil servant, who had been arrested and imprisoned by the Allied authorities, on regaining his freedom, found his flat occupied by a couple working for the Salvation Army, and when he was at last able to regain possession of it he found it in a condition of incredible filth.

A lady of English birth and married to an Italian, while her husband was lying seriously ill, received a visit from two young American officers, who told her that the family must clear out within twenty-four hours, as they needed the house for themselves, and that the furniture must be left in it. When she told them that her husband could not be moved from his bed and that in any case they would have nowhere to go, as the hotels were all requisitioned, the officers replied that that did not concern them and that they must have the house. But by a piece of good luck the American Ambassador, Alexander Kirk, who was a friend of the family, happened to pass that way and, on being told the story, at once requisitioned the house for the Embassy, thus enabling the family to stay in it undisturbed. It turned out afterwards that the two officers had no authority to requisition houses. These are but a few of many thousands of episodes of

[7] After the war Poletti returned to America, but was soon involved in law suits over his financial activities.

the same kind occurring all over occupied Italy during and immediately after the War.[8]

There were, of course, exceptions which deserve mention.
Two Italian ladies, mother and daughter, who had remained in
Rome throughout the war, on the occupation of the city by
the Allies, were visited by an American N.C.O., bearer of a
letter from some American friends of theirs who had commis-
sioned him to supply the ladies with anything they needed. He
was a pleasant, well-mannered youth, who in civil life was a
mechanic in a small-town garage. The ladies thanked him, but
said they had managed to get along and did not need anything.
He returned a week later and said to the ladies: "We were
told at home that we were being sent to Italy to bring civilization into the country; but from what I have seen I think that
even we have a lot to learn about civilization over here."

All persons who had been imprisoned for political offenses
under the Fascist regime had by now been liberated. With what
the French call "la mentalité des sinistrés" (the spirit of victims
of misfortune), they claimed every privilege and emolument as
theirs by right under the new dispensation. Together with them,
a considerable number of common criminals were released,
posed as political victims and, therefore, felt entitled freely to
loot the dwellings of Fascists or persons alleged to be Fascists.
This they were allowed to do with impunity; in many cases
they occupied these dwellings themselves. To this very day
some of these illegal occupations still persist. Even when the
rightful owners were at last able to reoccupy their dwellings
they usually found them stripped of every stick of furniture,
books, plate, and linen, and other valuables.

While the Italian Government was still at Salerno and had
enacted the notorious punitive law of May 26, 1944 (which
came into force on June 1st), "Colonel" Poletti, assisted by a
gang of Italian rapscallions, issued a decree of his own on June
26th, listing 25 categories of "Fascist criminals," who were to

---

[8] What happened in Rome was paralleled in other cities. See, for instance, John
Horne Burn's picture of life in Naples in 1944 in his vividly written book *In the
Gallery* (Harper Edition, New York, 1947).

be punished not for offenses against the Allied forces, but as Italians who had supported their own former legitimate Government. Scores of thousands of men were thus deprived of all employment in the public service or of the right to practice their own professions or trades, and many of them were arrested and interned in the Allied prison camps at Padula or Collescopoli.

Even this was not enough, and the Italian Government issued a yet more drastic decree on July 27, 1944, which became the basic law for the persecution of political opponents with retroactive effects. I shall deal with this and other similar measures in another chapter.

Count Sforza was now, as we have seen, appointed High Commissioner for the punishment of Fascists, and he held the appointment from June, 1944, to January, 1945, when he was succeeded by the Assistant High Commissioner, Berlinguer. Sforza slaked his lust for vengeance on all opponents, often issuing denunciations against them based on falsehood. He was so blinded by his factious spirit that in his public speeches he was apt to use the language of the gutter. On one occasion he defined the Fascists "sons of b——s."[9] The aim of the said law was not to "purify" but to punish, and Sforza claimed that, as the Fascist regime had been illegitimate from the very first and constituted a twenty-year period of non-justice, never having been legalized by a popular vote, all decisions taken by it and all sentences issued by its courts were illegal and void.[10]

For one gesture, Count Sforza deserves the particular remembrance of his fellow citizens. In the autumn of 1944, he asked the Moscow Government for a list of names of Italians whom it wished to have sent to Russia to be tried by it as "war criminals."[11] The Russian Government replied sending a list of only twelve names.[12] Sforza would have been better pleased

[9] Gorresio, op. cit., p. 285.

[10] This, of course, was untrue, as the Government had secured a large majority vote and all its laws had been passed by an elected Parliament.

[11] This was in harmony with Article 29 of the "long" armistice.

[12] Report of Ezio Maria Gray's trial in his pamphlet, La morte civile di Carlo Sforza (Rome, 1950).

to have had an opportunity to surrender some hundreds or thousands of Italians to the tender mercies of the Russian executioners and torturers.

Sforza now had all the members of the Senate, except about a score, deprived of their seats, on the charge of having supported the Fascist regime. This measure was wholly illegal, for the Senators had been appointed for life by the King on the proposal of successive Prime Ministers, according to the provisions of the Constitution of 1848, then still in force. They had been chosen for exceptional merits—for having held the highest offices in political life, in the armed forces, in the civil service, in diplomacy, in the judicature, or as experts in science, literature, the arts or general culture. Some of them had been nominated on Mussolini's proposal, but most of them on that of his various predecessors. In this connection, an episode dating back to 1938 (under the Fascist regime) is worth recording. In that year, a Fascist Senator had proposed to the Senate that Count Sforza, then living abroad and busily engaged in reviling not only the Fascist regime, but Italy in general, and inciting foreign Governments against his own country, should be expelled from the Senate. But a large majority of the Senators present, beginning with the Fascist President, Luigi Federzoni, opposed the proposal as being a flagrant violation of the Constitution. It was subsequently withdrawn. Nearly all these same Senators (including Federzoni himself) were among those now expelled on the order of that same Senator, Count Sforza.

The Government had been allowed to return to Rome on July 15th, but until August 15th it remained the "guest" of Poletti. Even after that date, it continued, of course, to be subject to the absolute control of the Allies, so much so that even the anti-Fascist extremist, Benedetto Croce, resigned.

Count Carlo Sforza, leading opponent of Mussolini and Fascism, in exile. He was a vigorous Anti-Monarchist Foreign Minister in the coalition cabinet of De Gasperi in 1947. He died September 4, 1952.

King Humbert II. He ascended the throne in 1946, left Italy after the referendum of June 2, 1946, and now lives in Portugal.

General Vittorio Ambrosio, Commander-in-chief of the Italian forces in the second World War, helped to plot the overthrow of Mussolini, 1943.

Benedetto Croce, Italian philosopher and historian,

CHAPTER XVIII

MILITARY AND PARTISAN ACTIVITIES

THE formation of an Italian army in the occupied provinces proved a slow business. Only thirteen badly equipped battalions, with very little artillery, were allowed to take part in the operations by the side of infinitely more numerous and admirably equipped Allied forces.

The Germans continued to retreat slowly and with many rear-guard actions. On August 4th they began to evacuate Florence, but fighting still went on in and around the city. When the last German units had departed, some partisan bands who, in spite of General Alexander's orders, had, as in the case of Rome, never risen against the enemy, now emerged from hiding and proceeded, under the orders of Professor Calamandrei of the *Partito d'Azione,* to shoot stragglers. The Fascists defended themselves vigorously until they were overwhelmed by superior numbers of Allied troops, after which many of them were murdered by the partisans, while others were tried by the newly created partisan tribunals and sent before firing squads.

One of the actions of the Germans relative to the evacuation of Florence was the destruction of some bridges across the Arno River. This was, indeed, deplorable, but the Germans tried to justify it on strategic grounds, namely, that it delayed the advance of the Allies. The Allied destruction of the great historic Abbey of Monte Cassino had no strategic justification whatever, for there were no German or Italian military forces in it at the time of the bombardment of the Abbey, and the Allied Command knew this before the order was given to start the bombardment. Moreover, the destruction of the Arno bridges, however regrettable, was one of the few instances of any destruction of historic or artistic monuments by the Germans or Fascists in Italy. On the other hand, the indiscriminate bombing of non-military objectives by the Allies destroyed innumerable ancient churches, palaces, libraries, and the like. The destruction of the famous San Lorenzo Basilica in Rome and of the church in Padua which contained the priceless Mantegna frescoes are only two instances out of hundreds of others of a similar nature.

On August 22nd, Alexander could claim that Florence was completely "liberated," but the atmosphere in the city was somewhat hostile. An American officer was heard to say that the Allies had found in the city not the expected "friends" of the Allies, but "the friends of Mussolini."[1]

The Allied attack on the "Gothic line" commenced on the 25th, and Kesselring resisted with such forces as were available, inflicting heavy losses on the attackers; the Italians fighting under him distinguished themselves in these actions, whereas those on the Allied side were only allowed to take part in some very minor operations.

In Northern Italy there were sporadic partisan activities. On August 9th the Milan GAP set off a bomb under two German trucks, killing a couple of passers-by, but no German soldiers. The German authorities, instead of rounding up the terrorists, seized 15 persons detained in the San Vittore prison and had them shot in the Piazzale Loreto.

The North Italian CLN, known as the CLNAI (Comitati liberazione nazionale Alta Italia), requested the Rome Government to invest it with delegated powers, and Bonomi agreed, entrusting it with the conduct of the war against the Fascist regime, a task for which it was totally unfit. Nevertheless, in September, it began to issue decrees, declaring that all the laws and other measures enacted by the RSI and the German authorities were null and void, and providing for the dismissal of all officers and officials of the RSI Government who might be on duty at the moment of "liberation." But the quarrels within its ranks were as bitter as those within the Rome CLN.

The Communist leaders now thought that the time was ripe

---

[1] Quoted by Tamaro, *op. cit.*, Vol. III, p. 232.

for a general insurrection in the territory of the RSI, and on October 5th they issued orders to that effect. But, if the Communists dominated the partisan units, their numbers in the population as a whole were very small. Even according to Communist sources, they were only 5,500 in Turin out of a total working-class population of 200,000, or 2 per cent. In Milan, the Communist street-car workers were 104 out of a total of 5,925, with only 4,000 Communists out of all the workers in the city; at Biella there were 400 Communists out of 40,000 workers. Throughout the whole area involved, with a population of 20,000,000, not more than 60,000 were Communists, or 0.33 per cent.

The attempt of the Communist leaders to induce the railwaymen to strike failed completely, and Kesselring publicly thanked the latter for their loyalty. The Communist manifesto of August 4th stating that the whole people were united in the struggle for "liberty" bore no resemblance to the facts, as any general revolutionary feeling was totally lacking.

During the period of sporadic strikes which occurred here and there, the Minister of the Interior, Buffarini-Guidi, was appointed by Mussolini High Commissioner for Lombardy, Piedmont and Liguria, and he intended to take drastic measures in the case of any further agitations. But Carlo Silvestri, who always exercised great influence over the Duce, warned him of the inadvisability of such action and urged him to cancel the appointment and leave all responsibility for the maintenance of law and order to the Prefects of the various provinces. To this the Duce agreed, with the result that no unusual measures were taken.

A letter written by one of the leaders of the *Partito d'Azione* containing the names of the members of the executive committees of the underground parties (the Communists excepted), fell into Mussolini's hands, so that he might have had them all arrested. But he only warned them, including Parri and Riccardo Lombardi, that they had better make themselves scarce. His Minister of Justice, Piero Pisenti, had previously informed Silvestri that Parri's conduct was very alarming, but his arrest was again averted. Pisenti then declared: "How many times have I intervened during the last fourteen years to save him!" adding: "We may say indeed 'nulla dies sine salvatione'."[2]

Another attempt was then made by Mussolini to bring Fascists and anti-Fascists together, and meetings with that object were held between delegates of both sides. At the same time, the Cardinal Archbishop of Milan, Ildefonso Schuster, tried to bring about an agreement between the CLNAI and the Germans behind Mussolini's back, and his representative, Don Giuseppe Bicchierai, met with the German Ambassador, Rahn, and General Lehmann for the purpose. A memorandum was sent by the Cardinal to Rome through the Papal Nuncio in Bern with a draft proposal to that effect. Of the parties represented on the CLNAI, the *Partito d'Azione*, the Christian Democrats, the Liberals and the Socialists were inclined to agree, but the Communists, dominating the whole body and thirsting for blood, bitterly opposed the plan and caused it to fall through.

One might ask what the partisans as a whole were doing at this time. Longo, always exaggerating everything, claims that he could then have inflicted a knock-out blow against the Germans, as there were 80,000 partisans behind their lines. If so, why did he not do so? The fact is that Kesselring's armies were slowly retiring line by line, often undisturbed by the partisans. Parri says that partisan action completely paralyzed the military efforts of the RSI, but General Alexander, while showering lavish praises on that action in his public utterances, admitted in private that it had merely a nuisance value and that the Germans only employed second-line troops against it.

The failures of the partisan movement were due not only to incompetent strategy, but also to the fact that, under Communist leadership, it was devoted chiefly to purposes of domestic policy, with the war as a mere pretext. The British writer, Mr. Julian Amery, rightly points out that their real object was not victory or "liberation," but the seizure of political power.[3]

[2] Silvestri, *op. cit.*, pp. 76 et seq.
[3] *The Nineteenth Century and After*, March, 1949.

The Communist leaders, it is true, camouflaged the actual character of the movement so as to secure the support of the other parties and instructed their followers (June, 1944) not to shout Communist slogans, but to sing patriotic songs and give an apparently national tone to their activities. But this deceived very few people.

The real nature of the partisan movement has already been described, but it is interesting to note that even Parri admits that its leaders (Communists and non-Communists), made the mistake of recruiting a number of men who had little stomach for fighting, not a few being common criminals. Many of them, including some of the leaders, were afterwards arrested for murder, robbery, rape, burglary, and other crimes, but in many cases the accused succeeded in securing acquittal. Those who did commit terrorist acts, like the authors of the Via Rasella outrage, or even ordinary crimes, usually managed to get released on the ground that their acts had been of a political nature.

The movement was further discredited by the fact that many of the partisans demanded pecuniary rewards, even if they had done nothing in the way of fighting. Moreover, they well knew that any activity on their part inevitably led to reprisals, often on quite innocent local inhabitants, but this they did not consider, on the usual principle that the end justifies the means. In many cases, however, they were caught and executed, and it must be admitted that not a few of those who had to face a firing squad died bravely.

The London radio and its Bari satellite were constantly urging the partisans to further violent activities, as in a message of September, 1944, including the murder of Fascist leaders.[4] But, as I said before, it was usually the Fascist rank and file who most often fell victims. Bottari[5] gives a list of 150 Fascist "spies" executed in various North Italian towns in one month,

[4] The Communists afterwards elected to Parliament always maintained that any acts committed by members of the Party were political and, therefore, deserved full immunity.

[5] *L'eccidio e il processo*, p. 9; quoted by Tamaro, *op. cit.*, Vol. III, p. 173.

while Silvestri[6] reports the case of Lieutenant Perretti of Aosta, whom the partisans wished to murder, and not having found him in his home, they murdered his father, mother and sister instead.

As to the numbers of the partisans at this time, it is again impossible to secure definite data. According to Parri, there were in North Italy, in the early months of 1944, 90,000 to 100,000, and in the summer of that year there were 100,000 others operating in more or less regular units in the mountains, and another 100,000 in small irregular groups scattered about the plains and in small towns and villages. These figures are enormously exaggerated. General Cadorna gives their number at not more than 90,000 in all, but even this figure may be excessively high; probably there were never more than 50,000 or 60,000 actually fighting. It was after the end of hostilities that their greatest activities began and their numbers underwent a huge inflation, soon reaching 200,000 to 300,000 and possibly even more. But, owing to the irregularity of their formations, many were only part-time partisans, operating for a few months or weeks, and then returning to their homes, while large numbers lived more or less permanently in idleness, fed and supplied, willingly or otherwise, by the local inhabitants, and only occasionally indulging in some petty military action.

Many of the partisan bands were composed almost wholly of Communists. According to some sources, the Communist partisans made up 48 per cent of the total, those of the *Partito d'Azione*, practically Communists, also, 31 per cent, the Christian Democrats, 14 per cent, the rest being made up of small groups. In the Valdieri district (Piedmont) and in the provinces of Modena, Bologna and Ravenna, the partisans were nearly all Communists. It cannot be too often repeated that everywhere it was the Communists who ruled the partisan roost, however few their actual number in some cases.

The anti-Fascists of all colors accused the RSI Government of having sold out to the Germans, whereas it actually paid a large monthly contribution to the Germans for war expenses in

[6]*Op. cit.*, p. 160.

Italy. It was, as we shall see, the partisans who were in the pay of foreign Governments.

In the early days of the partisan movement, when it was on a small scale, financing it was not a serious problem. General Operti, who handled the funds of the Italian IV Army in France, gave 180,000,000 French francs to the Piedmontese CLN, and the treasurer of the latter handed over a part of the sum to the Lombard CLN. Alfredo Pizzoni, treasurer of the Lombard committee, states that sums of money were brought in from Switzerland.[7]

Certainly, the activities of the partisans were much exaggerated by their leaders, and Longo declares that the movement constituted a vast "people's army" spread all over the country.[8] But that "people's army" never had any existence, and Silvestri writes that, in the winter of 1943-44, a few hundred German soldiers along the lines of communications and in the various towns were more than sufficient to secure what the German command wanted.[9] In many cases, the German forces did not trouble themselves much about the partisans, and in some districts left them undisturbed.

In the latter part of 1944, attempts were again made to unify the partisan movement under a general command, with a single military chief at its head and a political commissar and delegates of the various parties by his side. The CLNAI and the British Colonel, Holdsworth, of the "Special Force N. 1," which dealt with partisan affairs, invited General Cadorna to take over this command, but the partisan spokesmen were opposed to the idea, and would only accept Cadorna as a military adviser. The dispute dragged on for months, and was not decided in favor of Cadorna until almost at the end of the War.

Here and there, agreements for the exchange of prisoners and for the "neutrality" of certain districts were concluded between the Germans and the partisans. In some cases, the latter undertook not to attack the Germans, but only the forces

[7]"Il finanziamento," in *Mercurio,* December, 1945.
[8]*Op. cit.,* p. 114.
[9]*Contro la vendetta,* p. 147.

of the RSI.[10] An arrangement of this kind was made by the partisan forces at Imperia in Liguria, it being agreed to leave the defeat of the Germans to the Allies and to reserve their own forces for the task of establishing control over the country when the War was over, thus revealing the true Communist aims.

The RSI Government now raised a special force known as the "Brigate Nere" (black brigades) for police duties in its territory. At first, its members were carefully chosen, but later on undesirable individuals were admitted to its ranks, and some of them committed drastic acts of repression on the partisans, usually, however, as retaliation for previous brutal crimes on the other side.

The great majority of the partisans were, of course, Italians, but, as we have seen, even at the beginning of the movement there were also many foreigners among them, including some of the leaders, who could hardly be expected to care much about "liberating" or "saving" Italy. One of the leaders in the Cuneo province was a Frenchman known as "Lulu." At Ascoli Piceno one band was commanded by a Slav woman of the hell-cat type; of six partisans captured at Pegli, two were Slavs; the torturer of a member of the German Todt organization in the Casentino was a Russian, and a completely Russian unit operated in the province of Parma.[11]

With regard to the punitive expeditions carried out by RSI forces against the partisans, while Longo claims that they often achieved no results, Parri admits that they proved disastrous.[12] German reprisals were, as usual, ruthless, as in the case of Niccioletto in the Maremma, where they shot 83 miners and deported others; on June 21st they announced the execution of 400 prisoners and 110 deserters; on June 26th they deported 2,000 men to Germany for the blowing up of a bridge over the

[10] Ittolem, *La Divisione Fiamme Verdi*, p. 79; quoted by Tamaro, *op. cit.*, Vol., III, p. 193.

[11] According to Major Gordon Lett, in his book *Rossano*, in addition to British and Americans, there were in an international battalion in Liguria, Poles, Russians, Yugoslavs, French, Bulgarians and Dutch (as in the notorious International Brigades in Spain).

[12] In a lecture delivered on March 14, 1945.

Dora Baltea river in Piedmont; and on the same day several partisans, including their leader, Count Manzi of Trento, were executed at Rovereto in the Trentino.

Some partisan bands operating in the Susa and Chisone valleys, being pursued by the Germans, took refuge in France, but were there interned in a concentration camp by the French "maquis" forces, whom they had regarded as friends and allies, since an agreement had been previously concluded between the CLN and the French "résistance" command.[13] A similar agreement between the French and the Cuneo partisans led to the same result.[14] Only the "Rosselli" partisan unit found friendly treatment in France.

An attack by partisans in the Versilia area on August 12th, 1944, led to reprisals inflicted on the local population, but the partisans themselves escaped in good time. On the same day, in an operation conducted by the Decima MAS (a large former naval unit divided into numerous small detachments scattered over the country) there was an encounter with the partisans. In this, the commander of the whole force, Don Valerio Borghese, and the Secretary of the Fascist Party, Alessandro Pavolini, were wounded, but the partisans suffered heavy losses.

In September, the Allied Command ordered the partisans to sabotage all the main roads of Venetia and to hold the Alpine passes, as it was then rumored that the Germans were about to retreat. The Germans were not retreating, however, but attacked instead, putting several bands to flight, executing prisoners and burning and pillaging some villages. On Monte Grappa (in Venetia), 1,700 partisans had concentrated, and for some time were left undisturbed; but when they attacked a German unit in the district they were vigorously counterattacked; and, although they resisted gallantly, 700 of them were captured, of whom 264 were executed, while the rest managed to escape.

At Villamarzano (Province of Rovigo), a detachment of Fascist militia demanded that the bodies of four of their com-

---

[13] *Bollettino d'Informazioni* of the Communist Party.

[14] Bianco, *Venti mesi di guerra partigiana nel Cuneese*, p. 104; quoted by Tamaro, *op. cit.*, Vol. III, p. 159.

rades shot by the partisans be handed over for Christian burial, threatening to execute some partisans held as hostages if the request were refused. After waiting ten days in vain for an answer, they executed ten partisans, on one of whom was found the wrist watch of one of their own men. Later, they found the bodies of their comrades, bearing traces of having been tortured before their execution; in their indignation they court-martialed, condemned and executed 43 of the remaining prisoners.[15] These episodes give us an idea of the atrocious character of the civil war promoted, aided and abetted by the Allies.

In certain districts occupied by the partisans local administrations were set up by them, without any form of election, but calling themselves "independent republics." One of them, at Torriglia in Liguria, created in July, 1944, came to an end in September. The same thing happened at Alba sulle Langhe (Piedmont), and in the Carnia (province of Udine), where the municipal "giunta" held a meeting in the presence of the political commissar of a Communist band, while the members of the latter took to wholesale looting. But, in October, a mixed force of Germans, Italians, and Mongols in the German service began an offensive against the "republic." Most of the partisans took to flight after ordering the local inhabitants to resist with scythes and pitchforks, but the only attempt at resistance was offered by some partisans of the Osoppo division, although they, too, soon fled beyond the Tagliamento river. In the "republic" itself, the inhabitants did not resist at all, but the Mongols killed some of them and indulged in looting, until the Germans intervened to restore order.

The Ossola valley (just below the Simplon pass) had never been occupied by the Germans, except for a very small garrison in the town of Domodossola and a few isolated posts. Three partisan divisions and two units consisting of men belonging to various parties took advantage of the situation to invade the district, but allowed the German garrison to depart undisturbed. The foreign press magnified the episode as the beginning of a general rising for the complete "liberation" of all

---

[15] Bottari, op. cit., pp. 8-10.

Northern Italy. But the Allies failed to give the partisans the aid promised them, and the local inhabitants took no interest in the proceedings. The partisans created a republican administration, placing the Socialist, Dr. Tebaldi, who had just arrived from Switzerland, at its head. There was no trace of democracy in the set-up and the military command was entrusted to an attorney named Stucchi, with Paolo Scarpone as political commissar at his side.

Neither the RSI nor the German command could allow this musical comedy "republic" to continue to exist, and on October 10th one "Black Brigade," some men of the Republican National Guard, parachutists of the "Folgore" division, and a few Germans advanced on Domodossola. Resistance was very feeble, and on October 17th the governing "giunta" met for the last time at Ponte Formazza at the extreme northern end of the valley on the Swiss frontier. It thereupon broke up, conferring full powers on Dr. Tebaldi, who, however, fled back to Switzerland a couple of days later. Valiani (commissar of the *Partito d'Azione*) wrote that relations between the partisans and the local population were very bad, owing to the looting and other criminal acts of the former, and that the arrival of the Italo-German forces was warmly welcomed.

During the rigorous winter of 1944-45, the numbers of the partisans decreased considerably; many of them returned to their own homes, and others were ready to come to terms with the RSI authorities. But the Communists, as usual, strenuously opposed any such arrangement and, owing to their superior numbers and greater energy, they succeeded in preventing a peaceful solution.

In Central Italy, where the Allies had driven out the Germans, people's courts, composed almost wholly of Communist partisans, were instituted, and their proceedings against the Fascists were, as usual, mere travesties of justice. In Florence alone, 400 Fascists were executed after mock trials.[16]

The partisans who, during the winter months, descended

[16] Di Collegno-Signon, *I nostri e la guerra clandestina in Piemonte* (Turin, 1947), p. 116.

from their mountain fastnesses to the plains, devoted themselves chiefly to looting, with the result that the local inhabitants became ever more hostile to them, and sometimes the inhabitants appealed to the German or Fascist authorities to
defend them from the partisans.

In the field of military operations the partisans' spokesmen
talked about the "liberation" of Ravenna, Cesena, Forli and
other cities, although these places were only reached by them
after the British or American troops had arrived. In the provinces of Parma and Reggio Emilia and in Piedmont, German
and Italian forces destroyed the partisan organization in the
months of November and December, 1944. In January, 1945,
the German General, Karl Wolff, commander of the SS units in
Italy, announced that 9,000 partisans had been killed in three
months and 80,000 disarmed, probably a considerable exaggeration.

The British Colonel Stevens, who had intimate dealings with
the partisans, had little use for them. Although he sent Captain
Farran to the province of Reggio Emilia to form a mixed unit
of British, Russian and Italian partisans, Stevens stated that,
for fighting the Germans, they were of no earthly use.[17]

The leaders of the CLNAI delivered the worst blow at the
whole partisan movement by concluding an agreement with
the Allied Command, accepting the political conditions imposed on it in exchange for a large monthly subsidy. On November 14, 1944, four CLNAI delegates (Parri, G. C. Pajetta,[18] Edgardo Sogno[19] and A. Pizzoni) were conveyed by air to Mono-
poli in Apulia to confer with the Command of "Special Force
N. 1" and the local U. S. Command on questions concerning underground warfare. The negotiations dragged on for some time,
but were finally concluded, and an agreement was signed in
Rome on December 7th, whereby the CLNAI was to carry out

[17] J. R. Reynolds in the *Tablet*, September 22, 1945, and Roy Farran's *Winged
Daggers* (London, 1949), pp. 261, 278, 292, 300, 310; Tamaro, *op cit.*, Vol. III,
pp. 454-5.
[18] Now a Communist Deputy.
[19] Editor of the anti-Communist monthly *Pace e luce e libertà*.

all the instructions of the Allied Command in Italy.[20] When the Germans withdrew, the CLNAI was to provide for the maintenance of law and order and to safeguard all the economic resources of Italy until an Allied Military Command could be set up. The partisan bands, or "Volunteer Forces for Liberty" were to come under the orders of the same Allied Command. The Allies, on their part, undertook to pay 160 million lire per month to the CLNAI. General Maitland Wilson thereupon appointed General Cadorna commander of the "Volunteer Forces," a position which, however, he did not take over until February, 1945.

This agreement deprived the CLNAI of any right to pose as an Italian national movement, and the partisans became mere mercenaries in the pay and operating in the interest of the foreign powers whose forces were occupying Italy. They certainly did not contribute to driving the Germans from Italy, to overthrowing the Fascist regime, or to raising Italy's international status, but merely promoted, instead, the continuation of an atrocious civil strife.

Perhaps the most dramatic episode connected with the partisan military activities during the liberation period is that involved with what has come to be known as "the Marzabotto Affair." It is worth recounting as providing an example of true partisan bravery in battle and of the continuing power of the Communists in the conduct of war-crimes trials and in intimidating post-War Italian Governments.

By September, 1944, the Germans under Field Marshal Kesselring were retiring to make a final stand on the so-called Gothic Line along the Apennines north of Florence. Their rear and their supply lines from the North were being harassed by a partisan force of some 2,000 under the command of Mario Musolesi, known in partisan circles as "Major Lupo." His partisan detachment was called the Red Star Brigade. It showed more than usual initiative and bravery, and its depredations were especially effective since Allied airplanes had dropped for their use large quantities of arms and ammunition, includ-

[20] Tamaro, *op. cit.*, Vol. III, pp. 466-7.

ing machine guns and light artillery. Hence, the German General, Max Simon, decided that the Red Star Brigade must be wiped out. He chose for this important assignment a Unit of the crack 16th Panzer Division whose gallantry in battle was several times acknowledged by British Field Marshal Alexander. The officer placed in command was a professional soldier of Austrian birth (Bohemia, which in 1915 was a part of Austria-Hungary), Major Walter Reder, who had served with great bravery in France, Russia and Yugoslavia before being assigned to the Italian front.

Major Lupo's partisan force was concentrated around Monte Sole and Monte Salvaro between the Reno and Setta Rivers on the route from Florence to Bologna. Major Reder decided to attack the Red Star Brigade from all sides, and his Unit converged on it on September 29, 1944. The Italian partisans under Major Lupo fought bravely, but they were defeated and wiped out, Major Lupo being one of the dead. The partisans could have scattered and escaped in the brushy and mountainous country, but apparently Major Lupo decided to risk a desperate battle rather than abandon his large stock of military supplies. There is no evidence that Major Reder's forces engaged in any violence other than that required to overcome resistance and carry out the assignment of disposing of the Red Star Brigade. The small Italian town of Marzabotto was located some miles from the scene of battle and no fighting whatever took place there at the time that the Red Star Brigade was destroyed.

A few days later, one of Major Reder's men, Julien Legoli, an Alsatian collaborator who had enlisted in the Nazi forces, deserted to the Americans. To ingratiate himself with them, he made the utterly false charge that, before his attack on the Red Star Brigade on September 29th, Major Reder had informed his Unit that even civilians were to be given no quarter if they offered any resistance to the German troops, and that they were to be shot in reprisal if any of them fired on German troops. This mendacious report was passed on to General Badoglio, and Major Reder was listed as a "war-criminal," to be tried after the Germans surrendered.

Having been severely injured in battle in Hungary in March, 1945, Major Reder was released for a time after the German collapse. In September, 1945, he was arrested by the Americans in Salzburg when they learned that the Italians sought him as a war-criminal. He was held by the Americans for exactly two years under very harsh conditions in a prison camp. The American authorities satisfied themselves that the charges against Major Reder, based on Legoli's report, were not sustained by the evidence, and they turned him over to the British forces in Austria. The British made an even more thorough investigation of the Legoli accusations and reported that they were not supported by any valid evidence. Yet, they turned Major Reder over to the Italians on May 13, 1948.

The Italians held Major Reder in prison for over three years before bringing him to trial before a military court in Bologna in October, 1951. The Bologna trial was a farce dominated by Communist pressure. Bologna was a main stronghold of Italian Communists. Communist mobs besieged the courthouse. The prosecution was conducted by an ardent youthful Communist who was neither a lawyer nor a soldier but was given full leeway to vent his passion on the defendant. Legoli, whose false tale constituted the main basis for holding Major Reder at all, was not even called to testify. It is probable that he had already been shot by the French as a collaborator. Despite all this, the court dismissed five of the eight charges against Major Reder, found him guilty of three, and sentenced him to life imprisonment. If the court had actually regarded him as guilty on these three charges, it would most certainly have sentenced him to death. But it did not dare to acquit Major Reder for fear of Communist violence and reprisals. Major Reder appealed to the Supreme Italian Military Court in March, 1954.

In the interval between his conviction in Bologna in October, 1951, and 1954, Major Reder was mysteriously and abruptly accused of having driven the entire population of Marzabotto into a church there and burned them to death, along with their priest, after which the whole town was razed to the ground. The facts are that Major Reder never set foot in Marzabotto, and the only injury to the town during the war came from American bombardment as their forces moved northward against the German army. No such charge of massacre and destruction was made against Major Reder at the Bologna trial, whereas it would have constituted the main basis for the prosecution if anybody had then heard of it or believed him guilty of it. The charge was manufactured out of whole cloth *after* the trial by the device of transferring to Marzabotto the alleged destruction of the French village of Oradour, several hundred miles from Marzabotto, as a Nazi reprisal. The English lawyer, F. J. P. Veale, who has made the most careful investigation of the "Marzabotto Affair," declares that the alleged massacre "is nothing but a Communist fairy tale."[21]

In their effort to make the "fairy tale" stick, the Communists erected a stone mausoleum in Marzabotta on which are inscribed the names of those alleged to have perished in the massacre, including five priests and eighty women, a total of nearly 1800 persons. The names actually appear to be those of all the persons in the region who perished from any or all causes during the entire second World War. There is no evidence that any serious massacre or devastation took place in Marzabotta during the War, to say nothing of its having been carried out by Major Reder.

The Supreme Italian Military Court, also fearful of the Communists, denied Major Reder's appeal on March 16, 1954, and confirmed his sentence to life imprisonment. Had the Court really believed in the massacre story, it would doubtless have ordered a new trial and a death sentence would have been imposed.

One of the most astonishing items in regard to the Marzabotta Affair is the fact that the Italian Minister of the Interior, Mario Scelba, assumed to believe the massacre tale and affirmed its validity when denying an appeal for clemency in the Major Reder case made to him by the Austrian State Secretary, Herr Graf. Like the two Italian military courts which had

[21] F. J. P. Veale, *Crimes Discreetly Veiled*, (London, 1958), p. 165. The whole case is covered by Mr. Veale in Chapter V of this book.

passed judgment, Scelba, also, appeared to fear the Communist pressure against justice for Major Reder. The latter still languishes in an Italian prison after more than thirteen years of unjust detention.

The Americans and British, after apparently regarding Major Reder as innocent, followed the example of Pontius Pilate and washed their hands of the case by handing Major Reder over to the Italians. The post-War Italian Governments have not dared to challenge the Communist "fairy tale." Since Major Reder was of Austrian birth, the German Government under Chancellor Adenauer has not troubled itself about the case, and the Austrian Government has been too weak to press the cause of clemency and justice.

CHAPTER XIX

CRISIS IN THE ITALIAN CABINET

FROM the moment of its formation, the Bonomi Cabinet had been an abortion, and its whole history was a series of crises while the general conditions of the country were going from bad to worse. There was little or no respect for law and order, banditry became ever more general, and in this connection Allied soldiers and Italian rapscallions vied with each other, while the Italian authorities were powerless. The Prefect of Foggia complained that any Negro GI had more authority than he had. The mayors of the larger cities could not authorize the expenditure of any sum above 2,000 lire without the permission of the Allies. Those of some of the smaller towns of Apulia formed brigand bands of their own, which infested whole districts.

Sforza, although the Allies had vetoed his appointment as Minister of Foreign Affairs, fatuously laid down a series of plans for Italy's foreign policy, which he knew he would never be allowed to carry out. At the same time, he was ever servile towards all foreign Governments, and demanded that Italy should take the initative in "returning" Rhodes, Cos and the Dodecanese to Greece, to whom they had never belonged, but he quite forgot that they were then held by the Germans and that they were about to be taken over by the British.

In September, 1944, the first trials for Fascist "crimes" were staged, and were to go on for several years. The President of the above-mentioned High Court was to have been Marquis Casati but, when a speech of his lauding certain Fascist institutions was unearthed, the office was conferred instead on the judge, Lorenzo Maroni. This magistrate had formerly been an ardent Fascist, and a near relative of his told me that if he occasionally made some mild strictures on a particular measure of the Fascist Government, Maroni would go off the deep end, exclaiming that everything which the regime did was perfect. At the trial of Cesare Rossi, who had been the head of the Fascist Government's press bureau in 1922, the accused reminded Maroni that during the Fascist regime he had worn a black shirt under his judicial robes. He now, over-compensating, became a veritable Torquemada in prosecuting the Fascists, inveighing against them in the foulest language.

During the trial of Caruso, the ex-chief of police, a savage mob invaded the courtroom to lynch him and, as he could not be found at that moment, it seized Carretta, the ex-warden of the Regina Coeli prison in Rome, dragged him into the street and threw him into the Tiber, where he was drowned. Caruso himself was later condemned to death by the court, although no evidence of guilt was produced, and was executed. In October, Vincenzo Azzolini, Governor of the Bank of Italy, was tried on the charge of having surrendered the Bank's gold reserve to the Germans and, although it was proved that he had merely sent it to the North of Italy for safety (whence it was afterwards brought back to Rome), he was condemned to thirty years imprisonment. Sforza had demanded that he be shot without a trial, but later Azzolini was fully acquitted.

The ACC treated the Italian Ministers, appointed by the Allies themselves, with gross insolence. A certain measure demanded by the ACC had been submitted to the Minister, Giovanni Gronchi,[1] with orders to carry it out. When he called attention to certain serious defects contained in it, the Allied delegate rudely told him to draft it and enforce it at once. Gronchi then threw the document on the table and exclaimed: "You may draft the law yourselves. We are a defenseless people and can only accept your orders, but you cannot make us say that we approve of what we do not approve."[2]

The question of using a larger number of Italian soldiers was raised once more, and Bonomi asked that the 39,000 Italian prisoners then detained in France be drafted into fighting units,

[1] Elected President of the Republic in 1955. He had been an under-secretary in the Mussolini Fascist government.
[2] Barbara Barclay Carter, *Italy Speaks* (London, 1947), p. 100.

but he received no reply. The few existing Italian units were defined as "combat groups," although they were hardly ever allowed to do any fighting, and to each group a British liaison unit was attached to control it; they were, in fact, regarded merely as parts of the British army. On November 24th, the first of these groups passed through Rome on its way north, and was warmly acclaimed by the people.

With a view to obtaining some improvement in the food conditions, a request was made to the Allies for an increase in the inadequate supplies then available for the population. But the British Ambassador in Washington, Viscount Halifax, sent a note to the State Department, declaring that his Government insisted that the supplies sent to Italy should only suffice to prevent actual starvation and rioting.[3] President Roosevelt was a little less harsh towards Italy than British statesmen, possibly because he had to consider the votes of the hundreds of thousands of American citizens of Italian origin in view of his coming campaign for re-election. On September 26th, in fact, he announced that further supplies would be shipped to Italy.

The question of Italy's diplomatic representation was now raised again, and at the Hyde Park meeting it was decided that she would be allowed to send ambassadors to Washington and London. This concession was, however, countered by Eden's declaration, early in October, that Italy was to be deprived of all her colonies, not being deemed worthy of having any such possessions, thereby confirming Churchill's statement to the same effect of September 21, 1943.

In selecting men for the two Embassies, party considerations prevailed. The choice for Washington fell on Alberto Tarchiani as representing the *Partito d'Azione*. He was a third-rate journalist, but as he had been in the service of the U. S. Government, even before the armistice, for anti-Italian propaganda and other assignments, it was believed that he would prove acceptable to the American Government.[4] He was to remain at

---

[3] Viscount Halifax was reported to be a very pious Christian gentleman.

[4] This was probably a mistake. In wartime, governments make use of anyone who they think may be useful, however shady, but they do not respect them.

that post until 1955, and it does not appear that during those eleven years he ever rendered any service to his country.

For London, Count Niccolo Carandini was chosen as representing the Liberal Party, on whom a plum had to be conferred. His chief merit was that he was a rich man and brother-in-law of the anti-Fascist former publisher of the powerful Milan *Corriere della Sera*, Luigi Albertini. Incidentally, he was a gentleman, which Tarchiani never professed to be. Albertini had been removed from the editorship of the paper by the owners of a majority of the shares. He received a large settlement which enabled him to buy an estate near Civitavecchia. Here, he devoted much time to compiling a large and discursive history of the causes of the first World War which was especially hostile to Germany and Austria.

The United States Government acted wisely in appointing Alexander Kirk Ambassador in Rome. He had been counsellor in that capital for many years and several times chargé d'affaires, spoke Italian and other languages perfectly, was a man of the world and a brilliant wit, and had always been friendly to Italy and even to the Fascist regime, many members of which were his personal friends. The British Government also appointed a former counsellor to the Rome Embassy, Sir Noël Charles. He was not without ability, but was prone to let awkward cats out of the bag. .

In November, 1944, a Cabinet crisis of unusual gravity was imminent, and on December 1st Bonomi resigned, but the Allied High Commissioner in Rome, Admiral Stone, ordered him to resume his office, and he, of course, had to obey. On the 8th, he issued his list of Ministers, consisting of Christian Democrats, Liberals, Social Democrats, members of the *Partito d'Azione* and Communists. Of the latter, Mauro Scoccimarro[5] was appointed Minister for the "Liberated Provinces."

The air-bombing in Northern Italy continued to produce widespread devastation and ever more numerous victims among the civilian population. The raid of October 20th on Milan resulted in the deaths of 600 persons, and in one on Gorla, near

[5] Now a member of the Italian Parliament.

that city, a schoolhouse was hit, resulting in the killing of 200 children from six to ten years of age and of several of their women teachers. A broken-down old steamship plying on the Lagoon between Venice and Chioggia was sunk (100 dead); another small steamer on the Sebino lake was also hit (35 dead); on November 18th a large party of men, women and children hastening to an anti-air-raid shelter at Parma were machine gunned from a low altitude, many of them being killed or wounded; and a few days later 109 women were killed in an air raid on a hospital.

A disgraceful incident of factiousness occurred at Vicenza on November 10th, when, in consequence of a wireless message sent to the Allies by the local CLN, stating (falsely) that there were important military establishments in that beautiful city,[6] an air raid caused terrible damage and killed many victims. On January 4th, another needless raid on Verona resulted in the destruction of many priceless works of art and about a thousand victims. On the 16th, Carrara was bombed in consequence of a message from a traitor in British pay to the effect that a large number of Germans were concentrated in the city, whereas there were none at all at that time. At Aulla, some 300 persons were killed in an air raid at the end of that month.

It is not easy to understand the reasons for this wholesale butchery. If the object was to terrorize the population, it was of no use whatever, for victory or defeat depended on the German army and to a lesser extent on that of the RSI, and not on working men and women, peasants and school children. It may, perhaps, have been part of the Allied program for introducing higher civilization into Italy.

Another consequence of the Allied occupation was being ever more intensified, namely, the growth of criminality, both among the Italian population and the Allied forces, and deserters from the latter contributed to it in no small degree. Certain districts had become veritable hotbeds of crime and vice. The Tombolo forest near Leghorn acquired an unenviable notoriety as a gathering place for murderers, thieves, gangsters

[6]The culprits were arrested, and at their trial confessed their crime.

and prostitutes of all nationalities and races. The Italian police authorities were far too busy with political persecution to trouble about ordinary crime, and the Allied authorities did not care what went on.

Relations with the Allied Powers and with the ACC and the AMG were becoming ever more important, and for these a really brilliant man was needed as Minister of Foreign Affairs. But the newly appointed Minister of Foreign Affairs (and future Prime Minister), Alcide De Gasperi, was devoid of the necessary qualities. A native of the Trentino, but wholly detached from the patriotic Italian Irredentist movement of the province, he had been a member of the Austrian Reichsrat and, unlike the great majority of his fellow Trentini, had always been devoted to the Emperor Francis Joseph and to the Imperial and Royal Government. Throughout World War I, he had faithfully served the Hapsburg Empire, and only discovered his Italian origins when his native province became part of the Italian Kingdom. He was then appointed secretary of the Catholic *Partito Popolare* (the spiritual forebear of the Christian Democratic Party); but the publication of a letter written in October, 1914, by the Austrian Ambassador in Rome (Italy was then still neutral) to the Vienna Ministry of Foreign Affairs on De Gasperi's ultra-loyal Austrian sentiments. led to his forced resignation.[7]

During World War II, De Gasperi had been imprisoned for a short time on account of his hostility to the Government, and after his release he took refuge in the Vatican as a library assistant, emerging into the open only after July 25, 1943.

He joined the first Bonomi Cabinet as Minister without portfolio, and in the second he became, as we have seen, Minister of Foreign Affairs. He had only very slight knowledge of, or interest in, international relations and no patriotic feeling for Italy. He was hardly ever seen at the Palazzo Chigi, but spent most of his time and activities at the Christian Democratic

---

[7] The letter was first published in Vol. V of Field Marshal Count Franz Conrad von Hötzendorff's *Memoirs (Aus meiner Dienstzeit)* (Vienna, 1921), and reprinted in various Italian papers.

headquarters. The only matters on which he was really keen and of which he had considerable knowledge were party organization, electioneering and parliamentary cabala. He was a mild, timid, feeble little man, and his one merit was, that, unlike many of his colleagues then and after the War, he was personally honest.

The low esteem in which Italy was held in British circles appeared in the statement made by Churchill on January 18, 1945, that Great Britain had no use for Italy or for Spain, and Sir Noël Charles one day told an official of the Italian Ministry of Foreign Affairs that Fascist Italy had placed Great Britain in serious danger in the Mediterranean and forced her to tie herself very closely to Russia and the United States for reasons of self-defense. Hence, Italy must be reduced to such a weak condition as never again to be a menace. If war were one day to break out between Great Britain and Russia, the former would need Italy, but would have no use for the Italians.

During the fatal Yalta meeting, Bonomi sent messages to Churchill, Roosevelt and Stalin, as Italian affairs were also being discussed at the pleasant little Crimean health resort. Churchill then submitted his notes on Italy's future frontiers with Austria and Yugoslavia and proposed to support Russia's offensive through Austria into Central Europe.[8]

A new memorandum on Italian affairs was now presented by the President of the ACC, Harold Macmillan, and the High Commissioner in Italy, Admiral Stone, proposing some slight alleviation of the armistice conditions;[9] but if the form was somewhat altered, full Allied control was maintained and every measure of the Rome Cabinet continued to be subject to the approval of the ACC. Nothing was promised in the matter of better supplies of food and other necessary commodities.

Bonomi had also asked for some improvement in the deplorable conditions of Italian prisoners of war, and Macmillan replied that something might be done for their employment in the

---

[8]Tamaro, op. cit., Vol. III, pp. 468-9.
[9]Holborn, War and Peace, Aims of the U. S., Vol. II, p. 14; Robert Sherwood, Roosevelt and Hopkins (New York, 1948), p. 852.

interest of the Allied Commands; in a press conference, he spoke highly of the Italian contingents in the Allied ranks, and also expressed hopes for the action of the partisans, but evidently without much confidence.

Lack of food and other difficulties led to sporadic riots in various parts of Southern Italy, especially at Caulonia in Calabria. There were also underground Fascist movements, attributed mainly to Prince Valerio Pignatelli, who was afterwards arrested by the British authorities and interned at Padula (province of Salerno), but was believed to be in touch with various Fascist groups even while in prison. He was a man of heroic courage, a soldier in many wars, a journalist (at one time connected with the Hearst papers), and capable of exercising great personal influence over his supporters. His wife, a woman of exceptional intelligence and courage, cooperated with him in his political activities and was herself arrested by the British and interned at Terni, where she was subjected to the severest treatment until she managed to escape. Pignatelli was afterwards handed over to the Italian authorities, imprisoned by them at Procida and elsewhere, but at his trial he was fully acquitted. At Teramo, in the Abruzzi, the conscripts for the new Italian army were frequently heard singing Fascist songs, and at Ascoli Piceno, in the Marche, a group of ardent Fascists tried to wreck the local headquarters of the Communist party.

Fruitless negotiations were conducted by the Government with France over the repeal of the armistice concluded with that country in June, 1940.[10] The negotiations also failed to prevent the exclusion of Italy from the San Francisco Conference where the United Nations Organization was to be created, whereas France, which had held out against the Italo-German attack for only a week, was admitted to that body as a victorious power.

Amid the ceaseless spate of ferocious warfare, bloodshed and crime, there came on March 18, 1945, a public address by the Pope, advocating an end to hatred, ultra-nationalism, racialism and violence. A true peace, His Holiness rightly declared,

[10] Communiqué of March 3, 1945, in Tamaro, *op cit.*, Vol. III, p. 487.

should be based on justice and truth, but he failed to say how it should be achieved. In any case, the Allied Powers paid not the slightest attention to him, but proceeded relentlessly and ruthlessly in their policy of unlimited slaughter and devastation, without respect for any of the generally accepted principles of international law or of humanity, while preparing a "peace" in flagrant violation of all these considerations.

In the parts of Italy nominally under Bonomi's Government the political quarrels continued unabated. The upper classes, although mainly Royalist, avoided appearing to give support to the Monarchy, while the chief arguments in its favor were supplied by the appalling blunders of the demagogues at that time in power.

With regard to the eternal question of building up an Italian army to cooperate with the Allies, several of the above-mentioned "combat groups" were now actually formed, and some of them were sent North where they distinguished themselves in action when given a chance. But their effectives were very small, their equipment utterly inadequate, and the Allied authorities viewed them with disfavor, lest their courageous action might supply arguments in favor of better treatment for Italy in general.

CHAPTER XX

THE VENEZIA GIULIA AGAIN

L ET us now return to the situation of Italy's northeastern frontier, endangered by Tito's expansive ambitions.

The Allied Command wished to reach that area as soon as possible, so as to have a clear route for their armies through to Austria. But Tito, who then enjoyed the full support of Russia, snapped his fingers at the Western Powers and was determined to lay his hands on as much territory as possible. Great Britain and the United States were not willing to alienate Stalin and, still believing that it was possible "to get on with him," as Roosevelt was always saying, practically let him have a free hand.

With the break-up of the Italian armies and the subsequent withdrawal of the Germans, the path was open to Tito to push on towards the head of the Adriatic, generously supported as he was in arms, equipment and money by the British and American Governments. His aim was to seize Trieste, all the rest of the Venezia Giulia and, if possible, some parts of Venetia proper as well. That the great majority of the population of those territories was Italian and that the whole civilization was historically Italian were circumstances of no consequence to the Yugoslav dictator. He intended to set up a Communist State in Yugoslavia and expand its frontiers in all directions. Even the Rome Government did not raise any objections to his scheme and, blinded as it was by its hatred of Fascism, was ready to hand over any territory to Tito which he might ask for, while the local Italian Communist partisan bands were, of course, willing to play his game.

In the Carso, in Trieste, and in Istria, there were Italian partisan bands which Tito, with the help of the local Communist party and the CLNAI, had succeeded in bringing under the

161

command of the IX Slovene Corps. At first, few Italians were willing to join that unit, but a German decree for compulsory recruiting of labor in the area induced 3,000 of them to do so. They thus betrayed Italy, but were betrayed in turn by their new masters. Tito now sent agents into the Italian province of Udine to promote the annexation to Yugoslavia of all the territory between the Isonzo and the Tagliamento rivers, on the pretext that it contained some Slovene-speaking inhabitants, although these had always been patriotically Italian. Even the Gorizia partisans, although anti-Fascists, rejected the idea of annexation to Yugoslavia.

The Italians who had joined the IX Slovene Corps soon bitterly regretted having done so, for the Yugoslavs robbed them and mistreated them in every way. They were divided into battalions of forced laborers, compelled to perform the hardest work and ordered to fight against their fellow-Italians; many of their officers were murdered.[1]

Nevertheless, the CLNAI of the Venezia Giulia actually issued an appeal to all Italians to cooperate with the Yugoslav partisans, who were demanding the annexation of the whole area and butchering Italian prisoners of war, as well as many of the local Italian inhabitants.[2]

A few Blackshirt units under General Sommavilla and some of the regular RSI army under General Esposito undertook to defend the territories in question. But further complications ensued, owing to the action of the German *Gauleiter* in Trieste, Rainer, who seemed to be preparing the annexation of the area to Germany, although he had assured Mussolini's Minister, Biggini, that the German occupation was to be only temporary.[3]

Tito, at his conference with General Alexander at Bolsena (in Central Italy), had agreed not to go beyond Fiume, but without any real intention of respecting this undertaking, so little in harmony with his plans of unlimited expansion.

In the meanwhile, documents concerning Tito's intentions

[1] Statement in the *Bollettino della Brigata Garibaldi*, March 3, 1945.
[2] Tamaro, *op. cit.*, Vol. III, pp. 313-4.
[3] Hitler had said the same thing to Mussolini himself.

were sent by the Bishop of Trieste, Monsignor Santin, to the Pope and forwarded to the British and American Governments setting forth what the Yugoslavs intended to do, including a list of the Italians whom they had decided to murder. Roosevelt was impressed by this information, and gave orders that the provisions of the Bolsena agreement with Tito were to be suspended and that the whole of the Venezia Giulia was to be defined as the XII Region of Italy.

On the other hand, the Rome authorities insisted that an agreement with Yugoslavia was necessary, and ingenuously believed that Tito would respect it. The Secretary General of Bonomi's Ministry of Foreign Affairs, Renato Prunas, discussed the matter with the American Ambassador in Rome, Mr. Kirk, on August 5th and again on the 23rd, while the Italian Ambassador in Moscow took up the matter with the Russian Government, asking it to intervene to restrain Yugoslavia's excesses, and Bonomi discussed the matter with Admiral Stone on September 18th. Two Trieste citizens, Camillo Ara and Giorgio Pitacco, went around from one Allied command or office to another, visited the Pope, Prince Humbert, Bonomi, and various newspaper editors, to plead ardently for the cause of their city and province.

This state of affairs caused the deepest anxiety both in the RSI and in Monarchist Italy so far as public opinion was concerned. Togliatti did not, of course, consider the question from a national point of view, but he realized that the great majority of the Italian people were deeply affected by the danger of seeing the Venezia Giulia lost to Italy, and he indulged in the most acrobatic gymnastics in order to wriggle out of expressing any views which might offend either his Russian masters or the Italian people, of whom he expected one day to be the absolute ruler. In the end, however, he accepted the Russian-Yugoslav view in full, and suggested that Trieste should be given to Yugoslavia as war booty.

The other Italian Communist leaders made no secret of their sympathies for Yugoslavia as a Communist and Russian satellite state, and the "Garibaldi" Communist partisans had no hesitation in allowing themselves to be absorbed into the Yugoslav army, although they received little gratitude from Tito. Altogether, they amounted to some 16,000 men, of whom only 11,000 were repatriated, the rest having been killed in action or murdered by their Yugoslav "allies."

On landing at Bari, the remnants of these units were cordially welcomed by the people, but a curious incident illustrated the changed feelings of these repatriates. A woman presented a bouquet of red carnations to one of the corporals, who at first accepted it with thanks; but when the woman told him that the flowers were a tribute from the Italian Communist party he threw them away, cursing the Communists vigorously. "I have a son," he said, "but if I find that he has become a Communist I shall wring his neck as if he were a fowl." Likewise the Istrian, Ravnich, who had commanded a "Garibaldi" Communist unit in Yugoslavia, declared that after his experiences in that country he had become a reactionary.

The Italian Communists professed to be eager only for the establishment of friendly relations with Yugoslavia, and claimed that this could not be secured unless Italy handed over to that country all the territories in which there were any Slavs, even if only a tiny minority. When the brutal murders and ill treatment of Italians by Tito's gangsters were reported, they merely said: "We must do nothing which might offend those gallant Yugoslav fighters for freedom. . . . Italy has nothing to fear from the existence of a strong Yugoslavia on her eastern border, as the Yugoslav people have never had any expansionist aims against our country."

The only reason for that attitude was the fact that Tito's Government was Communist and that it enjoyed the full support of Russia. So, it was Italy's duty, apart from her own guilt in having been a Fascist State, to give him everything he asked for. They would willingly have handed over to him not only the whole of the Venezia Giulia, but the province of Udine as well, and perhaps Venice itself. Their ideal was to see the whole of Italy under Communist rule, and if, in the meanwhile, at least a part of the country was governed by a Communist so much the better.

Russia's aim was now to penetrate into the Mediterranean via the Adriatic ports, whereas the Allies, while ever ready to give Russia most of what she wanted, were eager to keep their own route open to Vienna and Southern Germany. Hence, they preferred not to see the Russians in Trieste. We shall see later how these contradictory aspirations were to be adjusted.

Churchill, in his speech in the House of Commons on January 17, 1945, while stating that the Bonomi Government would soon be menaced by many violent and aggressive politicians, with consequences which could not be foreseen or measured, added that Great Britain had no plans with respect to political combinations in Europe or elsewhere for which she needed Italy as an associate. "We have no need of Italy any more than of Spain, because we have no problems requiring the support of those Powers." In other words, he implied that, if Italy went Communist or went to the devil, Great Britain did not care two straws.

CHAPTER XXI

THE END OF HOSTILITIES

THE underground anti-Fascist groups in North Italy continued to develop and intensify their hate campaign, without contributing much to the defeat of the Germans, a task which was left to the advancing Allied armies. Their leaders were, however, preparing for the wholesale slaughter of their Italian opponents, but until the *Wehrmacht* and the forces of the RSI were completely defeated and all risks eliminated, the rebels lay low.

The Piedmontese CLN, on March 2nd, drafted a penal code of its own, whereby the members of Mussolini's Government and all other prominent Fascist leaders regarded as guilty of "the suppression of liberty" were to be executed without trial as soon as captured and identified, independently of any specific offenses rightly or wrongly attributed to them.[1] The Communists, whether members of the CLN or not, intended to secure full powers for themselves, to the exclusion of all other opponents of the regime. But, in the meanwhile, the masses showed no signs of carrying out any action at all.

Within the ranks of the partisans there was the usual lack of unity, and disputes were constantly breaking out, especially on the question of appointing a supreme commander for the whole movement. General Cadorna, strongly supported by the Allies, had at last succeeded in being invested with supreme authority, but his two seconds-in-command, Parri and Longo, had as much authority as he had, if not more, and many individual units continued to obey no one except their own local leaders.

At the end of March, 1945, during the absence from Italy of Cadorna and Parri, who were intriguing in Switzerland with various official and semi-official Allied representatives, the CLNAI attempted to weld the various partisan bands into more

[1] This was roughly the wording of Art. 2 of the legislative Decree of July 27, 1944.

regular military formations under a stricter discipline, but the effort failed completely. It was, indeed, very difficult for a number of men, accustomed to act more or less entirely on their own, or, in the case of the Communists, to obey only the orders reaching them from Moscow, to accept the authority of any single man or group of men who were not Russians.

The total number of partisans at this period, near the end of the War, is as difficult to estimate as it was in the early days of the movement. There were still no regular lists, and the numbers of each unit varied from day to day. The British military authorities estimated their total number at that time at about 90,000—more or less the same figure as that quoted by Cadorna —but it is a purely conjectural estimate.

The partisans who, in 1944 and early in the following year, had done some real fighting, now began, as Parri himself has admitted, to find themselves swamped by an ever-increasing tide of bogus partisans, who had never done any fighting but were determined to be in at the kill and get their share of the pickings, "hastening," as General Trabucchi writes, "to the help of the victors."[2]

While the Allies were slowly and painfully driving back the Germans, who had practically ceased to receive any more reinforcements or supplies from Germany, then invaded from both the Eastern and the Western fronts, the CLNAI again began to talk about staging a general insurrection behind the German lines. On March 29th, on the proposal of the Communist Under-Secretary for the "Liberated" Territories, and in the presence of an Italian in the British service, one Max Salvadori, the CLNAI leaders undertook to obey the instructions of the Allied Supreme Command to organize the insurrectionary movement and save the Italian industrial plants from being wrecked by the retreating Germans, after which they were to hand over their powers to the AMG. But the various parties within the CLNAI had no intention of relinquishing their authority or their political position for building up the framework of the restored Italian "democracy." What the leaders were really keen about

[2] *I vinti hanno sempre torto* (Turin, 1947), p. 149.

was to carry out their vendetta against all political opponents and eliminate the "anti-social" elements, i.e., not only the Fascists, but also all patriotic Italians, regardless of party. The Communists took the lead in drafting this plan.

For the moment nothing was attempted beyond a few isolated outrages, followed by the usual reprisals. In the streets of Milan and other towns, corpses of murdered men were found every morning. Following the wiping out of several Fascist families, the Fascists retaliated by dealing in the same way with the Arduino family, known to be anti-Fascist.

These deeds of violence had no effect on the general situation and, although the position of the RSI was evidently becoming daily more precarious, its gradual breakdown was due exclusively to the general military situation and to the advance of the Allied armies.

In Genoa, the Communists organized a "spy day," on which they killed 22 men, most of whom had never been guilty of any act of espionage. In Turin, 70 Fascists were murdered in one week; in Emilia, 1,052 in a month.

The story of the negotiations between Mussolini, Graziani, Cadorna, the German authorities and the Allies, through the mediation of the Archbishop of Milan, Cardinal Schuster, I have already told in another book, *Italian Foreign Policy Under Mussolini,* as also that of the departure of the Duce and the members of his Cabinet for the Valtellina, where they mistakenly believed that important Fascist forces were concentrated for a last stand. As we know, the final outcome was the butchery of the Ministers of the RSI, Ferdinando Mezzasoma and Ruggiero Romano; the Secretary of the Fascist Party, Alessandro Pavolini; the President of the University of Bologna, Professor Geoffredo Coppola; the head of the *Stefani* Agency, Ernesto Daquanno; the Prefect, Paolo Zerbino; the Under-Secretary, Francesco Barracu, and others, who were held up at Dongo on Lake Como and shot without trial.

It is, of course, impossible to say just what fate Mussolini would have met if he had been captured by the Allied armed forces, but he would certainly have escaped cowardly butchery by Communist partisans. He could have remained safely with

Cardinal Schuster in Milan, pending the arrival of Allied troops, but he was repelled by the revelation of what he regarded as treachery on the part of the Cardinal. At that critical moment, he was under the influence of Alessandro Pavolini, the last Secretary-General of the Fascist party. Pavolini was a fanatical Fascist of theatrical tendencies. He projected an imaginary heroic "last stand" in the mountainous area of the Valtellina in northern Italy, and convinced Mussolini that a large body of loyal Blackshirts were already there to rally around him. Mussolini made the fatal mistake of capitulating to Pavolini's fantastic blandishments. He and his ministers left for the North via Como, which was only thirty miles from Milan, on the afternoon of April 26th. It would probably have been possible for the party to push quickly to the Swiss border at Chiasso, only four miles from Como, if they had then intended to escape. But, for the moment, Mussolini was thinking of going on to the final Fascist rally in the North. Hence, he lost time by spending the night at Como at the southern end of the lake, and then proceeded up along the west side of the lake to Menaggio, where he expected to join Pavolini with the first large detachment of Blackshirts. Only a dozen showed up, instead of the hundreds or thousands expected.

Mussolini then realized that there was to be no dramatic "last stand," and that his only hope was to escape in another way. By this time, however, the partisans had heard of his movements and were on the lookout for him. It was easy to stop any group of cars on the narrow and winding lakeside road. On the 27th, the cars carrying Mussolini and the Fascist leaders joined a German transport column which was halted by partisans near Dongo. Mussolini and his mistress, Claretta Petacci, who later joined him, were seized, along with the others in the party. Mussolini and Claretta were placed in a peasant's cottage for the night near the small town of Bonzanigo, some miles from Dongo. News of the capture of Mussolini spread to the Communists among the partisans and to their leaders in Milan. It was apparently decided to murder Mussolini before he could fall into the hands of American troops, for an American armored unit had already reached Como.

The assassination was carried out by a fanatical Communist partisan named Walter Audisio, known in the underground as "Colonel Valerio." He apparently acted under the orders from Longo, and the latter presumably had been directed by Togliatti to murder Mussolini, if it were possible. At least, Togliatti so boasted later on. Anyhow, Audisio faked the authority to execute Mussolini and was permitted by the partisans who had originally captured Mussolini to go with three other heavily armed men in a car to the cottage where Mussolini and Claretta still remained on the early afternoon of April 28th. Audisio told them that he had come to liberate them, and they gladly followed his orders to get into the car. He drove them a short way down the road, and then ordered them to get out. Even then, they may not have realized that they were about to be shot, for they were ordered to walk ahead down the road toward the entrance to the Villa Belmonte overlooking Lake Como.

While there is no reliable evidence as to just how they met their death, the astute English lawyer, F. J. P. Veale, who has made a careful study of all the testimony, is inclined to think that they were shot down by machine gun fire from their rear by the four Communist gangsters—Audisio, "Guido" Lampredi, Lazzaro Urbano and Michele Moretti—before they realized that their end had come. It would thus seem that they met their end much as the victims of a Chicago gang war—not unlike the Capone Valentine's Day massacre in 1929. Claretta was murdered, as we shall make clear later on, because she was aware of the seizure of a large sum of Fascist money by the partisans the previous day. Later on, Audisio dramatized the murder by telling how he made the victims face him, announced his intentions, and then shot them. Others have claimed that Audisio merely organized the assassination, following out the orders of Longo and Togliatti, and that it was Michele Moretti who really murdered Mussolini and Claretta. It would seem most likely that the four Communist gunmen riddled them from behind their backs and that they died almost before they knew what was happening. At any rate, Audisio claimed personal credit for the murder and, on this basis, was elected to the

Chamber of Deputies. After Audisio and his fellow-assassins had returned to Dongo and murdered the remaining members of the Fascist party and their associates, the bodies of Mussolini and Claretta were removed to Milan and there hung up by their feet in the Piazzale Loreto.[3]

While the Communist partisans were eager to murder Mussolini before he could fall into the hands of the Allied military authorities, there is little doubt that the Allied leaders, including Churchill, were immensely gratified to have the partisans dispose of Mussolini. According to the terms of the Long Armistice (Art. 29), Mussolini and his principal Fascist associates were to have been immediately arrested and turned over to the United Nations to be tried as war-criminals. Despite this provision, it was realized that Mussolini, with his native intelligence and his vast body of information about European and Italo-American diplomacy from 1922 to 1945, would be likely to prove a very embarrassing witness in any war-crimes trial. Between the Allied Commands and the partisans, it was made certain that the large bundle of documents that Mussolini was known to be carrying when arrested was destroyed or carefully hidden away. These documents have never been recovered.

The body of Mussolini was secretly removed from the Piazzale Loreto, and the Italian Government only recently, after a delay of twelve years, allowed it to be given a Christian burial. This was earlier refused, in spite of the repeated appeals of the family, supported by large numbers of the most prominent men in Italy, including not a few of his former bitter opponents, owing to the fear that a funeral ceremony might give rise to striking demonstrations in memory of the murdered statesman. In September, 1957, Mussolini's body was finally given to his family and was then buried in the small churchyard of his birthplace, Predappio. There, the grave continues to be visited not only by his family but also by large crowds of still devoted admirers.[4]

[3] The most satisfactory account in English of the flight, capture and murder of Mussolini is contained in Chapter III of F. J. P. Veale, *Crimes Discreetly Veiled* (London, 1958).

[4] Claretta Petacci was buried in the cemetery at Verano. A prominent resident of

The partisan insurrection broke out in Milan on April 25, 1945, when there was virtually no one to rise against, or at least no armed forces. The German troops were either in retreat or shut up in barracks, offering no resistance, the German and Italian police had disappeared, and the Allied armies were on the outskirts of the city, but had not yet entered it. The anti-Fascists, Communists and others, talked of having "captured the Prefecture by storm," when there were only two policemen and two German soldiers in the building, and they said the same thing about the Muti barracks which were entirely empty.

I was in Milan myself at that time, and hour after hour, for many days, I watched the endless processions of partisans, armed with rifles or submachine guns, which they evidently did not even know how to hold, never having taken part in any military action, marching through the streets, repeatedly singing the same Communist songs. Numbers of men whom I had known previously to be ardent Fascists, now sported the tricolor brassard of members of the CLN and claimed that they had *always* been anti-Fascists. Many of the most active members of the CLN were women, whose appearance reminded one of the notorious "pétroleuses" of the French Commune of 1871, and some of them distinguished themselves afterwards by their savage ferocity—it was Kipling who said that "the female of the species is more deadly than the male" and, in times like those, women, no less than men, easily forgot all feelings of human kindness or Christian charity.

The Communists aimed, as they always had, at wiping out not merely the Germans, who were no longer there, or even the forces of the RSI which were broken up and disarmed, but the whole of the bourgeois class. The order was given to murder as many Fascists as possible and innumerable non-

Rome was present at the occasion, and he noted with some surprise that among many other wreaths there was one from Faruk, the deposed King of Egypt. Since he happened to know Faruk personally, he inquired why he sent the wreath. Faruk replied: "When I was deposed from the throne and exiled from Egypt, all the women I had known turned their backs on me and refused to see me again. Claretta Petacci remained faithful to Mussolini to the very end and shared his fate. Hence, I felt obligated to express my admiration for her fidelity and courage."

Fascists, as well, in order to have a free hand in setting up an Italian Soviet Government in Milan, which was to extend its authority to the whole of Italy at the earliest possible moment under Russian satraps.

In Milan, the slaughter began on April 25th, and the Allied forces, although within easy reach of the city, delayed their entry into it for several days, so as to allow the Communists a free hand to clear things up by getting rid of all who might have offered some resistance in the future, if not at the moment. Every morning when I opened the papers I read that a given number of corpses had been found in the streets murdered during the past night, almost all of them without a document of identity or a lira in their pockets, and many unrecognizable on account of the mutilations inflicted on them. When one morning it was announced that "only one hundred corpses had been found," the papers said that the situation was "improving." The same thing was happening on a smaller scale in innumerable towns and villages all over Northern Italy.

In Turin, the insurrection began on the night of April 25-26 and, on the morning of the 26th, the partisan columns were about to enter the city, but were held up by the British military mission. There was some fighting with a few German and Fascist units after which both groups withdrew undisturbed. A detachment of the "Decima MAS" surrounded in the Monte Grappa barracks, surrendered on the promise of being treated as prisoners of war, but they were massacred directly afterwards.

Longo wired to Togliatti that Northern Italy had been "liberated" by a popular rising, which was obviously untrue, as in nearly every case the partisans only appeared on the scene when the fighting was over. Likewise, the claim that the industrial plants had been saved by the action of the partisans was pure fiction—the result had been achieved through negotiations between members of Mussolini's Government and the German military authorities and by the intervention of the German Ambassador, Rahn.

On April 29th, the capitulation of the German forces—twenty

or twenty-two divisions with greatly reduced effectives—was signed at Caserta, the Fascist units being included, and came into force on May 1st. Field Marshal Graziani gave himself up to the Americans, who conducted him first to Milan, then to Florence, whence he issued the order of surrender to his Ligurian army.

The remaining 2,200 men of the "Decima MAS" refused to surrender to the partisans, but did so to the Allies, who granted them the honors of war. The "Lupo" and "Barbarigo" battalions, after a gallant resistance, which caused the partisans heavy losses, also surrendered to the Allies.

It will be noted that the Italian units who surrendered to the Allies were treated as prisoners of war, on the same footing as the Germans, whereas the Rome Government continued to regard them as "traitors" and refused to grant them any form of recognition until quite recent times, and even today they are not yet on an equal footing with other Italian ex-service men.

The end of hostilities marked the final tragedy of the Venezia Giulia. Trieste had been gallantly defended as long as possible by Italian forces commanded by General Esposito. But, with the end of the RSI, the area fell into the hands of the Yugoslavs, who demanded that it be surrendered to Tito unconditionally. On September 27, 1945, the governing committee of the Venezia Giulia Communist Party, acting under Russian orders, voted a resolution stating that the people of the region had repeatedly expressed the wish to be annexed to "democratic and federated Yugoslavia," and that "the region itself, together with the port of Trieste, constitute an indissoluble political and economic unit." As we know, the immense majority of the people of the Venezia Giulia had never asked for anything of the kind; even in earlier times they had bitterly hated the Slavs, but now that Yugoslavia was under the tyranny of the Communist adventurer, Tito, they hated them still more intensely.

On May 2nd, Tito's forces occupied Trieste and remained there for six weeks, treating the Italian majority with every form of oppression and deporting large numbers of them to

Yugoslavia, whence many of them have never returned. The Allies subsequently compelled the Yugoslavs to evacuate Trieste and a small territory immediately adjoining it, occupying the area themselves, while the Yugoslavs remained in the Trieste hinterland, in Istria, Fiume and Zara, and in all Dalmatia. A temporary settlement of a most unsatisfactory nature was arrived at, as we shall see, under the terms of the Peace Treaty with Italy in 1947, modified by later arrangements in 1954. The whole of the rest of Italy remained occupied by Allied armed forces until 1947.

Ever since the end of the War the partisans have continued to claim that it was they who had chiefly contributed to the defeat of the Germans and of the RSI forces in Italy, and the various Italian Governments which succeeded each other after April 25, 1945, have, for electioneering reasons, lent full support to this absurd claim. But all who have any real knowledge of the facts take a very different view. The following passage from Luigi Barzini, Jr.'s pamphlet *I Comunisti non hanno vinto* is significant:

> A few months after Tito's defection from the Kremlin in 1948, the Russian Ambassador in Rome, Kostilev, in a conversation with an Italian ex-partisan leader, who was at that time a member of the Communist Party, made him understand the reasons militating against an armed insurrection of the Communists. The Italian partisan had been extolling the contribution of his movement to the common victory, when the Ambassador brusquely interrupted him saying: "The partisans have done very little. The victory is due to the heroism of the Red Army. It is the Soviet soldiers who have destroyed Nazism, saved Europe, and even Italy, bear it well in mind, the Red Army alone." He thereupon turned his back on the Italian partisan.
>
> The latter remained disconcerted. Then he understood what had been said to him, viz., that revolutions must not be made at home, with one's own national heroes, because in such cases leaders like Tito acquire prestige and local authority, enabling them at times to act on their own authority. Revolutions must always be made in collaboration with "the evolution of the international situation," to lend support to the Soviet armies.[5]

[5] (Milan, 1955), p. 43.

CHAPTER XXII

HOW THE COMMUNISTS ACQUIRED THEIR INFLUENCE
IN ITALY

IF we wish to understand the status of the Italian Government after the end of the war, both during the years when it was still under control of the Allies and later when it had once more attained a measure of sovereignty and independence, it is necessary to ascertain how and why the Italian Communist Party acquired so much influence.

Today, we often hear Americans expressing anxiety and even consternation at the large number of Communists in Italy, at the power which they have seemed to wield over all the successive Governments in office since April 25, 1945, and the timidity or benevolence towards them evinced by the Christian Democratic Cabinets, in spite of the fact that their own supporters are by far the most numerous party. Who then originally conferred on the Communists the power which they still have over the policy of the Government, and facilitated their penetration into so many branches of the public administration?

I have already stated that the exiled Communists, then a very small number, were brought back to Italy during the Allied invasion under Allied auspices, that their leader, Palmiro Togliatti, was conveyed to Naples on an American ship, and that it was the ACC and the AMG which imposed on the various Prime Ministers appointed by those bodies the order to take into their Cabinets representatives of all the various anti-Fascist parties, including, above all, a certain number of Communists. Togliatti and Gullo were the first to enjoy that privilege, and others followed afterwards, while many Communists of lesser standing were placed in various key positions of the administration, always by Allied orders. The argument in favor of this policy was quite simple: "We, the Allies, are fighting in Italy against the Fascists. Are not the Communists their bitterest enemies? *Ergo,* we must support the Communists in every way, and leave them a free hand to wipe out as many Fascists as possible. If they incidentally wipe out a number of non-Communists as well, it cannot be helped." It is the same argument as was attributed to the Dominicans at the time of the Crusade against the Albigensians: that if among the heretics massacred there might be some non-heretics, it did not matter, as the Lord would recognize his own and reward them in Paradise.

A lecture delivered by Professor Thomas R. Fisher, who had been a lieutenant-colonel in the reserve of the American forces in Italy during the War, at the American Academy of Political and Social Science in Philadelphia, on Allied Military Government in Italy, reports various facts showing how authority was conferred on the Communists by the American command.

After a general criticism of the methods of the Allied Military Government, Professor Fisher states that "the lack of insight and planning for political parties and labor organizations was probably the greatest error, and was all but fatal. Italy may delay, but cannot escape political disaster if labor remains under Communist domination."[1]

Professor Fisher goes on to say "that the Italian Communist Party and the Italian General Confederation of Labor (C.G.I.L.) are one and the same thing was known to the ACC. When General Harold Alexander, through his proclamation N. 7, issued in July, 1943, dissolved the Fascist organizations, he also reinstated some pre-Fascist institutions, and among them the Italian General Confederation of Labor. The Communists lost no time in seizing this opportunity to infiltrate back of the Army lines. They came down the Adriatic coast from Yugoslavia, and generally made themselves 'useful' in organizing labor. The ACC very soon sent out orders to deal with the C.G.I.L. whenever possible." By October, 1945, "the head of every provincial labor office for the region of Lombardy was a Communist. There were 576 people employed in the labor

[1] Published in the *Annals* of the American Academy for 1950. Professor Fisher was then at Syracuse University in New York State.

offices of the Region of Lombardy, and by October, according
to the statement of the Regional Labor Officer, every one was
an enrolled Communist."

With regard to the large number of Communist votes in Italy,
Professor Fisher adds: "It is not wild to assume that Togliatti
and his C.G.I.L., which is a Communist labor party, would be
far weaker today had we been less co-operative, and stimulated
other labor organizations." The idea of encouraging non-Communist labor unions was then discussed, "but the Regional
Commissioner held that we could not interfere with the organization of labor, however ruthless the organizers were! The
Regional Commissioner, who was an American colonel, did not
wish to disturb the political situation; hence, he gave orders to
this writer (Professor Fisher), who was Regional Labor Officer, *to appoint no labor officer who was not recommended by
the Communist Party.*"

Here we see again how, while the American Government professed not to wish to interfere in any way in Italian politics, the
American authorities in Italy were steadily building up the
control of the Communists, now so strongly combatted by the
Washington Government, and enabling them to secure a far
larger share of the country's body politic than their actual
numbers, large as they are, would justify. The American authorities in Italy had been warned by responsible Italian sources
of orthodox anti-Fascist views of the danger they were pro-
moting. Alfredo Pizzoni, head of the CLNAI, a banker and a
non-Party man, had told the Regional Labor Officer: "For the
sake of God and of the Italian people, do not appoint Communists to all labor offices." But no attention was paid to him in
responsible quarters.

Is it surprising, then, that the results have been what they
are? The most anti-Communist Americans of today cannot
logically complain of what has happened and is happening in
Italy. An eminent Italian professor and ex-Minister told me
that, in 1945, a member of the American President's Cabinet
had said to him: "If you want a really sound man to be Prime
Minister of Italy you should choose Togliatti." That same pro-

fessor met that same American a year or two ago and reminded him of his previous statement, whereupon the latter exclaimed: "I was then utterly wrong, and for Heaven's sake do not tell anyone what I said to you in 1945!"

Other instances of the appointment of Communists to important public positions by order of the American authorities are also worth recording. After the Allied occupation of Milan, the *Corriere della Sera*, the most important paper in Milan and, indeed, in all Italy, had to be converted from a Fascist into an anti-Fascist organ. After being suspended for a short time, it was allowed to resume publication by the American authorities, but they placed the Communist journalist, Domenico Capocaccia, in charge of it.

The old-established *Stefani* telegraphic agency (founded in Turin as far back as 1853) was also closed down by the Allies because it had been under Fascist control,[2] and for some time Italy was not allowed to have any telegraphic agency at all. Several months after the end of the War, but while the country still remained under the control of the ACC, the journalist, Longoni, told some of his friends that he thought he could set up an agency again. The plan seemed an impossibility to most people; but, after prolonged negotiations, Longoni managed to secure the necessary consent of the Allied authorities, and the new "Ansa" agency started business. The condition imposed on Longoni was that he should appoint a Communist as "commissioner" of the agency, and another Communist (Renato Mieli) as "technical adviser."

As I said before, it was the ACC which imposed the appointment of Communists to Cabinet posts. Togliatti, who had at first been Minister without portfolio, later became Minister of Justice, in which capacity he was responsible for the most flagrant interference in the judicial administration and for innumerable miscarriages of justice.[3] Mauro Scoccimarro was

[2] Its director had committed suicide after the fall of the Fascist regime. Its last director was, as we have seen, one of the men murdered at Dongo.

[3] To mention only three cases, the soldiers Testorio and Sabelli, who had been condemned to death, one for having shot a prisoner trying to escape, and the other for supposed complicity in the case, had sent in appeals for pardon to the Head of the State, but Togliatti, as Minister of Justice, managed to prevent the appeals from

appointed, as we have seen, Minister of "Liberated" Territories, Giuseppe Moranino, who had murdered a number of Fascists and also several partisans who knew too much, became Under-Secretary for Defense,[4] and Gullo received the portfolio of Agriculture. The Communists who were given other appointments in the public service were legion. According to Edgardo Sogno's monthly review, *Pace e libertà*, there are today no less than 400 Communists in the Italian judiciary.[5]

The support of Communism in Italy by the American authorities may possibly be explained, apart from that Party's uncompromising hostility to Fascism, by the fact that the late President Roosevelt had for a long time had among his closest personal advisers several Communists and fellow-travelers, such as Alger Hiss and Lauchlin Currie, to mention only two of the most prominent, and that even after the President's death his policy of encouraging Communism survived, at all events for some time. "The evil which men do lives after them."

The American periodical *Life*, published a long, and, on the whole, accurate article on Communism in Italy, and the author asserted that "the onlie begetter" of their influence in the country is the Government of the United States. This is, of course, an exaggeration, for the British cooperated in the process of strengthening the Communist influence and forces in postwar Italy. Even though the Americans may have taken the initiative, the British did little or nothing to check the development and in many instances encouraged it. But the United States alone has paid the large bill for strengthening Italian Communism after 1944. When the Cold War began and the

reaching their destination until the two men had been executed. The third case was that of a political prisoner who, having lost an arm, had had it replaced by a wooden one; Togliatti gave orders that the wooden arm be removed and confiscated.

The propriety of appointing as Minister of Justice a man who had praised mass murders of innocent persons by the thousands as one of the finest achievements in all Italian history does not require further comment here.

[4] The judicial authorities applied to the Chamber of Deputies for authorization to proceed against him. This was granted, but means were found to enable him to escape to a satellite country (Czechoslovakia), where he is now living in safety as an honored guest. Proceedings were then instituted against him in the Florence Court of Assizes, and he was condemned to life imprisonment (*in absentia*) for a series of murders.

[5] He had published their names and standing in an issue of his review, and only one of them wrote denying his Communist connection.

American Government became alarmed at the growth of Communism in Europe, the United States poured approximately four billion dollars into Italy to keep the Communists from getting control of Italy and to support the non-Communist parties in the Italian Government. Britain, by this time, was borrowing money from the United States and accepting economic and military aid to keep its economy and defense in operation. The struggle against the Italian Communists still goes on. They rank second in voting power in Italy today. The American Ambassador to Italy, James D. Zellerbach, stated on a visit to the United States in March, 1958, that about the most that can be truthfully said is that the Communists are now "well under control."

That the control is still somewhat precarious may be discerned from the leftward trend in the Italian Government in the middle of 1958. This was evident from the make-up of the Cabinet of Premier Amintore Fanfani, who took office in July, 1958. Even the American periodical *Time*, which has been a strong partisan of the post-War Italian political system and policy, was moved to observe: "Not since Italy became a Republic after World War II had an Italian Government leaned so far to the left."[6]

An interesting and cynically amusing item on the responsibility for the growth of Italian Communism was supplied by the American newspaper columnist, Drew Pearson, in a column written in Rome and published in American newspapers on May 12, 1958. Mr. Pearson tells of his visit to Mussolini in 1923 and of the boast of the latter that he had banished Communism from Italy forever. Mr. Pearson attributes the growth of Italian Communism after 1945 to this action of Il Duce: "Banishment of Communism or any political party by force never pays, and Italy now has the biggest Communist party of any country outside Russia." Now, Mr. Pearson is one of the warmest supporters of the banishment of Fascism from Italy and of Nazism from Germany. He has as yet failed to tell us how he reconciles this with his well-known hatred of Fascism and Nazism and his obvious desire that neither of them will be revived and prosper.

[6]*Time*, July 14, 1958, p. 24.

CHAPTER XXIII

TREATMENT OF ITALIAN PRISONERS OF WAR

THE rules for the treatment of prisoners of war have been laid down in various international agreements, accepted and applied by all civilized countries for many decades. Prisoners of war are entitled to be adequately fed, provided with medical assistance, allowed to send to, and receive messages from their families, and to receive religious assistance; they shall not be compelled to perform work of military utility to their captors, may not be humiliated in any way, and their political opinions should in no way be taken into consideration.

In World War II, these prescriptions were in many cases generally disregarded, although treatment varied from country to country and from camp to camp. A few instances concerning Italian prisoners will illustrate these points, showing how, at least in this connection, civilization has declined instead of progressing.

The conditions of Italian prisoners in East Africa are described in a book written by one of them, the journalist and reserve officer, Franco Piccinni, entitled *Africa senza sole* (Sunless Africa).[1] He was interned successively in several British camps in Kenya. Some of the prisoners belonged to the regular army, others to the Fascist militia, the latter, however, being in wartime on a footing of absolute equality with the regulars. For the members of the militia their own regulations prescribed that they should always salute their superiors with the Roman salute (raising the right arm). The commandant of one of the P.O.W. camps in Kenya, Colonel Tucker, had forbidden the militia prisoners to salute in that way, regarding such action as evidence of wicked Fascist sentiments. As some of them, in obedience to their regulations, did so salute, they were put in

[1](Rome, 1949).

irons for whole days on end, and a group of them, after having spent some time in prison, were deported to a camp near the coast, where every form of punishment was inflicted on them, including almost total lack of drinking water in a tropical climate. In any case, the mere fact of dividing prisoners of war into two categories, according to their political opinions, and treating those whose views were disapproved of with exceptional severity, was a crass violation of the elementary and conventional laws of war.

At the Burguret camp, where many prisoners of Fascist sentiments were interned, the British authorities let loose among them a number of common criminals, expressly imported from the various Ethiopian prisons, and left them free to commit the grossest acts of barbarity on the prisoners. They had taken good care that no British officer should be present during these proceedings, although, of course, nothing could be done in that or any other camp without the knowledge and express permission of the authorities. The affair raised such a scandal that the British Government sent out a commission of inquiry. But the commissioners asked the prisoners if they had *seen* any British officers during the troubles; they had, of course, to reply in the negative, and were then asked to sign statements to that effect; those who refused to do so were detained as prisoners for several months longer than those who had signed. They were all prevented from giving any further evidence.

A camp at Mandone in Somaliland had been reserved for the women and children of Italian civilian settlers in Ethiopia, who had been deported there on the pretext that the natives might attack them, although they had always been on the best of terms with the latter. These internees were robbed of all the valuables they had on them, except the women's wedding rings. But in one case a woman was deprived even of her ring because it had a tiny diamond in it, and the British inspection officer said that it was worth over £20. When the woman was asked if she had any other valuables she replied: "We Italian women have given our gold to our country, but we did not know that

we were expected to give alms to George VI."[2] The officer
was so astonished that he returned the ring to the woman, saying: "Keep it; it is we who are giving alms to Mussolini."

The treatment of Italian prisoners of war in British camps in
Italy varied. I came upon various youths who had been captured immediately after the armistice, tried by British military
courts and condemned to long terms of imprisonment on the
charge of having sent or having intended to send military information to the Germans, or of being about to commit acts of
sabotage.[3] The trials were usually conducted with all proper
formalities, but the charges were often preposterous and the
charge sheets were not communicated to the defense counsel
until the very last moment. In one case, a boy had been sentenced to death for offenses of the above nature, but when his
counsel pointed out that he was under eighteen years of age
and that by Italian law no one under 18 could be executed, the
execution was suspended. He was, however, detained as a prisoner until he had reached his 18th year and shot the next day.

The intrepid naval commander, Don Valerio Borghese, underwent experiences in a British prison camp which are also
worth recording. On his surrender to the Allies, he was conveyed to a special camp at Cinecittà near Rome, operated under the auspices of the British Intelligence Service and reserved
for alleged "war criminals," Italians and Germans. Prisoners
were treated there far worse than in other camps; they were
deliberately starved, prevented from having any correspond-
ence with their families, who did not know where they were
or even whether they were alive or dead, and they were refused
religious assistance and visits from members of the International Red Cross. No distinction was made between officers and
men, and even officers of high rank had to perform the hardest
and most humiliating duties—Borghese himself often had to
carry away excrement buckets for a couple of miles under the

[2] During the Ethiopian war, when the Italian Government was short of gold, the
people were asked to contribute gold ornaments, and large numbers gave their gold
wedding rings, which were melted down and deposited with the gold reserve of the
Bank of Italy.

[3] It is unlikely that boys of 17 could have any valuable information to send.

blazing sun. They were constantly subjected to endless grilling cross-examinations, especially about the *Sicherheitsdienst* (secret service), of which they knew nothing. The N.C.O.'s and privates in charge were mostly Palestine Jews or Maltese of the worst character.

On one occasion, General Alexander visited the camp and, among others, he asked Borghese if he had any complaints to make. He replied describing the above incidents, but the General's only remark was: "You are all criminals." After six months, as absolutely no charge materialized against him, Borghese was handed over to the Italian authorities and interned at Procida.

Before Borghese had fallen into British hands his wife, Donna Daria, and their children had been living on a small island on the Lago d'Iseo. There, a British major came to cross-examine her, and the conversation was as follows:

Q. What are your political opinions?
A. The same as those of my husband.
Q. What are your husband's political opinions?
A. You had better ask him, yourself.
Q. Where is your husband now?
A. I have no idea.

Thereupon, she was arrested and carried off to a prison at Modena, having been obliged to leave her children behind on the island (the eldest a girl of twelve), with no one to look after them. Fortunately, a lady living in the neighborhood took charge of them until they could be sent off to Florence. Donna Daria Borghese did not remain long at Modena because, strangely enough, an Italian Communist prison guard told her that it was not right for her to be there, and enabled her to escape.

A number of Italian soldiers and sailors, who had passed through the lines and were captured by the British were interned in a P. O. W. camp at Santa Maria di Capua Vetere, near Caserta. Every now and then one of them would be taken out of the prison and shot without trial on the island of Nisida.

They were buried there without any ceremony, and not in a cemetery. Among others, this was the case of four men of the "Decima MAS," and the commander of the unit, the above-mentioned Don Valerio Borghese, afterwards had the bodies exhumed and given proper Christian burial.

Many prisoners were deported to the United States. There too, their conditions varied from camp to camp, and various episodes in this connection are described in a book by Lieutenant Roberto Mieville, who had been taken prisoner in North Africa, with the English title (although it is written in Italian) of *Fascists Criminal Camp.*[4] On reaching Newport on August 4, 1943, he and his fellow prisoners were asked if they were prepared to collaborate with the Allies and sign an "I promise" document to that effect. Those who refused were transferred to the P. O. W. camp at Hereford, Texas, specially reserved for non-collaborating prisoners. On one occasion, a number of Comanche Indians in United States uniforms were brought into the camp and proceeded to bludgeon the prisoners with baseball bats. It afterwards transpired that this penalty had been inflicted on the prisoners because they had been (quite falsely) accused of having set fire to one of the tents in the camp. On April 21, 1944, a notice was posted up in the camp, stating that those who refused to sign the "I promise" paper would be severely punished, that their release would be delayed longer than that of those who signed, and that their families in Italy would suffer serious consequences.[5]

Sometimes, however, the refusal of the prisoners to collaborate aroused the admiration of the Camp Commandant, Colonel Calworth. On hearing of the refusal of a group of prisoners to collaborate and of their admission that they were Fascists, he said: "Real soldiers, these boys." It was a case of "Even the ranks of Tuscany could scarce forbear to cheer!"

The prisoners were repeatedly searched by the M. P.'s who robbed them of their few belongings, including photographs

[4]Rome, 1947. Mieville was elected to the Chamber of Deputies in 1948 and again in 1953. He was killed in a motor car accident in 1955.

[5]This is quite in the best Russian Bolshevik style. As we know, imitation is the sincerest flattery.

of their families, which were apparently regarded as dangerous implements. One officer who tried to prevent a photograph of his mother from being taken from him was severely beaten.

In October, 1944, some of the non-collaborators were locked up in isolation cells and fed on bread and water for weeks, in some cases for months. When a prisoner who was a general protested against these measures as illegal, he was told by the camp commandant: "War is war, and the Geneva conventions do not apply in the United States."

At the Fort Bliss camp, non-collaborating prisoners were sometimes forced to race round and round for hours as a punishment. On one occasion, a certain Lieutenant Strohm, attached to the camp, on seeing one of the prisoners lying down utterly exhausted and incapable of moving, shouted at him: "Get up, you dog!" and beat him with a club. One of the other prisoners, named Lunardi, protested at this action and struck the officer down, whereupon the Comanches fell upon Lunardi, who defended himself vigorously and struck several of them down, until he was overwhelmed by numbers. He was then taken before a commission of American officers, who ordered him to ask pardon. On his refusal, he was beaten so savagely that he lost his memory and died within a month.

The American press finally heard of these matters, and published accounts of them. A young American naval officer, John Henry Holt, wrote a letter to *Life* (November 5, 1945), stating that he had lost the fear of death on Guadalcanal, lost his best friend at Okinawa, lost a leg at Iwo Jima and lost his faith in American democracy after reading of the treatment of Italian prisoners of war. He ended up his letter with the question: "Why have I been fighting?"

Italian prisoners of war in the French camps in North Africa were likewise subject to brutal treatment. In Russia, of course, the treatment of Italian prisoners was even worse. For instance, at the Krinovaya camp, south of Voronezh, there were from 25 to 30 thousand prisoners, of many nationalities, including 10,000 Italians at one time. They were literally starved and although there were no epidemics, men died of hunger, gangrene, frostbite, and dysentery, or were murdered by the prison guards. As many as 500 died in one day.

In every Russian camp there were political commissars, assisted by Italian Communists, who lectured the prisoners constantly on the beauties of Communism. A special anti-Fascist school had been created in Moscow where a small number of Italian officers and soldiers were trained for propaganda purposes. The perpetual cross-examinations of the prisoners were veritable nightmares; the men questioned were always being threatened with penalties of all kinds—life imprisonment and even death. Men who undertook to fight on the side of the partisans were promised early repatriation—which never came. None of the prisoners were allowed to communicate with their families.

In this connection, the conduct of Edoardo D'Onofrio (now a member of the Italian Parliament) deserves to be recorded. He visited the Italian prisoners' camps in Russia to conduct Communist propaganda, and the prisoners who rejected his advances and continued to proclaim their loyalty to Italy were at his instance subjected to third-degree treatment, tortured, and deported to the worst camps. These facts came out in a libel action instituted by D'Onofrio against an Italian paper which had published the story of his actions, and they were all proved true in court.[6] Even the number of Italian prisoners of war in Russia is still unknown.[7]

Another extraordinary circumstance connected with the late War was that even diplomats of enemy countries, who in past wars had been treated with every consideration, were in some cases confined in concentration camps, and in others actually imprisoned. Several of those accredited to the Holy See had, on the arrival of the Allied forces, to take refuge in the Vatican

[6] Fabretti, *Redivivus;* quoted in Tamaro, *op. cit.,* Vol. III, p. 668; and Arnaldo Cappellini, *Inchiesta sul dispersi in Russia* (Milan, 1949), and the proceedings of the D'Onofrio trial.

[7] Long after the end of the war the Russian Embassy continued to deny that there were any more prisoners of war left in Russia, whereas every now and then a few more managed to escape or get released, and all of them declared that there were still others left, although the great majority had died of starvation, disease or savage ill-treatment.

as its guests, while those accredited to the RSI were interned at Salsomaggiore.

Far worse was the fate of the diplomats who fell into Russian hands. When the Soviet forces occupied Rumania and Bulgaria, the Italian representatives in those countries were arrested without any pretext, conveyed to Moscow, and imprisoned there for years. The wife of the Italian Minister in Bucharest, Armando Odenigo, had insisted on following her husband to Russia, but she was interned in a different place of detention and died there a year later; he did not hear of her death until his own release. The Italian diplomats were kept in separate prisons in Moscow and never saw one another during the whole time of their detention, nor received any news of their families in Italy. They were continually cross-examined on various questions; one of them, the Italian consul in Bucharest, told me that, having been asked for a list of the anti-Fascist Italians in that city, he replied that there were none at all, the Italians in Rumania being either Fascists or devoid of all political opinions. A few days later, he was presented with a statement on the subject and asked to sign it; but, as he was asked to say in it the exact contrary of what he had really said, he refused to do so.

During their detention the imprisoned diplomats had some interesting experiences. While they never saw each other, they often had as cell companions Russians of all classes: members of the Government who had fallen from grace, managers of large industrial concerns, generals, university professors, railway and street-car employees, working men, peasants, and others. From their conversation with these incarcerated Russians they acquired more knowledge about what was going on in Russia than anyone else, except the most high-ranking Communists.

At last, after six long years of beastly food and filthy prison clothes, the diplomats were informed that they were to be released. They were conveyed by train to Vienna, but detained there in the Russian zone of the city for a couple of weeks longer, and then, finally, escorted to the Sudbahnhof, whence trains for Italy depart, and handed over to the Italian authorities. A curious detail is that they were each given by their ex-jailors huge hampers of food. When they expressed their surprise at these gifts, as the journey to Italy took only ten hours, the Russians told them that on reaching Italy they would find no food at all.[8]

Another incident of the kind was the arrest by the British at Merano of a distinguished Irish citizen, Hon. Charles Bewley. He was formerly Irish Minister to the Holy See and later to Berlin, but for some years past he had been no longer in the service. No charge was preferred against him, but he was cross-examined by his jailors as to what he knew about the Secret Service, and when he replied that he knew nothing about it, he was told that if he answered in that way he might be detained for an indefinite time. He replied that they might detain him until Domesday, but that he could not tell them anything. Bewley had to spend many months in five or six different concentration camps in Italy before he was released.

A few words should be said about the above-mentioned British concentration camp at Padula.

It was a large group of buildings covering an area of over five hectares, formerly a monastery famous in the history of Southern Italy dating from the fourteenth century, and dedicated to St. Lawrence. It is situated in the province of Salerno.

At the beginning of 1944, the British military authorities took possession of it and turned it into a concentration camp where at different times some 20,000 Italians, including not a few women, were interned for longer or shorter periods. The internees, with few exceptions, were not prisoners of war, but civilians. The well-known Italian writer Giorgio Nelson Page, who had been an official of the Ministry of Popular Culture and was interned in Padula for many months, has published a detailed and vivid description of the camp in a book entitled *Padula.*[9]

---

[8] This account is based on Armando Odenigo's book, *Priginni moscovite* (Bologna, 1955), and on my own conversations with him and his fellow prisoners.
[9] (Rome, 1956).

Independently of the treatment of the prisoners by British officers and N. C. O.'s, which was often harsh, brutal and humiliating, the most striking feature of the situation was the fact that at Padula all those thousands of Italians were interned without any specific charges having been preferred against them; and, with very few exceptions, they were never tried. The only reason for their detention was that they had served the legitimate Government of their country and supported the existing regime which had been brought into power by an overwhelming majority in a Parliament freely elected before the advent of that regime. But they were regarded as opponents of the countries with whom their own country was at war.

We thus see here still another expression of the policy of the Allies who claimed the right not merely to fight against Italy, which they had invaded merely as a military operation, but of imposing on her a form of government agreeable to themselves, regardless of what her inhabitants might wish. I need not to repeat that this conduct constituted a gross violation of the elementary and generally recognized principles of international law, and even of common justice and equity, all the more heinous when applied by nations who were (or professed to be) inspired by the principles of democracy.

To quote a single instance of how the choice of Italian citizens to be interned at Padula was often made, I shall mention the case of Professor Giulio Quirino Giglioli of the University of Rome. This man, an archaeologist of world-wide reputation, had been arrested and interned at Padula because, among his many publications, he had written some articles proving that the ancient civilization of Malta was partly of Roman origin. This was evidently regarded as a serious menace to the integrity of the British Empire, which could only be safeguarded by imprisoning this dignified and elderly scholar.

One case of poetic justice is cited in Page's above-mentioned book on the Padula prison. One of the British officers in that prison who had made himself especially odious and hated because of his brutalities was a Captain Davidson. After the War and the closing of the Padula prison, he was met on the streets of Rome by two of his victims, Count Carlo Del Bono and Prince Vittorio Massimo. They invited him to a restaurant where he became intoxicated, and later went with them to the home of some of their friends. Here, in his maudlin condition, he tried to take gross liberties with some of the ladies present, whereupon, the men there beat him up thoroughly and put him out on the street in his half-naked condition.

CHAPTER XXIV

PARTISAN MASSACRES AFTER THE END OF HOSTILITIES

FROM April 25, 1945, onwards there were three Governments operating in Italy: the Rome Government under Bonomi's Premiership; the Allies represented by the ACC and the AMG; and, in the North, the CLNAI, nominally acting on behalf of the Rome Government, but actually under the direction of the partisans, especially the Communist partisans.

The Rome Government was still devoid of any real authority, and the Allies continued to exercise full powers everywhere, but for a few weeks they allowed the partisans a free hand all over North Italy.

I have mentioned the activities of the partisans during the War when their numbers amounted, according to Cadorna, to about 90,000. When hostilities came to an end, hordes of men who had taken no part in the movement before then joined its ranks, thus leading to an impressive inflation. The total rose to 200,000 men or even more. According to some sources, before many months had passed about 700,000 partisan certificates had been distributed, in many cases obtainable on payment of a small fee.

It was thus that during the five or six weeks following the end of hostilities the movement assumed its largest dimensions, and its members began murdering a very large number of men and women who were or were alleged to be Fascists. The total number of the victims has never been accurately ascertained, as no records were kept. The present Government takes good care to keep the matter secret. The murderers themselves, although then and even now enjoying full immunity for any act committed at that time which might remotely be defined as being of a political nature, were not too eager to leave evidence of their crimes, lest at some future time they might be called upon to answer for them. The figures given for those killed vary between 50,000 and 300,000. A few years ago the Minister of the Interior, Mario Scelba, stated, in answer to a question in Parliament, that the total number only amounted to 1,732; but this figure, fantastically low, probably referred to a few non-Fascists who had been murdered by mistake; the other victims, having been Fascists, did not count. Among the "mistakes" of this kind were the murders of three men who had been mistaken for the Fascist ex-Minister of the Colonies, Attilio Teruzzi, to whom they bore some slight resemblance![1] Similarly, a peaceful trader near Modena was murdered because he had been mistaken for General Mario Roatta. In many cases, whole families were wiped out, including small children, while every document or scrap of paper and every stick of furniture in the houses of the victims were carried away, so that no evidence of the deed could be traced. Some of the homicidal episodes which occurred at that time are typical and worth recording for their brutality.

The Emilia region shows the highest percentage of murders, especially in the so-called "death triangle" in the provinces of Bologna, Ferrara and Modena, where the Communists were very numerous. In the city of Bologna, one of the victims was the chief of police, who was seized and shot dead before the town hall, although he was known to be a very kind-hearted man against whom no charges were ever preferred. Immediately afterwards, a group of partisans entered a hospital, and seized, tortured and murdered several of the women patients. In a street in the same city, several Fascists, including two women, were murdered, the women having first been raped. At Pieve di Cento (province of Bologna), six brothers and a sister were carried off from their home and have never been heard of since; when their mother was trying to find the bodies of her children, she was attacked and beaten by the wife and daughter of one of the murderers. At Galliera, in the same province, 13 men alleged to be Fascists were carried off from their homes and murdered. On May 24, 1945, a disabled war

[1] Teruzzi himself was imprisoned at that time; he had been condemned to thirty years imprisonment, but was subsequently released, and died of illness ten days later.

veteran (from World War I), Vittorio Vaccari, and his brother Guerrino, also a war veteran, were seized near Verona, where they happened to be residing, conveyed to their home town of Crevalcuore and murdered. At Castelguelfo (Bologna), a war widow named Zanelli was carried away from her home by partisans, was brutally beaten and tortured and her tongue was cut out.

Piedmont provides many cases of the same kind. At Colle Umberto on May 19, 1945, 19 men were murdered. At Arona (Novara province), a man was seized on April 24th, and although the local CLNAI testified in his favor, he was shot the next day. In the town of Novara, an agreement had been concluded between a partisan unit and one of the Muti battalions (Fascist) for an exchange of prisoners, but, while the partisans were released, the Muti prisoners were murderd. At Nichelino (Turin), Agostino Gastaldo, a member of one of the Black Brigades, was seized, tortured and shot, and in the same place the nurse, Margherita Audisio, was also murdered. At the Graglia sanctuary, a battle had taken place on April 26th, and, as the war was then ended, the Fascists surrendered on the promise that their lives would be spared; but 24 men and 5 women auxiliaries (stenographers, clerks, cooks, etc.) were locked up in a building and murdered on May 2nd. At Alessandria, the partisans seized 53 men from the local prison on May 10th; they had been demanded by the Savona partisans; and they were carried off in trucks towards Savona, but, during the journey, 38 of them were murdered at Colle di Codivona. For some reason, two partisans of the escort also disappeared and were never heard of again, and not all the bodies of the 38 murdered men were identified.

In Lombardy, apart from the butcheries in the city of Milan, there were innumerable victims in other towns and villages. On April 25th a medical student who had volunteered for service with the RSI, Emilio La Pera, was captured, together with 15 other students, in a village near Brescia, and while 14 of them were shot at once, La Pera and another, who had been wounded in action, were conveyed to a hospital in Leghorn and murdered there. Antonio Balzanetti, also a volunteer in the RSI forces, was arrested on the same day and imprisoned at Bergamo, where he was tortured, and, although not murdered, he died of his injuries a few days later.

Some members of the staff of the State Printing Office in Rome had been transferred to Milan to set up a plant for printing currency notes, against the danger of German-printed occupation notes (a danger which was averted by the action of the RSI Finance Minister, Domenico Pellegrini-Giampietro). They had joined the fighting forces as volunteers and taken part in some minor engagements, but they surrendered their arms after the end of hostilities. They were then seized by a detachment of partisans, commanded by Vincenzo Moscatelli (later a Senator), and eleven of them, including some women clerks, were carried off and murdered at Pieve Vergnate.

On April 28th, some airmen, surrounded by an overwhelming body of partisans in the air force barracks at Gallarate (Milan), surrended with the honors of war. But the following day the officers, including the commander, Major Visconti, were conveyed to Milan, shut up in the cavalry barracks and then shot.

A vivid picture of the post-war days in Milan is given by Carlo Simiani in his book *I giustiziati fascisti dell' aprile 1945*:[2]

> The first days in Milan were terrible. Many citizens talked of the probability that a new reign of terror was being prepared. . . . Executions were carried out in double-quick time. Firing squads were rare; machine gun volleys were simpler. No one troubled about illegality. . . . People's courts existed, but in many cases only in name. Quick and cruel forms of justice produce morbid effects on simple minds in times of revolutionary frenzy. . . . Murder reached its culminating point after the slaughter of Mussolini and the other Fascist leaders. . . . In many cases the murders were the result of love affairs, or vendettas, without a shadow of political motive; poor wretches meeting with an unscrupulous commander were put to death. There were cases of persons seized merely in order to extort money from them, after which they were released even if deserving punishment.
>
> Thousands of persons were put to death without having undergone any form of trial, without any possibility of appeal, nearly al-

[2] Milan, 1949.

ways without religious rites. Very rarely were they allowed to send farewell messages to their families. . . . A foreign official stated that at Sesto San Giovanni (near Milan) 4,000 persons had been killed, while a French paper put the number in that town as high as 10,000.

Any attempt to arrive at the truth is impossible, as all witnesses are afraid of speaking out.

When the Germans and the Fascist authorities had disappeared, innumerable armed brigades and bands of partisans arose, searching for a nonexistent enemy. The older and authentic partisans were flabbergasted, but could do nothing. At first, the partisans were very few, but now they were innumerable. It was a hodgepodge of uniforms, ranks and weapons of all kinds. . . .

Many industrial experts, engineers, et al., all excellent men, were murdered, such as Ugo Gobbati of the Alfa Romeo, Siliveri, manager of the Marelli Company, a man esteemed by everyone, and many others who had taken no part in politics, Giacomo Grazioli, head of the Grazoli plant and a pioneer of industry, Scoloni and Mazzoli, engineers of the Breda works at Sesto, Weber of Bologna, Vischi of the Reggiane at Reggio Emilia, were all murdered.

The moderating orders of the CLNAI existed merely on paper.

In the province of Como, 1,200 persons were murdered, in that of Varese 300, in that of Brescia 1,700, but when, later, the Fiamme Verdi (partisans consisting of regular officers and men) arrived, order was restored. In the province of Bergamo, there were 53 murders, in that of Mantua 1,500, at Lecco 37, in all Lombardy 10,000![3]

These atrocities were nearly all committed by men who had become partisans *after* hostilities had ceased.

On April 26th, five masked men armed with machine guns broke into a house inhabited by a family of six persons, all perfectly innocent; they threatened to kill the head of the family, an honest tradesman, but they gave him to understand that if he paid them a large sum of money his life would be spared. While the partisans were searching for money, the masks fell off the faces of two of them, and the tradesman recognized them as two notorious rascals living in the district. For this reason the whole family was murdered and the house looted.

Venetia was also the scene of many excesses, especially the Northeastern districts, where there were gangs of Yugoslav partisans on the prowl.

On May 2nd, 40 youths were murdered in a cemetery at Valdobbadene (province of Belluno), and in the province of

[3] This figure is evidently exclusive of the city of Milan.

Treviso there was a spate of murders between April 24th and May 6th, many of the victims having been first tortured, while all were robbed of everything they possessed. At the baths of Recoaro, six officers and two soldiers were murdered, and on the night of April 25-26th two men were seized, tied together, and buried up to their heads near the river Brenta, after which their skulls were bashed in. Their remains were unearthed some time afterwards.

In the province of Modena, a woman was burned alive, a girl tortured in her father's presence, a woman school teacher tortured and killed. In the coastal districts of Emilia, some Slavs who specialized in revolutionary activities had placed themselves at the head of the local CLNAI, whom they trained in the methods of Balkan savagery.

Immediately after the end of hostilities, a motor coach belonging to the Papal Assistance Commission was conveying sixty persons, many of them refugees, from Brescia to Rome, all of them provided with regular passes from the CLNAI and having no charges against them. After reaching Concordia (in Emilia), the vehicle disappeared, together with its passengers, and was never heard of again. The corpses of some of the passengers were found murdered some time later, but of the others no trace was ever found. The episode came to be known as that of "the phantom coach."

On the evening of June 18, 1945, ten young gangster partisans entered a prison in the same area, and, after having disarmed the wardens, proceeded to shoot down the prisoners who were detained there while their papers and identity were being verified (no charges against them). Thirteen of them were killed outright, while three others, seriously wounded, hid under the corpses and afterwards managed to escape and tell the story. From the prison at Comacchio (province of Ferrara), a dozen prisoners were seized, conveyed by truck to the nearby cemetery and shot.

On May 9th, four partisans entered the Mirandola prison, and conveyed the prisoners, including a woman, by truck towards Modena, but on the way shot them dead. While cleaning the blood stains from the truck one of the partisans told Dr. Carlo Testi, president of the local CLNAI, that the men had been shot while trying to escape (the usual story), but the doctor, having found that the woman, although dying, was still alive, talked to her. The partisans feared that he might have learned too much, and the next night, while on his way home, he was shot dead to prevent him from making damaging revelations.

On May 1st, Riccardo Agnoletto, who had been the Prefect's commissioner in the town of Lonigo (province of Vicenza), was arrested there on the charge of having had some deserters shot, beaten within an inch of his life and robbed of all his possessions by a gang of Communist partisans. The charge afterwards proved wholly devoid of foundation, but the prisoner was tried, by order of the local CLNAI composed of Communists, before a people's court sitting in the Piazza Garibaldi of Lonigo, likewise composed of Communists. A mob of the worst characters of the town and district howled down any attempt at defense, and Agnoletto was condemned to death and shot by a firing squad composed of Communist partisans who had taken no part whatever in partisan operations during the war.[4]

On May 5th, at Salesina (province of Padua), the local town clerk was tortured to death, and five other men were murdered, their bodies being afterwards cast into a ditch. In the same province, on April 25th, the commander of a small garrison at Grantana, a disabled veteran of World War I, had left his men free to return to their homes, while he remained alone in the barracks. The next morning he was seized by partisans, one of his eyes was gouged out, and he was then murdered. At Codenigo (Padua), 200 men of the RSI National Guard were captured by partisans commanded by the notorious Arrigo Boldrini, and all but three were murdered. In another part of Venetia 93 persons, including some women, were likewise murdered.

At the end of the war there were several detachments of the

[4]The whole story is told in the Rome *Secolo* for June 14, 1955, with the names, addresses and occupations of the members of the local CLN, of the "judges" of the people's court, and of the firing squad.

RSI forces at Oderzo (Udine). They negotiated their surrender through Dr. Sergio Martin, of the local CLNAI, and the partisan leader Agostino Mascherelli, on condition that their lives be spared and that all should be released, except such of them as might be proved after trial guilty of actual offenses. The partisans had formally promised a local priest that in any case none of the prisoners would be executed, but on April 30th all the 104 men were shot without any form of trial. At the end of April a number of partisans had made their headquarters at Magnacola Carbonara, where they murdered 400 persons, after having tortured several of them.

I have mentioned only a few instances of the innumerable cases of slaughter. It should be noted that, with few exceptions, they all occurred *after* the end of hostilities, when there were no Italian or German forces or authorities in operation, and when the Allied police were either absent, or, if present, took no interest in any acts of violence unless committed against the Allied armed forces. The great majority of the murderers were Communists acting under the orders of the Kremlin, then regarded by the Western Allies as a centre of virtue and civilization.[5]

Important historic parallels to the butcheries of Northern Italy in the spring of 1945 are the Massacre of St. Bartholomew (1572), where only a few thousand persons were slaughtered; the massacre of tens of thousands of Irish by Cromwell in 1649-50; the Reign of Terror during the French Revolution, the victims of which are estimated at about 20,000, spread over several years; the French Communard uprising of 1870-71, in which 15,000 to 30,000 Parisians lost their lives; the massacres by the Reds in the Spanish Civil War, where the number of the victims is unknown; and the massacres by Franco and the Nationalists at the close of the War. Of course, the number of persons murdered in Russia since the Revolution of 1917, and that of the victims of the Chinese civil war after 1945 were far

[5]Many details have been recorded in the press, and a collection of the most striking facts have been published in a pamphlet issued by the *Secolo*, entitled *No al 25 aprile—si alla pacificazione* (Rome, 1955).

larger, amounting to many millions, but Russia and China cannot fairly be compared to European countries.

During and after World War II, only the French "Résistance" movement offers a parallel to the events in Northern Italy in the matter of atrocities, and there the number of victims was probably as large, running to over 100,000. But there is one important difference between the two bloody episodes. In Italy, the majority of the murders were committed by Communist criminals, operating in the streets and fields, in most cases under the orders of their own leaders, who were in turn obeying those of their masters in Moscow. The number of persons executed in Italy after more or less regular trials was far less. In France, although there, too, a great many murders were committed in the same way as those in Northern Italy, the number of victims of monstrously unfair and summary trials, conducted by more or less regular law courts, was enormous. According to Alfred Fabre-Luce[6] and Sisley Huddleston,[7] the French victims of the "Liberation" reached over 100,000, the majority of them executed after a judicial death sentence. Another difference is that, in Italy, the slaughter lasted only a few weeks, whereas in France the judicial murders went on for years, and are not yet ended, as we note in occasional reports in the papers of executions to this very day. The one thing that the massacres had in common in both countries was that they were committed mainly as a result of Communist influence, pressure and activities.

Writers of Leftish tendencies, sympathetic with the Italian partisans and the French "Résistance," have sought to minimize the slaughter during the liberation period. Alexander Werth, in his book, *France, 1940-1955*, bitterly smears Huddleston and denies that there is any evidence that 100,000 Frenchmen were directly or "judicially" murdered. The French Left, after the reaction set in against the "glorious days" of the 1944-1945 massacres, have also sought to suppress the facts. But, in the long run, not even the French Left could bury the facts. In "A

---

[6] Alfred Fabre-Luce, *Histoire de la Révolution européenne* (Paris, 1954).
[7] Sisley Huddleston, *France: the Tragic Years* (New York, 1955).

Letter from France," published in the radical periodical, *Freedom*, June 19, 1958, André Prunier thus contrasted the transition from the Fourth to the Fifth French Republic with that from the Third to the Fourth: "Instead of killing 130,000 'traitors' and marking naked girls with swastikas for 'bad conduct'; instead of acting as political gangsters, patriotic pimps, and 'victorious' braggadocios, the committeemen of both ultra-'Gaullist' and 'Communist' description behaved like decent persons, respecting each other with even an excess of scruple which could not be attributed to mutual fear."

The occurrences described above simply prove that if large numbers of criminally inspired men, many of them emerging from the gutters of the underworld, fully armed and not restrained by the fear of the police or any other public authorities, are let loose on an unarmed population, atrocities without number are inevitable, especially when criminals or men of criminal tendencies are told that they are acting from high political motives, and know that they can secure pecuniary profit by looting the property of their victims, occupying their dwellings, securing their appointments, getting rid of competitors, or receiving rewards from their parties. In fact, as soon as some form of authority was restored, the murders ceased, save in exceptional cases.

The attitude of the Communists towards the events described above may be summarized in a comment on them pronounced by their leader, Togliatti, in a public speech delivered a few years ago. "Those events," he said, i.e., the slaughter of scores of thousands of unarmed men and women by armed Communist partisans, "constitute the finest page in the history of Italy."

Legal proceedings were instituted against some of the authors of many of these crimes. But, owing to the amnesty decrees enacted by the post-war Governments, even the most notorious scoundrels often had their sentences quashed or reduced to trifling proportions, on the plea that the offenses in question had been consequences of the state of war. Not a few of the worst criminals, mostly Communists or fellow travelers, were afterward elected to the Senate or the Chamber of Deputies, and if today none of them are actually members of the Government (as was the case in the immediate post-war period, largely through the orders of the Allied Military Government), they still exercise considerable influence and enjoy large emoluments. It has been noted, however, that quite a number of the criminals thus acquitted have subsequently committed other crimes, and have been arrested, tried, and condemned, without being able to benefit by the post-war amnesties which are no longer in force.

Nothing could better illustrate the abasement and transformation of human values, interest, and world concern during the liberation period than the public apathy to the murder of 50,000-100,000 Fascists, men, women and children *after* the hostilities had ceased and when those killed were doing nothing to oppose the public order maintained by the Allies, and the world-wide excitement and indignation which had been expressed when *one* Socialist deputy, Giacomo Matteotti, was abducted on June 10, 1924, and died while being worked over by the stooges of Fascist extremists.

Matteotti was a wealthy landowner of Rovigo, an ardent Socialist, and a vigorous opponent of Mussolini and Fascism. The irresponsible Fascists who plotted the abduction and death of Matteotti had two motives for the dastardly act. It was rumored that Matteotti and the Socialists were about to publish documents exposing these particular Fascists. In a speech of June 7, 1924, Mussolini had indicated that he was contemplating offering two cabinet posts to Socialists. The Fascists who abducted Matteotti wished to prevent the publication of the documents and to drive a wedge between Mussolini and the Socialists. It appears that Matteotti actually died of a heart attack while being terrorized by underworld characters employed by these Fascist extremists. Whatever the cause of his death, it was a foul deed, and nobody in Italy was more shocked over it than Mussolini. Those known at the time to be involved were arrested, convicted, and imprisoned.

The responsibility for the act has been carefully investigated by the reputable anti-Fascist journalist, Carlo Silvestri, and the able Polish writer on Italian affairs, Roman Dombrowski, also an anti-Fascist. They both agree that Mussolini had neither any advance warning of the plot nor any responsibility whatever for the deed, and he was deeply distressed about it to the day of his death. A leader of the Fascist extremists responsible for the abduction of Matteotti, Giovanni Marinelli, confessed his complicity on the night before he was executed following the Verona Trial of January, 1944. The survivors of the 1924 episode were retried before an anti-Fascist court in 1947. One of the accused was acquitted and the other imprisoned for political reasons. As Dombrowski summarizes the facts: "Nothing could have done more to clear Mussolini of the charge of murdering Matteotti than the trial itself." As an anti-Fascist propaganda stunt, it was "a palpable failure." Even the Socialist leader, Nenni, then Vice-Premier, was opposed to reopening the question in 1947.

The abduction and death of Matteotti in 1924 produced a great outcry. Indeed, it was probably the outstanding international political incident of the year. It was exploited in every possible manner known to publicity and propaganda by Socialists and radicals, not only in Italy but throughout the civilized world. They were ardently joined by expatriate Italian foes of Mussolini and Fascism. Mussolini was portrayed as a foul and brazen murderer. Fascism was represented as founded on blood and fury and flourishing on assassination. Radicals throughout the Western World urged their governments to break off diplomatic relations with Fascist Italy. Some even went so far as to urge military intervention to unseat Mussolini by force.

Yet, the murder of 50,000-100,000 Fascists by Communist or Communist-directed partisans *after* the War was over passed virtually unnoticed by world opinion. There were plenty of newspaper correspondents in Italy at the time, but either they reported little or nothing about these massacres to their home papers or these papers refused to print the news submitted to them. Virtually no information about these many bloody weeks appeared in the newspapers of Britain, France, the United

States or other civilized countries. Citizens of those countries who happen to read this book are likely to gain their first information concerning the sanguinary events from the preceding pages of this volume. We shall leave it to these readers to draw their own conclusions from this experience.

In marked contrast to the summary speed and complete illegality with which the partisans moved against Fascists and other conservatives after the War was over has been the delay and deliberation with which flagrant crimes involving Communists have been handled. A conspicuous example is that relating to the so-called "Dongo gold trial."

When Mussolini and the loyal members of his RSI Government left Milan at the end of April for the Valtellina, where they hoped to make a last stand, they brought with them the reserve funds of the RSI and of the various public departments for the purpose of being able to continue to carry on government business. They also had with them a considerable amount of money and other valuables which were the private property of Mussolini, individual Ministers, and their staff. The total is estimated to have been about 90 million dollars.

On reaching Dongo, the column was held up by the Communist-directed "52nd Garibaldi Brigade," and Mussolini, the Ministers, and those accompanying them were murdered by the partisans operating under Communist orders. All the money and other valuables which they had brought with them were seized and confiscated by the partisans. This booty should then have been handed over to the representatives of the Rome Government which, aside from the Allied Commands, was the only legitimate authority in Italy after the RSI had ceased to exist. But, with the exception of small sums, everything seized at Dongo was turned over to Communists, led by Dante Gorrieri, and found its way into the coffers of the Communist party and, in part, into the pockets of some of its leaders. Pietro Terzi, who commanded the partisan group that seized the booty from the Fascists, admitted that he and his band handed over the Dongo treasure to the Communist partisans on the ground that "the Communists had fought harder than anybody else." This explains the remarkable resources of the Communist party after the War. The Rome headquarters of the Communist party are popularly known as "the Palazzo Dongo."

The Communist partisans did their best to cover up both the robbery and the amount and disposition of the "treasure." There is no doubt that this was the reason why Audisio either shot Claretta Petacci himself or had her murdered by Moretti. She knew of the treasure and its seizure by the partisans. When a partisan leader, Luigi Canali, known as "Captain Neri," protested against irresponsible robbery and insisted that the Communist leader, Dante Gorrieri, sign receipts for the money given him, Neri disappeared along with his receipts, and no trace of his body was ever found. His fiancée, a female partisan known as Gianna, who had been present with him at the time of the robbery, inquired as to what had become of Neri. She, in turn, disappeared without a trace. Gianna's friend, Anna Bianchi, started to look for Gianna. She was kidnapped by Communist partisans, tortured and thrown into Lake Como. Her father then swore vengeance on her murderers, whereupon he disappeared and his body was never found. Many other partisans who were present at the time of the seizure and disposition of the Dongo funds disappeared, but it is difficult to know who were murdered by the Communists and who made their way to foreign parts with a portion of the seized booty.[8]

Nothing was done about this violence and scandal for a number of years. The first move was made by a military judge, General Zingales, who uncovered rather sensational evidence about the episode and the confiscation of the funds. Even so, the Government, presumably as a result of Communist pressure and threatened blackmail, held up the proceedings and placed Zingales on the retired list. Finally, as the result of further publicity and the pressure of an aroused public opinion, a trial of those involved in the Dongo affair was started at Padua early in April, 1957. It appears likely to drag along through appeals and counter-appeals for months or years. It has seemed curious

[8]For a good account of the seizure of the Dongo "treasure" and the murders and disappearances which followed, see F. J. P. Veale, *Crimes Discreetly Veiled*, p. 85ff.

to many that the Government, as the injured party in connection with the confiscation of funds, has not constituted itself what is known in Italian criminal law as the "parte civile" to cooperate with the prosecution. Those accused of the murders and robberies are 35 in number. They include the Communist, Dante Gorrieri, who was made a member of the Chamber of Deputies to give him immunity against punishment for his crimes, Pietro Vergani, and Pietro Cambaruta, all of them, quite independent of the Dongo affair, men with very shady records. Michele Moretti, who, some believe, actually murdered Mussolini, has disappeared. As Mr. Veale observes: "Moretti is now either living in luxury in foreign parts on his share of the Dongo loot or is lying at the bottom of Lake Como with a Communist bullet in the back of his head."[9] No proceedings have been started against Walter Audisio for the assassination of Mussolini or the dastardly murder of Claretta Petacci, who was killed to prevent her from revealing the treacherous, deceptive and brutal manner in which Mussolini was assassinated and the partisan theft of the Fascist treasure seized at the time. Even Roman Dombrowski, who has no sympathy for the Fascists, denounces the act as "common murder."

This frantic desire of Audisio and the Communist partisans to cover up their crimes explains why they shot all those captured at the same time that Mussolini was seized, including Geoffredo Coppola, an eminent Greek scholar and president of the University of Bologna, and Ernesto Daquanno, director of the *Stefani* News Agency. This was also notoriously "common murder." So far did Audisio and the partisans carry their guilty precautionary violence that they even murdered the innocent drivers of the Italian cars that had brought Mussolini and his party from Milan to Dongo. As Dombrowski observes: "That circumstance cannot be ignored by any historian who attempts to understand the atmosphere of those last days of April, 1945."[10] The shocked mayor of Dongo, Giuseppe Rubini, rebuked Audisio and his fellow-murderers in forthright fashion

---

[9] Veale, *op. cit.*, pp. 87-88.
[10] Roman Dombrowski, *Mussolini: Twilight and Fall* (New York, 1956), p. 222.

when he remarked: "You have lost an unusual, a unique, opportunity to begin a new period in our country's history by applying principles of civilization." The "atmosphere" of the liberation era is still further revealed by the fact that, far from being tried and executed as a common murderer, Audisio became a popular hero and was elected to the Chamber of Deputies.

In addition to the funds seized by the Communists at Dongo, a large quantity of other government property vanished into thin air after the cessation of hostilities. The government depots were filled with all kinds of goods, such as 50,000 meters of woolen cloth for army uniforms, 25,000 motor vehicles, and arms of all kinds. These matters are not being dealt with at the Padua trial, but separate trials have been instituted in several Italian cities. Here, too, important facts are being revealed. With regard to the arms, as I have pointed out previously, many of them were seized and concealed by Communists for possible later use in their hoped-for revolution. Very frequently, large and small caches of arms are discovered by the police and seized by the military authorities. It is significant that none of the persons responsible for these concealments of arms, although well known to the authorities, have been prosecuted by the Government.

CHAPTER XXV

ANTI-FASCIST LEGISLATION

WITH the end of hostilities on April 25, 1945, the "liberation" of Italy may be regarded as having been completed, although few Italians realized anything of the kind, for it was not visible to the naked eye.

The Italian Government at the time and for a couple of years longer, until the signing of the Peace Treaty in 1947, continued to be under the complete control of the ACC and the AMG, supported by the Anglo-American armed forces. Its policy must, in consequence, be regarded as the logical continuation of that preceding the end of the War. The only difference is that, after the War, the Government's nominal authority was extended to the whole of the peninsula, except the province of Bolzano and the Venezia Giulia, still directly under Allied military administration.

The chief, we may say the only, real activity of the Government was the continued persecution of its political opponents, of course with the approval and encouragement of the Allied authorities. When I say "political opponents" I mean only the Fascists, because members of other parties, even if of a definitely seditious and revolutionary nature, were not only protected, but were actually represented in the Cabinet itself, and not prevented from committing acts of violence of all kinds, including wholesale slaughter.

Most of the legislation dealing with these matters had been enacted before the end of the War by a series of decrees which, although of fundamental importance and severely restricting the elementary rights of the citizens, had had no Parliamentary approval, there being then no Parliament or representative institutions of any kind, while the Government itself had been appointed, as we have seen, by order of the Allied Commands and kept in power at their good pleasure.

The basic measures were those laid down in the already mentioned legislative decree of July 27, 1944, supplemented by that of April 22, 1945. The essential feature of these provisions was their retroactivity, as they inflicted the severest penalties, including death, for acts which were not crimes when they were committed.[1]

Immediately after April 25th, and in some cases in occupied Italy, even before that date, the so-called "people's courts" arose, not in consequence of any Government measure, but made up of men with no knowledge of the law, self-appointed or chosen by the local CLNAI, nearly all of them Communists and most of them with very unsavory criminal records. They followed no formal rules of procedure, applied no existing laws, but seized any person whom they wished to get rid of, tried him, often in a few minutes only and giving him no opportunity for defense, condemned him to death and had him taken before a firing squad. No record of these "courts" has been kept, and it is impossible to ascertain how many persons were executed by their decisions; but the number was undoubtedly very large.

The above decrees set up a High Court of Justice to try persons of special importance, and its decisions, even if they imposed the death penalty, were not subject to any appeal. They also created a series of Extraordinary Assize Courts for dealing with offenders of lower rank. These Courts, too, could inflict capital punishment, but their decisions were subject to appeal before the already existing Court of Cassation. The High Court consisted of three career judges and four "popular" judges, selected from lists of known anti-Fascists, usually Communists devoid of all knowledge of the law. The Extraordinary Assize Courts were composed of a career judge as president and four "popular" judges, selected in the same way as those of the High Court. The public prosecutors were also selected in the same way by the CLNAI.

[1] The only parallel to this retroactivity is to be found in the measures enacted by the Neapolitan Bourbon Government (aided and abetted by the British Admiral Nelson) after the revolution of 1799. The account of those events, recorded in Pietro Colletta's *Storia del reame di Napoli dal 1734 al 1815*, is strikingly like that of the events which I have described.

Since in both the High Court and the Extraordinary Assize Court sentences were issued on a majority vote, it was with the "popular" judges that the decision actually rested, and death sentences were thus issued without limit, although it must be said that not all of them were carried out, for the decisions of the Extraordinary Assize Courts were, as we have seen, subject to appeal before the Court of Cassation and were often quashed. But, by a decree of August 6, 1944, no appeals to the Court of Cassation were allowed even against the sentences of the Extraordinary Assize Courts in the case of persons who had organized Fascist squads and committed acts of violence, or led the insurrection of October 28, 1922, whereby the Fascist regime had come into power, or had promoted the *coup d'état* voted by Parliament on January 3, 1925,[2] or who had by "important acts" contributed to maintain the Fascist regime in power, or had committed other crimes for Fascist motives or availed themselves of the political situation created by Fascism.

Article 2 of the decree of July 27, 1944, declared that all the ex-members of the Fascist Government and all those holding important offices in the Fascist Party, regarded as guilty of having annulled public liberties and constitutional guarantees, compromising the fate of the country and having led to the present catastrophe, were liable to life imprisonment and in the more serious cases to the death penalty. The same penalties were declared applicable to the judges and public prosecutors of the Fascist Special Tribunal, the editors of political newspapers, and field officers in command of Black-Shirt units with political functions. All persons who, after September 8, 1943, i.e. after the signing of the armistice, had committed offenses against the military defense of the State, by intelligence or collaboration with the "German invaders," were to be punished according to the provisions of the war-time Military Criminal Code, which could also inflict the death penalty. This measure applied to all those who, as Ministers, high officials or officers, had served Mussolini's RSI Government.

It is obvious that many of these charges were purely conjec-

---

[2] A decision which reinforced the Fascist regime.

tural, incapable of proof, or based on merely political opinions. The clause concerning "important acts" (*atti rilevanti*), invented by Count Sforza, has no legal significance whatsoever, but it played a very relevant part in a number of the political trials during the two years following the end of hostilities. Moreover, not a few of the offenses in question had been committed a long time ago, twenty or more years previously, and the accused persons had already been tried and either acquitted or condemned and had served their sentences. But no account was taken of these facts, and the accused were tried again for these same offenses, an astounding violation of elementary principles of justice. Of the amnesties granted under the Fascist regime those in favor of Fascists were annulled, while those in favor of non-Fascists were maintained.

A legislative decree of October 10, 1945, abolished both the High Court and the Extraordinary Assize Courts, and the offenses within their jurisdiction were submitted to the newly-created Special Sections of the Assize Courts, composed in the same way as the Extraordinary Assize Courts. But on March 31, 1947, these Special Sections also ceased to operate, and the cases which would have been dealt with by them were referred to the ordinary Assize Courts, which also handled offenses of a non-political nature.

It would be interesting to ascertain how many persons were actually executed in consequence of the sentences of these courts. We know of a few such cases, but the total number of these executions is regarded as a top secret by the authorities, who refuse to supply any figures, probably for the following reason:

One of the most bitter strictures brought against the Fascist regime by its opponents was the creation and functioning of the Special Tribunal, instituted in 1927 to try political offenders, and described as an instrument of tyranny, operating in disregard of law or justice. Actually, its duties were carefully laid down by a law voted by Parliament, it applied the provisions of the ordinary Criminal Code, was presided over by men of high standing, and the accused were given every opportunity for defense with their own counsel and witnesses. An eminent British publicist and historian told me, after attending a trial before this Court, that the accused appeared to enjoy the same facilities for defense which they would have enjoyed in a British criminal court.

After the War, the judges, prosecutors, investigating magistrates and other officers of the Special Tribunal were arrested in view of prosecutions to be held against them under the anti-Fascist legislation then enacted. But they were *all* acquitted without being tried, because it was proved that their conduct had been perfectly legal.

When we come to actual figures we find that, in the 17 years of its existence, the Fascist Special Tribunal had issued a total of only 65 death sentences. Of these, 52 were for acts of espionage in behalf of the enemy during the War, for criminal violence committed during the black-out, all wartime offenses liable to the severest penalties in every country. Of the remaining 13 death sentences, one had been inflicted for a common crime of peculiar atrocity (the murder of a whole family). This leaves twelve executions for purely political crimes (murders or attempted murders committed for political motives) or considerably less than one per annum.

We thus find a very good reason for concealing the number of executions carried out in consequence of decisions by the new anti-Fascist courts. The large number of the latter would, in fact, have made a very bad showing when compared with that of the executions under the Fascist Special Tribunal.

Moreover, while the proceedings before the Special Tribunal were perfectly regular and conducted in strict conformity with the law of criminal procedure, the same certainly cannot be said of these before the anti-Fascist courts. One instance of the latter, recorded by the eminent attorney, Titta Madia, in a speech delivered in the Chamber of Deputies (of which he was a member) on November 19, 1953, is typical of many others. Four men were being tried before an Extraordinary Assize Court for collaboration with the Germans. When the President of the Court began to read the decision arrived at, it was realized that only two of the accused would be condemned to death, and a mob, composed of the rapscallions of the city and neighborhood, specially imported for the purpose, began to howl with such savage vehemence that the terrified judges retired into chambers once more and emerged a few minutes later to read their altered decision, condemning all four of the accused to death.[3]

In that same speech, Titta Madia also spoke of the trial in Verona of Castellino, Glissenti and others; on that occasion, one of the accused was shot dead in court by a policeman who was presumably there to protect the prisoners against mob violence. Even where the judges were not subjected to political pressure by the Government, the courts were so definitely under mob rule that the normal course of justice was impossible.

Another Fascist institution which came in for a vast amount of abuse, and was one of those suppressed under Article 30 of the "long" armistice, was the OVRA, a police organization about which the most lurid stories were told. It was, however, nothing more than the regrouping of the political sections of the ordinary *questure* or provincial police departments which had existed for generations. Information of a political nature thus collected was systematized and passed on to the Chief of Police in Rome, who acted upon it or ignored it, according to circumstances. Its chiefs were all members of the regular police service, but, of course, like all police officials, they had a number of private informers. Immediately after the end of the War all the OVRA officials were arrested with a view to subjecting them to trial.

In the summer and autumn of 1945, lists of the alleged informers of the OVRA were from time to time issued to the press, but these communiqués were always followed by further statements to the effect that the lists in question were neither complete nor official, and that the real list would be issued later. In fact, it soon came to be said, cynically, that very shortly another list would be published containing the names of all Italian citizens who had *not* been informers of the OVRA! The

[3] This sentence was quashed, however, by the Court of Cassation.

definite official list never materialized, because Pietro Nenni, head of the pro-Communist Socialist Party and at that time a member of the Government, had the whole of the OVRA file submitted to him. When he returned it to the judicial authorities, many of the documents contained in it had been mysteriously spirited away. According to the Rome weekly, *Il Merlo Giallo,* whose editor, the late Alberto Giannini, had been a fellow-exile with Nenni in France during the Fascist regime, Nenni himself had been in touch with the OVRA, which had secured the names of many Communists and other anti-Fascists, together with detailed accounts of their activities. It would have been very awkward if these communications had been published. Hence they were eliminated from the OVRA file. The *Merlo Giallo* statements have never been disproved.

The OVRA officials, after being detained in prison for many months, were all released without trial, as nothing illegal was ever proved against them. The chief of the political police during the War, under whose authority the OVRA operated, Guido Leto, was in fact not only released but reinstated in his post at the Ministry of the Interior.[4]

In addition to the trials of persons who had been prominent in the Fascist regime or had committed acts regarded by the post-war Government as criminal, we have seen how a whole series of measures were enacted to deprive all those who had been Fascists or pro-Fascists, even if they were only obeying the laws of the land, of their positions in the civil service, diplomacy, the fighting services, university chairs, teaching appointments in the schools, and so on, while professional and business men registered as Fascists were in many cases to be struck off the rolls and excluded from all their activities, even if they had committed no illegal acts. These measures, which had begun under Allied pressure during the War, punished men for conduct which was admittedly not criminal, but was merely regarded as undesirable under the new dispensation. Such persons were also deprived of their right to vote for several years.

[4] Guido Leto himself has published an interesting and detailed account of the OVRA—*Fascismo e antifascismo* (Bologna, 1951).

The enforcement of these Star Chamber provisions was entrusted, as said before, to a special High Commissioner for Sanctions against Fascism, a position first held by Tito Zaniboni, the
would-be murderer of Mussolini, and subsequently by Count
Sforza, who was afterwards succeeded by his worthy second-
in-command, Mario Berlinguer. In carrying out their duties
these men, especially the two latter, committed the most monstrous acts of injustice.

The result of this policy was to deprive the country of most
of its best and most honest officials, who had been spared by
the previous "clean-up," substituting for them persons inferior
to them in every way and in many cases of very doubtful antecedents. Not a few officials were dismissed through the intrigues
of rivals who, having a pull with the powers that be, were determined to secure their jobs.

It must be admitted, however, that the Council of State, the
highest administrative tribunal in the country, composed of
officials of exceptional merit and ability, to whom the dismissed
officials appealed, reinstated large numbers of them, in spite
of political pressure. I remember attending a meeting of the
Council to hear the appeals of 25 officials of the Ministry of
Foreign Affairs, friends and former colleagues of mine, who
were all reinstated. The Minister of Foreign Affairs at the time,
Count Sforza, tried to oust them once more by placing them on
the retired list, but on a second appeal nearly all of them definitely secured redress for their wrongs.[5] The whole of this procedure proved very expensive for the State, as it not only had
to pay the dismissed officials their arrears of salary during sus-
pension, but, having appointed successors to the dismissed
men, found itself, after the decision of the Council of State, in
a number of cases with two officials for every post involved.

Not content with punishing or getting rid of innumerable
persons who had served the past regime, the new Government
was determined to seize as much of their property as possible.
Lurid stories had been spread about concerning the huge sums

---

[5] I may say that this measure was not applied to me, as I had retired from the
Foreign Office because of the age limit before the War.

illegally accumulated through political influences by the leading Fascist personalities, members of the Government, or of the various boards and committees of the Fascist Party. A decree of May 31, 1945, added to that of July 27, 1944, provided for the confiscation of all property acquired in that way. In every province an *ad hoc* commission was set up, composed of Government officials and outsiders, to inquire into all increments of the property owned by the persons mentioned, alleged to have been acquired through Fascist influences. The measure could be applied also to the parents and descendants of the above persons, and even to their mistresses, if any. Those accused of possessing illegally acquired wealth were actually expected to prove that it had not been so acquired. The law remained in force until December 31, 1952, after which no new cases were taken up, although proceedings still in course of inquiry were continued.

The results proved very disappointing to the authorities. Instead of the vast sums which they had hoped to confiscate, only a very small amount was secured. The exact figures have been kept a strict secret, but it is said that no more than about one billion lire (about $1,500,000) was collected, most of it in comparatively small sums, and in nearly all cases still under appeal. It is remarkable that not one of the leading Fascist personages, Ministers and Party "big-wigs" was proved to have secured wealth by illegal means and most of them had remained poor men, even when they had had the responsibility of handling large sums of public money. The same cannot be said of many of their successors under the various postwar Italian Governments.

On the other hand, the cost of the administration of the organization set up in the attempt to confiscate illegally acquired wealth is estimated at about eleven or twelve billion lire. It has evidently not been a good piece of business for the State—or the taxpayer.

According to the measures enacted against Fascism by the Government of Badoglio and his successors, all who had served in the armed forces of the RSI were regarded as traitors to

the legitimate Government of Italy and as having acted on behalf of the German "invaders." These measures deprived all
such persons of the right to remain in the Italian armed forces
or to secure pensions on retirement.

When a group of officers of the "Tagliamento" Legion put
in an application to be regarded and treated as regular combatants, the Milan Military Court rejected this application,
denying that the RSI was a *de facto* Government.

The said officers thereupon appealed to the Supreme Military
Court, the highest tribunal of its kind in Italy. This Court, on
April 26, 1954, issued a decision reversing that of the Milan
Court. It declared that all the laws and decrees against Fascism
had come into force exclusively through the orders of the Allied
Command. The Italian Government thus exercised its powers
only *sub conditione*, within the limits laid down by the said
Command. It could not operate, of course, in the Center or
North of Italy, not yet under Allied occupation, and in those
areas all legal authority was vested in the RSI. That State
could not be regarded as a subject of international law, but
it enjoyed full legal personality before those States which had
recognized it. It was indeed a *de facto* Government, and exercised full authority under Italian laws and decrees and operated through Italian offices and officials, courts and police.
Field Marshal Kesselring's ordinance of September 11, 1943,
subjecting the territory of Italy to German legislation, was re-
voked on September 23rd, when the new Italian Fascist State
came into being. The Italian authorities were, no doubt, often
subject to German pressure, but they functioned regularly,
and the RSI had its own armed forces under its own commanders, even if the high Command was German.

It may be said, the Court added, that the commands of units
who did not obey the orders of the legitimate Government
violated the provisions of the Italian wartime military Penal
Code, which punishes any activity prolonging hostilities during
an armistice. But this does not eliminate the quality of belligerents vis-à-vis the Allies, to which all combatants are entitled.
Never in history has this character been refused to troops who

did not accept surrender. According to Article 40 of the provisions annexed to the Hague Convention on the laws of war, it cannot be denied that the members of the armed forces of the RSI retained their character as regular belligerents. Therefore, the Allies in Italy, in agreement with the legitimate Italian Government, treated the combatants of the RSI captured by them as regular prisoners of war.

The Hague Treaty on the laws of war and also the Geneva Convention of December 8, 1949, recognize as combatants, entitled to be treated as prisoners of war, members of volunteer organizations, acting outside or within their own territory, provided that:

a) They had at their head a commander responsible for his subordinates;

b) they wore fixed distinctive emblems, recognizable from a distance;

c) they bore arms openly;

d) in their operations they acted in conformity with the laws and usages of war.

The Italian partisans, as we have seen, did not conform to the provisions under a), b) and d).

Thus, according to the decision of the Supreme Military Court, the members of the armed forces of the RSI were legitimate belligerents, whereas the partisans were not.

This decision reversed a whole body of laws, decrees and regulations enacted by the "legitimate" Government of Italy. It remains to be seen if and how the Government now in control will give effect to it.

In the course of time many of the most flagrant injustices committed by the various Governments succeeding each other after July 25, 1943, have been mitigated or corrected in practice, either through the action of the ordinary judiciary, or through changes of heart or "crises de conscience" on the part of some of the more influential members of the Cabinet and higher officials. But there has not as yet been any definite reversal of the anti-Fascist CLN policy, whose authors are ashamed of confessing their iniquities and prefer to let the worst provisions merely fall into abeyance. The above-quoted decision of the Supreme Military Court will inevitably affect a whole body of measures concerning members of the armed forces of the RSI, and by implication they cannot fail to react in the long run also on non-military men who have suffered gross injustice. But it will be many years before the effects of the CLN spirit are wholly eliminated or forgotten.[6]

[6]The decision was published in a pamphlet by Piero Pisenti, Minister of Justice in the RSI Government, *Revisioni in cammino* (Milan, 1955).

On the dictation of new forms of government by the Allies as a policy of the liberation after the second World War, see J. D. Montgomery, *Forced to be Free* (Chicago, 1957), which deals especially with the situation in Japan and Germany.

CHAPTER XXVI

SOME SPECIAL CASES OF POLITICAL PERSECUTION

A FEW typical instances of the manner in which some men
who had particularly distinguished themselves for their
patriotic activities, of a kind regarded as unorthodox after July,
1943, were treated, are worth recording. One of them is that of
Baron Carlo Emanuele Basile.

A Sicilian by origin, but long associated with Lombardy,
Basile was a man of good family and exceptional culture. He
had served with true gallantry in World War I, and again in
the Ethiopian campaign. He had held various positions in the
Government service and in the Fascist Party, of which he was
an ardent supporter, and during World War II he had been for
a time Prefect of Genoa, where he had saved large numbers of
workmen from being deported to Germany for forced labor.
Later he was appointed Under-Secretary of War in Mussolini's
last Government (RSI), a position which he held until the end
of hostilities.

On April 25, 1945, he was arrested by the partisans, brought
before a "people's court," charged with having been a Fascist
and a patriot and, after a bogus trial, he was condemned to
death. But he was saved at the last moment through the intervention of an ex-officer who had served under him (in the
Ethiopian campaign) but had become a partisan of some influence. Although disagreeing with Basile's politics, he was
personally devoted to his old chief. On hearing that Basile
was about to be shot, he hastened to the scene of the coming
execution and declared that that particular "court" was not
entitled to try Basile for reasons of territorial jurisdiction.

Basile was then taken back to the Milan prison of San Vittore,
and was later tried before the Extraordinary Assize Court in
that same city. He was there charged with not having prevented

the deportation of Genoese workmen, and condemned to twenty years' imprisonment. The public prosecutor appealed to the Court of Cassation, as he considered this sentence too mild. The Court of Cassation quashed the Milan decision and ordered a new trial to be held at Pavia. There whole truckloads of false witnesses were brought into the courthouse, they howled down the defense counsel, prevented any witnesses for the defense from speaking, and threatened a general strike throughout Italy if the prisoner was not condemned to death. The terrified judges did condemn him to death, but this time it was he who appealed to the Court of Cassation, which quashed the Pavia sentence and ordered a new trial to be held in Naples over a year later (August, 1947). There it was the public prosecutor himself, Riccardo Seravo, who applied for Basile's acquittal, which was forthwith granted by the Court.

But the Communists all over Italy set up such howls of protest against the decision that the then Prime Minister, De Gasperi, with the lack of courage which had always distinguished him, most illegally had Basile again arrested on the very same charges of which he had been acquitted by the Naples Court. He was once more imprisoned and detained for several months longer, until, at a new trial at Perugia, he was again fully acquitted, and this time definitely released. He had thus undergone some five trials, had been twice condemned to death and once to twenty years' imprisonment, and had spent seven years in nineteen different jails. His property had been confiscated, but he was afterwards able to have it returned to him, although the furniture and the valuable library of his villa on Lake Maggiore had been looted. All through his vicissitudes he never lost his calmness or his sense of humor, as I am able to attest, having been his fellow-prisoner both in Rome and at Procida.[1]

Another case worth recording is that of Ermanno Amicucci. A native of the Abruzzi and a journalist by profession, he had been elected a member of the Chamber of Deputies, and was appointed Under-Secretary in the Ministry of Corporations

[1] The details of this case were supplied to me by Basile himself.

from 1939 to 1943, during which period he had dealt efficiently with various important economic problems. He was always known to be one of the most moderate and well-balanced of the Fascist leaders. On the formation of the RSI he gave his full adherence to it and, while he held no official appointment in the Government, he was selected for the editorship of the Milan *Corriere della Sera.*

When, after the end of hostilities, Mussolini and the other members of his Government left Milan, hoping to reach the Valtellina, Amicucci followed in his own car. But during a wayside halt near Cadenabbia, where he got out for a few minutes, the chauffeur fled with the car and the baggage, and Amicucci was arrested by partisans, taken to the San Vittore prison in Milan, and there told that he had been condemned to death without a trial and without any charge having been preferred against him. When he was taken before a firing squad his execution was held up, owing to the absence of the commander of the squad, and he was conveyed back to San Vittore. On May 30th, he was brought to trial before the Extraordinary Assize Court in the same city. The charge against him was the publication of a pamphlet entitled *Partita aperta* ("An Open Question") consisting of sixteen of his articles reprinted from the *Corriere della Sera* during his editorship, dealing with events from November 4, 1943, to December 17, 1944, in which he had defended the action of the RSI and of Mussolini in the attempt to retrieve Italy's honor after the armistice of September, 1943. Amid the shrieks of the mob he was condemned to death but, on his appeal to the Court of Cassation, the Milan sentence was quashed, and a new trial ordered at Brescia for September 25th. The public prosecutor only demanded that he be condemned to twenty-four years' imprisonment, but the Court raised the penalty to thirty years. A second appeal to the Supreme Court resulted in his acquittal, on February 18, 1947, after a detention of twenty-one months and four days.[2]

Even more striking were the vicissitudes of Field Marshal Rodolfo Graziani. One of the finest soldiers in the Italian army

[2]These details were given to me by Amicucci himself.

and a man of magnificent bravery, he had distinguished himself in World War I and in several African campaigns. He had brilliantly commanded the southern force in the Ethiopian War, for which exploit he had been created Marquis of Neghelli, and he fought gallantly in North Africa in World War II. After a period without any command in Italy, he felt it his moral duty, on the signing of the armistice, to give his support to the newly-created RSI Government in order to recreate an Italian army for the defense of at least a part of Italy against the Western invaders, as well as to protect the country against possible German reprisals. He was appointed Minister of Defense and given the command of the Ligurian army, fulfilling these duties with ability and intelligence.

After April 25, 1945, he surrendered to the Americans, was interned by them in the San Vittore prison in Milan, then conveyed to a P.O.W. camp near Florence, then to another in Algiers, and finally handed over to the Italian authorities, who imprisoned him at Procida. As he was still suffering from the attempt on his life at Addis Ababa, where a bomb had been thrown at him, leaving over three hundred fragments in his body, he was removed to a Naples clinic.

He was subjected to a trial before a civil court on October 11, 1948, but, after seventy-eight hearings, the judges declared themselves incompetent, owing to the military nature of the charges against him, and he was brought before a military court in Rome on March 21, 1949. He was brilliantly defended by Prof. Francesco Carnelutti, Giacomo Augenti and Giorgio Mastino Del Rio. They proved, among other things, that the charge of having collaborated with "the German enemy invaders" was without foundation, inasmuch as Badoglio's Government was so completely under the control of the Anglo-American forces that the declaration of war against Germany was null and void, and there had, thus, never been any war with Germany.

The Court, on May 2, 1950, nevertheless condemned Graziani to nineteen years' imprisonment for "collaboration," but admitted that he had acted "for reasons of exceptional moral and social value" and granted him various extenuating circumstances, whereby the sentence was reduced to a few months' detention. The actual wording of the decision was tantamount to a full acquittal, but the Court was afraid, for political reasons, to say so openly. On the other hand, for moral and political reasons, it did not dare to declare him guilty, and he was released very soon afterward. What was particularly noticeable was that not a single witness was found to give any evidence of any sort against him.[3]

On leaving prison he retired to private life, surrounded by the devoted affection of his family and friends, until his death in 1954. His family had asked that the funeral service be celebrated in the Church of Santa Maria degli Angeli in Rome, as had been done in the case of many other eminent military leaders, such as Field Marshal Diaz and the Duke of Aosta. But the authorities declared that this was not possible, as the Vicariate of the Rome diocese had refused its permission. The Vicariate at once announced that it had never raised any objection of the kind, thereby proving that the official statement was a lie. The service, held in another church, was attended by an enormous crowd, which also lined the route along which the funeral procession passed for scores of miles. In every town or village between Rome and Arcinazzo, in the province of Frosinone, where he was to be buried, the whole population turned out to do homage to the dead hero. It was a wholly spontaneous popular demonstration which had been in no way prepared.

On the occasion of Graziani's death the American weekly *Time* published an account of his career, filled with vulgar abuse and with the most shameless falsehoods. I addressed a letter to the editor correcting the grossest misstatements, but it was not published.

Another case which deserves to be recorded was that of Commander Don Valerio Borghese. A member of one of the

[3] Graziani's case is set forth in his own book *Ho difeso la patria* (Milan, 1947), in a volume containing his defense by his lawyers, Mastino del Rio, Augenti and Carnelutti, and in the actual record of the Court's decision. See also a volume entitled *Graziani*, by several authors, published by the *Rivista Romana* (Rome, 1956).

greatest Roman princely families, he had joined the Royal Navy and had distinguished himself for his magnificent courage and marvelous technical skill in World War II, especially in the attacks at the head of the above-mentioned unit known as the "Decima MAS" on Alexandria and Gibraltar, sinking or damaging a number of British warships. After the armistice, he joined the RSI Government and commanded a unit of the same name, but operating on land and divided into a number of small detachments scattered about in various parts of the RSI territory, where they distinguished themselves in many engagements.

After the end of hostilities Borghese surrendered to the Allies and, while he and the men who were with him were given the honors of war for their magnificent courage, he himself was interned for many months in a British P.O.W. Camp near Rome, and then handed over to the Italian authorities. He was detained a long time at Procida, was tried and finally released, but deprived of his rank as an officer and of the right to vote, although he was not deprived of his medals for valor. Since then, he has devoted himself mainly to assisting the men formerly under his command, securing work for them and trying to get their rights as soldiers recognized. The book in which he tells the story of the exploits of his unit, entitled *La Decima MAS*, published also in England and in the United States under the title of *Sea Devils*, has been an amazing success in all three countries.

The case of General Niccolò Bellomo is worth recording as one of the first trials of an alleged "war criminal." After the armistice of September, 1943, Bellomo was one of the few Italian generals who kept his control over a part of his troops, and, acting under the orders of his superiors, he resisted the German attempt to occupy Bari, being wounded several times during the action. He then held the city until it was taken over by a British force.

In 1944, he was arrested by British orders on the charge of having had two British officer prisoners shot at Torre Tresca near Bari in 1941, while he was in charge at a P.O.W. camp.

The officers had escaped from the camp, but had been caught and brought back to it. They again tried to escape, and the General ordered the guard to fire on the would-be fugitives, one of whom was killed in the attempt and the other wounded. Bellomo was detained for over a year at Padula while awaiting trial, treated with great harshness and forced to perform the most humiliating duties, such as cleaning the latrines. That his execution had been already decided on before the trial appears from a remark made to him while in prison by a British captain. The general was arranging a small crib sent to him by his family for Christmas in 1943, and the captain, seeing him so engaged, said to him: "You are quite right in doing this, as it will be your last Christmas on this earth."

The trial was held from July 23 to 28, 1944, and ended in a death sentence. This sentence was not, however, carried out at once. Bellomo's family made every effort to secure a pardon or a reprieve, and sent a petition to General Alexander to that effect. But no reply was received and the sentence was confirmed; General Bellomo was conveyed to the island of Nisida in the Bay of Naples and, on September 11th, he was taken before a firing squad and executed.

That Bellomo was not a man of ruthless severity is proved by an episode which had occurred some months before the affair at Torre Tresca. He had then conducted an operation against a party of British paratroopers who had descended on the Vulture area and shot two Italian civilians. Orders came to the General from Rome that all the captured paratroopers were to be shot, but he refused to carry them out, because he had ascertained that the civilians shot by the British were armed. On his communicating this fact to the Rome authorities, the order to execute the paratroopers was rescinded. The subsequent execution of this gallant officer can only be regarded as an act of mean and illegal vindictiveness.

I have limited myself to a few of the most striking instances of the postwar treatment of the really fine men in Italy. But a whole volume could be filled with similar cases.

One other prison experience, although of small importance

in itself, I wish to record; first, because it happens to have been my own, and, second, because it is characteristic of hundreds of thousands of others, illustrating the utter disregard of the elementary principles of justice on the part of the post-war Governments. We must remember that at the time of which I shall now speak—1945-46—Count Sforza was still on the rampage and Palmiro Togliatti was Minister of Justice.

I had retired from the public service, having reached the age limit shortly before the War. But when Mussolini set up his new Government, I felt it my duty, disgusted as I was with the *coup d'état* of July 25, 1943, and above all with the ignoble armistice of September 3rd-8th, to serve the man and the party again, especially in their then difficult circumstances. I thus accepted an appointment with the new Government, first in the Ministry of Popular Culture in Venice and later in my old department, the Ministry of Foreign Affairs, in its Milan office. On April 25, 1945, my work naturally came to an end, but I had to remain in Milan for some weeks more until I could find means of returning to Rome. Fortunately, nothing happened to me or to my colleagues in that office during those weeks of slaughter, because nobody discovered us.

I managed to return to Rome on May 24th, and for a few weeks things went on normally. Then Sforza discovered my whereabouts. He had a particular grudge against me for my activities in Great Britain and the United States in defending the Italian cause and striving to improve relations between those countries and Italy, while Sforza himself was busy libeling not only the Fascist regime but Italy itself. Hence, he ordered my arrest on June 20, 1945.

No particular charge was preferred against me, but I was detained first in the Regina Coeli prison in the capital. On July 22nd, the non-political prisoners in that same jail mutinied in the hope of effecting their escape, and although they were not able to do so, they set fire to a part of the building. The next day the Minister of Justice (Togliatti) came to the prison to conduct an inquiry. He definitely assured the political prisoners that none of them would be transferred elsewhere on account of the mutiny, in which they had taken no part. But on the 24th he broke his promise and had all the political prisoners handcuffed and conveyed by truck first to Naples and then to the island prison of Procida.[4]

There I was detained for nearly a year. Conditions at Procida were not too bad, as the prison was airy, the climate excellent, the views of the Bay of Naples very beautiful, and the jailors, from the head warden downward, deferential toward persons who might one day or other again acquire influence. Moreover, I found myself in the company of many of the finest men in Italy, military heroes such as Field Marshal Graziani, Commander Borghese, Prince Pignatelli, General Gambara, the ex-Ambassadors Jacomoni and Suvich, the ex-Minister of War, General Pariani, the journalist Amicucci, ex-deputies or members of the Government, such as Ezio Maria Gray, Giacomo Acerbo, and Baron Alessandro Sardi and hundreds of other interesting personalities.

On June 28, 1946, I was released without a trial, as no charge against me had materialized. Many others were released on that same day or a little later; others who had been condemned were pardoned and others were afterward tried and acquitted.

Along with many others, I had been deprived of freedom for over a year for no reason at all, and the whole procedure had been thoroughly illegal, so much so that we asked ourselves whether we were not freely entitled to commit some crime punishable with a year's imprisonment, as we had a prison credit to our account!

Two small details may also be recorded. On being arrested all our valuables had been taken from us and deposited in the Regina Coeli prison, to be returned to us on liberation. A few weeks later we were informed that the prison had been burglarized and all the prisoners' valuables stolen. It was obvious that the burglary had been arranged by the prison staff, as no outsider could possibly enter the building without permission, and most of the victims of this theft were convinced, rightly

---

[4] The transfer of prisoners from one prison to another involved them in serious difficulties and expenses, as they were detached from their defense counsel.

or wrongly, that, as the Minister of Justice was a Communist, the burglary had been ordered from above and that all the valuables found their way into the coffers of the Communist Party—or into the pockets of specially favored individual Communists. None of us was able to get any redress. The other item was the following: As I said before, I was arrested on *June 20, 1945*. But when, on my release, I consulted my file at the Palace of Justice, I found that the first document in which my name was mentioned bore the date of *June 24*. That meant that at least one document had been abstracted, so as to prevent awkward inquiries. I am convinced that that document was my order of arrest.

CHAPTER XXVII

THE END OF THE MONARCHY

THE Monarchy, as we have seen, had encountered opposition during the War, especially after the events of July 25, 1943, from two opposite quarters. On the one hand, the Fascists and other supporters of Mussolini could not forgive the King for having dismissed the Duce and having him arrested (or having allowed him to be arrested) in the grounds of the Royal villa. On the other hand, the Communists, Socialists and other Leftists were hostile to Monarchy on principle. Nevertheless, a great many Italians, regardless of party affiliations, and including not a few Fascists, were in favor of the Monarchy as an institution, apart from the errors or faults, if such they were, of Victor Emmanuel III, believing it desirable to maintain the one existing political institution which was above and independent of party politics.

In view of these contrasting attitudes, the various parties in power favored the holding of a referendum to decide on the maintenance of the Monarchy. A decision on this matter had been taken, and under the terms of the Decree of June 25, 1944, it was laid down that, after the liberation of Italian territory, a Constituent Assembly should be elected by universal suffrage to decide on a new Constitution for the State. But under Article 3 the members of the Government were to swear not to take any measure prejudicial to the solution of the institutional question (i.e., the choice of Monarchy or Republic) until after the meeting of the Constituent Assembly. Therefore, the decision to hold a referendum on the Monarchy on June 2, 1946, at the same time as the election of the Constituent Assembly, was in itself illegal, in addition to the fact that the country was still under Allied occupation. There was at the time no elected body entitled to make decisions on the matter, for the Chamber of Deputies had been dissolved and the Senate had been abolished by Count Sforza when he deprived all the Senators, except about a score, of their seats. Moreover, the country was in a state of political and administrative chaos, so that there was no guarantee that any type of election could be held under conditions such as would insure decisions corresponding to the true will of the people.

But the Minister of the Interior, Giuseppe Romita, for reasons of his own which had nothing to do with political principles, decided that the referendum should be held at once. "Now or never," he said—as he was sure that at that time he could secure the result he desired (a Republic), whereas in a calmer atmosphere he feared that he might not be able to achieve the decision he wanted.

A few dates should be remembered. On May 9, 1946, King Victor Emmanuel III abdicated in favor of his son, Prince Humbert, who until that date had been Royal Lord Lieutenant, but who now, on May 10th, became King Humbert II. Victor Emmanuel had previously agreed unwillingly to the holding of a referendum on the Monarchy, a measure forced on him by the Cabinet. But in his proclamation of May 31, 1946, on the eve of the referendum, the new King had declared that "if the Monarchical institution is confirmed . . . I hereby undertake that, as soon as the Constituent Assembly has carried out its duties, the question which you are asked to answer on June 2 shall be submitted to the Italians once more—in the form which the people's representatives will propose." The advocates of the Republic made no such statement, but got a clause inserted in the new Constitution whereby the Republic was declared eternal.

The conditions under which the referendum was held were not such as to guarantee a free vote, nor would they enable the whole of the people to take part in it, despite universal suffrage.

In the first place, the provinces of Bolzano and of the Venezia Giulia, with 1,254,977 inhabitants, were arbitrarily prevented from voting at all until sometime after the referendum. Second, there were still 300,000 non-repatriated prisoners of war, and several hundreds of thousands of Italian soldiers outside Italy, unable to vote. Third, all persons who had held any office or position under the Fascist regime, and all officers who had served under the RSI, amounting in all to some hundreds of thousands, had been deprived of the right to vote. Fourth, there were many scores of thousands of political prisoners who also could not vote. Fifth, on the very eve of the referendum, many thousands of persons known to be Monarchists were arrested on bogus charges or no charge at all, merely to prevent them from voting, and then released immediately after June 2nd.

The manner in which the referendum campaign was conducted violated all the elementary principles of free government. The electoral organization was placed in the hands of CLN members, in many provinces largely Communists, in others almost illiterate persons. Large numbers of voters known to be Monarchists were prevented by violence or the threat of violence from approaching the polling booths. From all parts of the country protests poured in by the thousands concerning episodes of this kind. In another connection, Ferruccio Parri, the ex-Premier, declared in a speech in Turin that only a Republican Government could hope to secure favorable conditions in the Peace Treaty (we shall see later how this hope was realized) or obtain the necessary supplies of foodstuffs from the United States. Among the more ignorant parts of the population the Republican propagandists assured their hearers that, once the Republic was established, all taxation and compulsory military service would be abolished. In many cases women were induced to put their voting mark under the Republican emblem (the head of a woman) on their ballot papers, having been told that the emblem represented the Queen.

Here are a few details of the many thousands of protests showing how the referendum campaign was carried out, according to the sworn statements of a number of local committees.

In the environs of Turin and in other cities of Piedmont, Monarchist advocates were not allowed to speak. Everywhere acts of violence were committed to prevent free expressions of opinion.

In Emilia, where the number of acts of violence immediately after the end of hostilities had been enormous, it was impossible for Monarchist opinion to be expressed, nor could Monarchist posters be put up on the walls.

In Liguria, intimidation was general, and the King himself was attacked in Genoa by a savage mob as he was coming out of the Prefecture in his car.

In Florence, and in Tuscany, in general, there was organized intimidation to prevent any free expression of opinion in favor of the Monarchy.

Similar conditions obtained in many other parts of Italy.

In his report on the referendum, Professor Agostino Padoan concluded that "the electoral organization of the referendum had been based on fraudulent figures—population and numbers of voters—deliberately arranged for issuing a corresponding number of false electoral certificates, thereby depriving the returns of all value."

Large numbers of citizens entitled to vote never received their ballot papers because the authorities had failed to distribute them, or received them too late. In Reggio Calabria, out of some 350,000 registered voters, 60,362, or 17.25 per cent, never received them; in Messina, the same thing happened to 16,000 voters out of 115,000, or 14 per cent; in Catanzaro to 169,000 out of 1,080,000, or 16 per cent. Altogether, about 15 per cent of the voters throughout Italy were unable to vote for this reason. On the other hand, many voters received several ballot papers and were thus able to vote more than once. Apart from the generally chaotic conditions of the country and of the administration at that time (in many of the electoral sections the election officers and the tellers were illiterates and others were chronic drunkards, some suffering from delirium tremens), the confusion was not purely accidental, and the voters who failed to receive their ballot papers were usually known in advance to be Monarchists, while those who secured more than one ballot were Republicans.

At the Ministry of the Interior large numbers of Monarchist votes were deliberately suppressed, and every form of malpractice was indulged in to falsify the returns. According to a statement made by Dr. M. G. Rutelli, Inspector of the State Printing Institute, on May 31, 1946—twelve days before the vote—some police officers, on the strength of information received, searched the lithographic section of the Institute and came upon a number of blocks which appear to have been used for printing false ballot papers assigned to voters who had been killed in the troubles during the previous year and whose names had been used for swelling the Republican vote.

The result of the balloting, as announced, was as follows:

For the Republic, 12,672,767; for the Monarchy, 10,688,905—a majority of 1,983,862 votes for the Republic.

It is calculated that the total number of votes returned, despite the immense number of persons who, for one reason or another, were prevented from voting, was about one million larger than that of the citizens actually entitled to vote; this means that, apart from the large number who were prevented from voting at all on one pretext or another, there were at least one million bogus votes.

According to constitutional practice the results of the referendum, as in the case of any election, should have been proclaimed by the Court of Cassation after the reports of all the electoral offices had been sent in and carefully verified, an operation requiring a considerable amount of time, especially in view of the chaotic conditions of the country. But the Minister of Justice, the Communist Togliatti, ordered the Court merely to verify the number of votes according to the returns of the election sections, without troubling about their genuineness or completeness. In the circumstances, the Court, in spite of the scathing remarks of the Procurator General, Massimo Pilotti, one of the greatest jurists in Italy, and of several of its other members, was forced to issue the returns at once without further investigation. We do not know to this day what the true figures of the referendum were.[1]

We must, therefore, conclude that the referendum, as it was carried out and as its figures were manipulated officially, in no way represented the will of the majority of Italian citizens. We do not know by what considerations the "onlie begetter" of that referendum, the Minister of the Interior, Giuseppe Romita, was inspired. But he will certainly be remembered by future generations as the author of one of the most colossal frauds in history.

The Republic thus instituted has up to the present done nothing to excuse its illegitimate birth unless we admit, as some ironical observers do, that it has the merit of justifying the Monarchical system. As the eminent Spanish philosopher, Miguel de Unamuno, who had been a Republican all his life, said, after the Republican regime had been set up in Spain: "What a beautiful thing the Republic was—under the Monarchy!"

The Allied officials in Italy exhibited an attitude of hostility toward the Monarchy from the time of the Armistice of 1943. They made no effort to assure honesty and fairness in carrying out the referendum. The inference was that they regarded Monarchy as an archaic and effete institution, out of touch with the times and overdue for discarding.

This is not the place to debate the relative virtues of Monarchy and a Republic. But contempt for Monarchy as an institution does not proceed with much grace or propriety from the British or Americans. Monarchy has never been the recipient of more devotion and sentiment in Britain in modern times than since the outbreak of the second World War. Nor have American political leaders ever shown greater deference and respect for the British Monarchy than in the period between the visit of George VI to the United States in June, 1939, and that of Elizabeth II in October, 1957. Monarchy can hardly be a detestable political relic for Italy and the indispensable cornerstone of political life for Britain.

[1] Full details of how the referendum originated and how it was carried out are given in the valuable pamphlet by Professor Niccolo Rodolico and Count Vittorio Prunas-Tola, *Libro azzurro sul referendum 1946* (Turin, 1953).

CHAPTER XXVIII

THE PEACE TREATY

W E now come to the concluding phase of the "liberation" of Italy, summing up all the others preceding it, namely, the Luxembourg Peace Treaty of February 10, 1947, drawn up by the victorious Powers (including France, to whom that adjective can only be applied by an acrobatic stretch of imagination). It was imposed on Italy without giving her delegates the possibility of discussing its terms or getting a comma altered —much as the disastrous Treaty of Versailles had been imposed on the Germans in 1919.

Two years after the end of the War, "two tragic years," as Attilio Tamaro writes, "which followed the defeat of Italian arms and the fall of Fascism, filled with slaughter, ruin and the shame of foreign invasion, sullied by the most atrocious civil war and concluded with a blood-bath unequalled in Italian history, the victors decided to inflict on Italy a final *coup de grâce,* imposing on her a treaty contrary to her dignity, her honor and her interests as a great nation. She had lost; her sufferings were beyond all imagination; and they punished the Italian people with a sentence of extreme harshness."[1]

Here are the chief provisions of the Treaty. The introductory paragraphs at once define the character of the instrument:

> The Union of Soviet Socialist Republics, the United Kingdom of Great Britain and Northern Ireland, the United States of America, China, France, Australia, Belgium, the Bielorussian Soviet Socialist Republic, Brazil, Canada, Czechoslovakia, Ethiopia, Greece, India, the Netherlands, New Zealand, Poland, the Ukranian Soviet Socialist Republic, the Union of South Africa, and the People's Federal Republic of Yugoslavia, hereinafter referred to as "the Allied and Associated Powers," of the one part, and Italy, of the other part:
>
> Whereas Italy under the Fascist regime became a party to the Tripartite Pact with Germany and Japan, undertook a war of aggression

[1] *La condanna dell'Italia nel trattati d' pace* (Bologna, 1952), p. 9.

and thereby provoked a state of war with all the Allied and Associated Powers and with other United Nations, and bears her share of responsibility for the war; and

Whereas in consequence of the victories of the Allied forces, and with the assistance of the democratic elements of the Italian people, the Fascist regime was overthrown on July 25, 1943, and Italy, having surrendered unconditionally, signed terms of Armistice on September 3 and 29, of the same year; and . . .

If the "democratic elements of the Italian people" had really contributed to the overthrow of the Fascist regime and consequently taken part in the war against Germany, how was it that Italy should be subjected to this humiliating treaty?

Whereas after the said Armistice Italian armed forces, both of the Government and of the Resistance Movement, took an active part in the war against Germany, and Italy declared war against Germany as from October 13, 1943, and thereby became a co-belligerent against Germany; and

Whereas the Allied and Associated Powers and Italy are desirous of concluding a treaty of peace which, in conformity with the principles of justice, will settle questions still outstanding as a result of the events hereinbefore recited and will form the basis of friendly relations between them, thereby enabling the Allied and Associated Powers to support Italy's application to become a member of the United Nations and also to adhere to any conventions concluded under the auspices of the United Nations . . .

As we know, Italy's application to become a member of the United Nations was for a considerable time flatly rejected, even if some of the members supported it; here we have another of the host of promises made to Italy, and then broken.

. . . have therefore agreed to declare the cessation of the state of war and for this purpose to conclude the present Treaty of Peace and have accordingly appointed the undersigned Plenipotentiaries who, after presentation of their full powers, found in good and due form, have agreed on the following provisions:

Part I on the Territorial Clauses (Section I—Frontiers) proceeds (Art. 2) to deprive Italy of various districts on the French frontier, calculated to open the roads to an invasion of Italy from France, on the Little St. Bernard Pass, on the Mont Cenis Plateau, on Mont Thabor-Chaberton.

Article 3 deprives Italy of a large area on her Northeastern frontier in favor of Yugoslavia immediately behind Gorizia[2] and Trieste, and including Istria, and, under Article 11, of Zara and various islands.

Under Article 14, 1. Italy cedes to Greece in full sovereignty the islands of Rhodes, Cos and the Dodecanese (which had never belonged to that country).

In Part II (Political Clauses) are contained some of the worst provisions, inasmuch as they constitute inadmissible interferences in Italy's domestic policy. Article 15 is worded as follows:

> Italy shall take all measures necessary to secure to all persons under Italian jurisdiction, without distinction as to race, sex, language or religion, the enjoyment of human rights and of the fundamental freedom of expression, of press and publication, of religious worship, of political opinion and of public meeting.

During the Allied military occupation many of these freedoms were shamelessly violated, especially that of political opinion, as anyone suspected of Fascist ideas was liable to every form of persecution. The Italian Government carried out these measures for many years after the War with the full approval of the Allies. Only the Communists enjoyed full respect for their every form of activity, both under the Italian laws and under the Allied measures.

> Art. 16. Italy shall not prosecute or molest Italian nationals, including members of the armed forces, solely on the ground that during the period from June 10, 1940, to the coming into force of the present Treaty, they expressed sympathy with or took action in support of the cause of the Allied and Associated Powers.

This means that Italy was not entitled to punish in any way traitors acting in the interest and/or in the pay of her enemies in war time. Never in all history has such a clause been imposed on any country. The postwar Italian Governments actually would probably never have punished even the most flagrant acts of treachery, but to have such a policy forced on the coun-

[2] The frontier is so near to Gorizia that in many cases it cuts houses and farms in two.

try and written down in black and white, is unheard of in decent public relations. The clause made a most deplorable impression on the great mass of Italian public opinion, and notorious traitors such as the late Count Sforza and Randolfo Pacciardi[3] are commonly alluded to as "Article 16."

Article 17 is hardly less intolerable. It states in fact:

> Italy, which, in accordance with Art. 20 of the Armistice Agreement, has taken measures to dissolve the Fascist organizations in Italy, shall not permit the resurgence on Italian territory of such organizations, whether political, military or semi-military.

Here we have a definite declaration by foreign Powers of the political systems which Italy shall or shall not establish, regardless of the wishes of the Italian people. Moreover, Article 17 is almost a complete contradiction of Article 15.

In addition to the various territories filched from Italy under the clauses of the Treaty, an abortion was created in the shape of the Trieste Free Territory. Article 21, in fact, provides as follows:

> 1. There is hereby constituted the Free Territory of Trieste, consisting of the area lying between the Adriatic Sea and the boundaries defined in Arts. 4 and 22 of the present Treaty. The Free Territory of Trieste is recognized by the Allied and Associated Powers and by Italy, which agree that its integrity and independence shall be assured by the Security Council of the United Nations.

> 2. Italian sovereignty over the area constituting the Free Territory of Trieste, as above defined, shall be terminated upon the coming into force of the present Treaty.

> 3. On the termination of Italian sovereignty, the Free Territory shall be governed in accordance with an instrument for a provisional regime drafted by the Council of Foreign Ministers and approved by the Security Council. This instrument shall remain in force until such date as the Security Council shall fix for the coming into force of the Permanent Statute which shall have been approved by it. The Free Territory shall thenceforth be governed by the provisions of such Permanent Statute. The texts of the Permanent Statute and of the Instrument for the Provisional Regime are contained in Annexes VI and VII.

[3] Who was at one time actually Minister of Defense.

4. The Free Territory of Trieste shall not be considered as ceded territory within the meaning of Art. 29 and Annex XIV of the present Treaty.

5. Italy and Yugoslavia undertake to give to the Free Territory of Trieste the guarantees set out in Annex IX.

The creation of this Free Territory was the result of a compromise between the proposal of Yugoslavia (supported by Russia), which demanded outright annexation, and the intensely anti-Slav and pro-Italian feeling of the great majority of the inhabitants. The Allied Powers did not care much about the wishes of the inhabitants, but they were afraid that annexation to Yugoslavia might lead to serious riots, the armed intervention of Yugoslavia, supported by Russia, and perhaps a new war. But the contraption thus set up, apart from its injustice, was one of the most preposterous arrangements ever conceived. In spite of the disastrous results of the creation of the Free City State of Danzig by the Versailles Treaty—the immediate cause of the outbreak of World War II—the great world statesmen now created another and even more monstrous arrangement for Trieste. Only years later was Trieste reunited with Italy, but with serious limitations.

Under Article 23 Italy was deprived of all her colonies, in spite of the fact that the country's most difficult problem was her superabundant population, a considerable section of which had found possibilities for settlement in Libya and East Africa. In her colonies, moreover, Italy had not only provided for a number of Italian farmers and other workers, but had greatly improved the conditions of the native population. These territories were now to be handed over to native administrations, obviously unable to cope with the great economic difficulties facing them without the financial and technical support of the Italian Government and people. This, of course, counted for nothing. The object was not to provide for the native population, but to punish Italy. The story is told of a foreign visitor to Tripoli (neither an Italian nor an Englishman) who, while visiting the city and its environs, was told by his Arab guide: "Everything which you *see* here was made or imported by the

Italians. Everything which you *do not see* has been carried off by the British."

Article 45 deals with the question of "war criminals" as follows:

> 1. Italy shall take all necessary steps to ensure the apprehension and surrender for trial of:
> a) Persons accused of having committed, ordered or abetted war crimes and crimes against peace and humanity;
> b) Nationals of any Allied or Associated Powers accused of having violated their national law by treason or collaboration with the enemy during the war.
>
> 2. At the request of the United Nations Government concerned, Italy shall likewise make available as witnesses persons within its jurisdiction, whose evidence is required for the trial of the persons referred to in paragraph 1 of this article.
>
> 3. Any disagreement concerning the application of the provisions of paragraphs 1 and 2 of this article shall be referred by any of the Governments concerned to the Ambassadors in Rome of the Soviet Union, of the United Kingdom, of the United States of America, and of France, who will reach agreements with regard to the difficulty.

We see here again, as in connection with the Nuremberg trials, that only the Axis countries were supposed to have produced war criminals. The inhabitants of the others were all innocent little lambs. In this way, treason against the Allied nations was infamous and must be punished, whereas treason by Italians against Italy was, as we have seen under Article 16, a meritorious action and those who committed it must be adequately protected and encouraged.

Under Part IV (Naval, Military and Air Clauses), all Italian fortifications on the frontiers toward France and Yugoslavia must be destroyed or removed and their reconstruction is prohibited. In coastal areas within 15 kilometers from the French and Yugoslav frontiers, Italy shall not establish any new nor expand any existing naval bases or permanent installations. Even along the Apulian coast (Article 48.6) "Italy will not construct any new permanent military, naval or military air installations, nor expand existing installations." Under Article

49 the islands of Pantelleria, the Pelagian Islands and Pianosa "shall be and shall remain demilitarized."

In Sardinia, all permanent coast defenses, artillery emplacements and their armaments and all naval installations which are located within a distance of 30 kilometres from French territorial waters were to be removed to the mainland of Italy or demolished within one year from the coming into force of the present Treaty. In both Sicily and Sardinia all permanent installations and equipment for the maintenance and storage of torpedoes, sea mines and bombs were to be demolished or removed to the mainland of Italy within one year of the coming into force of the present Treaty (Arts. 49 and 50).

Under Articles 52, 53 and 54, Italy's armaments were reduced to a minimum, and she was prohibited from possessing any atomic weapon, self-propelled or guided missiles, guns with a range of over 30 kilometers, etc., while Article 55 forbade her to confer officers' or N. C. O.'s rank on any officer or N. C. O. "of the former Fascist Militia or of the former Republican Army, in the Italian Navy, Army or Air Force or Carabinieri, with the exception of such persons as shall have been exonerated by the appropriate body in accordance with Italian laws." No such limitation, of course, applied to partisans, even if guilty of an unlimited number of murders.

Under Article 61, the Italian army was reduced to a maximum of 250,000 men, including 65,000 to 70,000 Carabinieri. The naval personnel must not exceed 25,000 officers and men (Art. 6), while the number of warships was limited (Annex XII) to 2 battleships, 4 cruisers, 4 destroyers, 16 torpedo boats, and sundry minor craft, all of them old and out of date. On the other hand, Italy was compelled to place at the disposal of the Governments of the Soviet Union, the United Kingdom, the United States of America and France 3 battleships, 5 cruisers, 1 sloop, 7 destroyers, 6 torpedo boats, 8 submarines and various smaller craft.

The air force was reduced to 200 fighter and reconnaissance aircraft and 150 transport, air-sea rescue, training and liaison aircraft, while all aircraft, except for fighter and reconnaissance aircraft, must be unarmed, and the personnel limited to 25,000 officers and men.

Italy was thus left practically disarmed, with her frontiers open to invasion, while her neighbors were armed to the teeth and free to invade Italy at their good pleasure.

Under Article 74 Italy was to pay $100,000,000 in reparations to Russia, $125,000,000 to Yugoslavia, $105,000,000 to Greece, $25,000,000 to Ethiopia, and $5,000,000 to Albania.

In the matter of private property, everything belonging to the United Nations or their nationals in Italy shall be returned (Art. 78), whereas under Article 79 "each of the Allied and Associated Powers shall have the right to seize, retain, liquidate or take any other action with respect to all property, rights and interests which on the coming into force of the present Treaty are within its territory and belong to Italy or to Italian nationals, and to apply such property or the proceeds thereof to such purposes as it may desire, within the limits of its claims and those of its nationals, including debts, other than claims fully satisfied under other articles of the present Treaty. All Italian property or the proceeds thereof, in excess of the amount of such claims, shall be returned."

Paragraph 4 of this article tells us that "no obligation is created by this article on any Allied or Associated Power to return industrial property to the Italian Government or Italian nationals, or to include such property in determining the amounts which may be retained under paragraph 1 of this Article. The Government of each of the Allied and Associated Powers shall have the right to impose such limitations, conditions and restrictions on rights or interests with respect to industrial property in the territory of that Allied or Associated Power, acquired prior to the coming into force of the present Treaty by the Government or nationals of Italy, as may be deemed by the Government of the Allied or Associated Power to be necessary in the national interest."

Other articles of the "Diktat" impose further restrictions and limitations on Italy.

Altogether, from reading the text of the Treaty one may well ask oneself what Italy gained by her "co-belligerence" with the Allies. But it must be admitted that the servile, abject and incompetent manner in which Italy's representatives handled Italian interests was not calculated to secure any attenuation of the attitude of the victors or even their respect. The former United States Under Secretary of State, Sumner Welles, with particular reference to the Adriatic clauses, defined the Treaty as unjust and not calculated to promote the development of democracy in Italy, inasmuch as it had made possible Soviet expansion in the Adriatic through the advantages conferred on Yugoslavia. Senator Henry Cabot Lodge, in the Committee on Foreign Relations of the American Senate, defined it "an ignoble and inacceptable solution," constituting "a veritable sentence of death on Italy as a nation."

Italy was condemned because she had been in the past a Fascist State, and it was here that the Italian delegates gave their case away by attributing all the troubles to Fascism. Three of her judges—Great Britain, the United States and France—had only a hazy idea of what Fascism really was, and the fourth, Russia, only knew it as the one really dangerous enemy of Communism.

In the course of time, many of the worst clauses of the Treaty have been allowed to fall into abeyance or have been definitely eliminated, and the Western Powers, to use the language of the London police court reports, may be compared to the prisoners in the dock held up to be judged for drunk and disorderly conduct, "who seem keenly to realize the disgraceful position in which they find themselves." But it is late in the day, and a great deal of the harm done still remains. It will take many long years before it is wholly eliminated—and forgotten.

To this Treaty we may apply the indictment pronounced by the Virginians on the State of West Virginia, when it seceded from Virginia proper during the American Civil War, namely, that "it was conceived in rape and born in sin."

CHAPTER XXIX

CONSEQUENCES AND CONCLUSIONS

THE events leading up to and following the "liberation," as set forth in the preceding pages, lead to several conclusions.

The first and most obvious is that a totalitarian, mechanized and industrialized war has not only caused the death or maiming of many millions of human beings and a vast destruction of wealth, including innumerable works of art of priceless value, but has also dehumanized whole communities in many countries.

To limit ourselves to Italy, we have seen how a great many Italians, Germans, Britons, Americans and others, by no means all cruel and barbarous by nature, committed crimes of all kinds and seem to have lost all sense of spiritual values. It is difficult to decide who have been the worst offenders, but it is safe to say that the most heinous infamies were committed by those who had the best opportunities for committing them. In Italy, this was the case of: (1) the British, the Americans and the Germans against the Italian people, reduced to helplessness after the armistice of September 8, 1943; and (2) of the Italian Communist partisans, especially after April 25, 1945, against Fascists and other honest citizens, when the Communists, acting under the orders of Russia, were armed to the teeth and unrestrained by any police or other authorities, and their victims were wholly unarmed. Even many non-Communist partisans were guilty of similar actions.

A second conclusion is that never before have there been so many and such gross violations of the universally accepted laws of war with respect to the treatment of the civilian population, prisoners of war, and even diplomats. The civilians were treated as serfs, *"taillables et corvéables,"* without any regard for their

246

human rights or their property, unlimited looting being allowed and practiced, not for military purposes alone, but because members of the occupying forces of all nationalities considered themselves entitled to take what they wanted for their own convenience and personal advantage. Diplomats who, in all past wars, were treated with all possible consideration in view of the functions assigned to them under international law, were imprisoned, tried and condemned, or put into concentration camps.

Thirdly, the belligerent governments and their military authorities did not limit themselves to fighting their enemies but, assuming the character of pinchbeck crusaders, interfered in domestic, political and economic policy, supported one political party against another, and imposed on the inhabitants of the occupied territories specific forms of government in harmony with the views and interests of the victors, regardless of the wishes and rights of the people in question. Fascism may have been a good thing or a bad thing for Italy, but it was the privilege of the Italians to establish and maintain it or to get rid of it, not the function of governments, armies or peoples of other countries. At the same time, the attempt to impose democracy on Italy was accompanied by a large dose of humbug, as the methods practiced bore very slight resemblance to what is generally regarded as representative government and democracy. The attitude assumed by the invaders reminds us of Dr. Samuel Johnson's dictum regarding religious belief: "When I say religion, I mean Christianity. When I say Christianity I mean Protestantism. When I say Protestantism I mean the Church of England."

A fourth conclusion is that the policy adopted by the Western Powers in Italy effectively opened the doors to Communism. Those Powers thought that they could use Communism for their own purposes and policies, but they soon found that they had raised up a Frankenstein monster which they were incapable of controlling. This was the worst crime of all, and it reacted during the War, as every man in the street realized that it would. Today even the great statesmen (so-called) of the

World are beginning to discover that it was the most dangerous policy for all concerned.

The War failed to bring any lasting benefit to any civilized people, and today victors and vanquished are all in the same boat, all are suffering, even if in different degrees. A very keen and experienced British politician, soldier and publicist, the late Sir Arnold Wilson, wrote to me on the eve of World War II: "If a new war does break out, Russia will be the residuary legatee." Never have truer words been written. No country, in fact, except Russia, has secured any permanent advantage whatsoever from the War or from the manner in which it was conducted. The only consequences for other European countries are gall and wormwood, dissatisfaction and hatred, poverty and unhappiness, and the threat of extermination.

To return to the case of Italy, what are the results of her "liberation"? We find a country completely wrecked by 1945, many of its cities and villages reduced to heaps of rubble, communications on their beam ends, agricultural production reduced to a minimum of what it was and of what the people needed, industrial plants not only seriously damaged, but deprived of most of their foreign and domestic markets, the armed forces almost non-existent and the frontiers open to any foreign invader. Class war, which had been all but eliminated, now raised its ugly head with greater violence than ever before.

At the same time, Italy found herself with a Government imposed on her by foreign invaders, composed of men far inferior to their predecessors of the pre-1943 days, in political capacity, honesty, culture, courage and the sense of dignity, and a civil service, from which the best men had been, at least temporarily, eliminated and replaced by far less competent officials. She still has a Parliament in which party intrigues and combinations are the be-all and end-all of political activity. A large army of unemployed, never before dreamed of, constituted—and still constitutes—a dead weight on the country's economic life, while the opportunities for emigration of the growing population are less than ever before. The sound financial system of the pre-war period has not only been shattered by war losses and the vast cost of repairing the damages, but the able financiers of the past regime have been replaced by inexperienced amateurs. With great difficulty and at a high cost the value of the currency has been maintained fairly well—one of the few assets on the credit side of the Government's policy—but the budget deficit and that of the trade balance are still alarmingly high.

Above all, nothing has been done to restore Italy's moral status and to give her a dignified international policy, the present regime having only distinguished itself in this field by an attitude which the late ex-Premier V. E. Orlando defined as "a lust for servility."

The one post-war political leader who may be regarded as something of a statesman, Giuseppe Pella, who, as Premier for a few months in 1953, gave evidence of a real grasp of the country's needs and of how to face them, was very soon ousted through the intrigues of political rivals drawn from his own party. The Cabinets which succeeded his have been, as usual, composed of second-rate politicians devoid of much knowledge of economic problems or of international affairs. They have been mainly interested in Parliamentary combinations and are still inspired by the spirit of vindictiveness against all men associated with the past regime.[1]

If we wish to make a comparison betwen the pre-war regime and that of the present day, we may cite a conversation between the late Emilio Bodrero, one of the finest men in Italian public life and of the highest standing, a professor of philosophy, a fine classical scholar, a distinguished man of letters, a volunteer officer of amazing courage in World War I, and an old and distinguished friend of his who had been an uncompromising anti-Fascist from the very beginning of Mussolini's premiership. The conversation, which took place in 1946, when Bodrero, under the new regime, had been ousted from his university chair and all his political activities, and even deprived of his Parliamentary vote, was as follows:

[1] Pella returned to office in the Zoli Cabinet as Assistant Premier and Minister of Foreign Affairs, but he was again ousted when Amintore Fanfani became Premier after the elections of May, 1958.

The anti-Fascist: "You, Professor Bodrero, have been a Fascist deputy, I think?"

Bodrero: "Yes, I have."

The anti-Fascist: "You have also been a Fascist Senator?"

Bodrero: "Yes, that is the case."

The anti-Fascist: "You have, I understand, also been a member of the Fascist Government?"

Bodrero: "Yes, I have been twice Under-Secretary for Education."

The anti-Fascist: "That may be so, but you have never been such an ardent and uncompromising Fascist as I am today."

The remarks of this anti-Fascist are typical of the sentiments of immense numbers of men formerly opposed to the Fascist regime, but who now see what an anti-Fascist regime really is. The former may have had its defects—it certainly had many— but they now appear mere trifles when compared with those of the regime in control today.

I may be asked by my American friends whether, even admitting the deplorable faults of the policy of the United States Government and especially of the late President Roosevelt towards Italy, before and during the late War, the help conferred on her later by the American Government and by various organizations through the Marshall Plan and in other ways, has not to some extent mitigated the damage wrought. My answer can only be in the affirmative, and no Italian can forget the generous manner in which the American Government and people came forward to try to enable Italy to get on her feet again, or the measure of success which has attended those efforts. Nevertheless, they have not been, and perhaps could not be, enough to make good all the material havoc wrought, or offset the rehabilitation and strengthening of Communism in Italy, nor can they make us forget the bitter anti-Italian campaign conducted for many years by that same Government, by the press, and by a large part of American public opinion. It may have been "all sound and fury," but it certainly did not "signify nothing"—it did signify a great deal in its effects at the time and thereafter.

And, in any case, would it not have been better if that campaign and that material havoc had never occurred, and if the generous aid afterward afforded to Italy had not been necessary? I venture to think that even the American taxpayer today will give an affirmative answer to that query. It may be answered that Italy did declare war on the United States. But who prepared the situation leading to the War? The answer is to be found in a whole library of books by eminent American and British revisionist writers, to which I would refer the reader.[2]

The best hopes for Italy are: (1) that in the domestic field every trace of the miasmas of the CLN spirit be wafted away, that every politician and official associated with that system be cleared out of Italian public life; and (2) that, in the international realm, the Italian people be allowed to work out their own salvation without any imposition of authority from the outside—from the West or from the East. In these ways the Italians, with their own characteristic fund of common sense and unlimited capacity for hard work, will find solutions for their problems, and will contribute, together with all the civilized Powers of the world, to the effort to resist any attempt at aggression by the Communist East.

When foreign friends ask me what I think of the Italian situation of today, my reply is: The mere fact that, in spite of the various governments in office since April 25, 1945, the country still manages to exist, proves that it still has dynamic possibilities and that its people have not lost their old qualities. This should enable it to carry on in the hope of better things to come.[3]

May the past provide a lesson for the future—for the Italians and for all other peoples.

Sir Walter Scott, at the end of Chapter LXVII of *Waverley*,

[2] See *Select Bibliography of Revisionist Books on the Two World Wars and their Aftermath* (Oxnard Press-Courier, Oxnard, California, 1957).

[3] It should not be forgotten that such prosperity as has been revived in Italy since 1945 has been based in considerable part on over four billion dollars in economic aid given to Italy by the United States to prevent conditions from becoming so bad that the Communists might take over the government of Italy. Mussolini received only $100,000,000 in foreign financial aid, an emergency loan in that amount from the American banking house of J. P. Morgan and Company.

in speaking of Colonel Talbot's refusal to intercede in favor of the Highland chieftain, Fergus MacIvor, and save him from being executed for his share in the Jacobite rising of 1745, adds the following comment:

> Such was the reasoning of those times, held even by brave and humane men towards a vanquished enemy. Let us devoutly hope, that, in this respect at least, we shall never see the scenes or hold the sentiments that were general in Britain sixty years since.

Scott had begun to write *Waverley* in 1805, exactly sixty years after the '45, and he was no doubt sincere in his belief in the moral progress attained by mankind during those sixty years. Had he lived 150 years later and witnesed the events of World War II and after, his judgment, I am convinced, would have been far less optimistic.

INDEX

A

AAC. See Allied Advisory Council
ACC. See Allied Control Commission
AHC. See Allied High Command
AMC. See Allied Military Commands
AMG. See Allied Military Government
Abruzzi, the, 2, 81
Abyssinia. See Ethiopia
Acebo, Giacomo, 229
Acquarone, Duke Pietro d', 4, 7
Acquisto, Salvo d', 113
Action, Party of. See Party of Action
activities, military and partisan, 135-51
Addis Ababa, Duke of. See Badoglio
Adenauer, Konrad, 150
Adige, Alto, 111
Adriatic Sea, 161, 165, 177, 245
Advance to Barbarism, by F. J. P. Veale,
   v, xvii
Advisory Council, Algiers, 92, 97
Africa, North and East, 1
Agnoletto, Riccardo, 199
Albania, 90
Albertini, Luigi, 155
Albertolli, Pilo, 113
Albini, Umberto, 117
Alexander I of Russia, 68, *note*
Alexander of Tunis, Field Marshal Earl,
   29-31, 75, 96, 123, 135, 136, 138,
   148, 162, 177, 185, 227
Alfiero, Dino, 6
Algeria, *x*
Algiers Mediterranean Council, 69, 92
Allied Advisory Council, 104
Allied Control Commission, 30, 31, 49,
   69, 72, 95, 98-99, 105, 116, 153,
   157, 158, 161, 176, 177, 179, 193,
   209
Allied High Command, 30
Allied Military Commands, 69, 85, 105,
   143, 146, 167, 171
Allied Military Government, 30, 92, 128,
   157, 167, 203, 209
Allies; hatred of, by Italians, 24
   in Rome, 122-34
Alps, 143
Alto Adige, 111
Ambrosio, General Vittorio, 1, 2, 4, 5,
   7, 10, 28, 69, 74
Americans; attitude toward Italians, 24
   praise of Mussolini, 56-57

Amery, Julian, 138
Amery, Leopold S., 55
Amicucci, Ermanno, 8, 222-23, 229
amnesties, 212
Anders, General Wladyslaw, 122
Anfuso, Filippo, 8-9
   book, *Roma-Berlino Salò*, 12 *note*
Annunciation, Order of the, 3
Anti-Fascists. See Fascism
Anzio, 96, 99, 103, 112, 123
Anti-Royalists, 67
   See also Monarchy
Aosta, Duchess of, 130
Aosta, Duke of, 13, 130, 225
Apalachin, New York; meeting at, 23,
   note
Apulia, 99, 146, 152, 242
Aquila, 12
Ara, Camillo, 163
Arangio-Ruiz, Professor, 117
Ardeatine Fosse, 111, 113-14, 122
   See also Via Rasella
Arduino family; massacre of, 168
armaments; reduction of, 243
Armellini, General Quirino, 87, 109, 111
armies, Italian, two, 3, 74-76, 159, 160
Armistice with France (1940), 159
armistices, "long" and "short," 15, 17-
   20, 36-47, 66, 72, 74, 75, 81, 89,
   92, 104, 171, 214, 238
Assembly, Constituent, 116, 118, 231
Atlantic Charter, *viii, xiii-xv, xviii*
atomic bombing, *xi*
atrocities by partisans, 193-208
Audisio, Walter ("Colonel Valerio"),
   170, 206-08
Augenti, Giacomo, 224, 225, *note*
Augusta, 15
Austria, 157, 158, 161
   Anschluss with Germany, 70
   "liberation" of, 70
Axis, *xvii*
Azione, Partito d'. See Party of Action
Azzolini, Vincenzo, 153

B

Bacini (author), *Roma prima e dopo*,
   129, *note*
Badoglio, Marshal Pietro, *xviii*, 1, 3, 4,
   7, 8, 17-21, 27-30, 33, 35, 36, 38,
   47, 48, 51, 52, 65, 67, 68, 71-73,

76, 84, 87, 97, 98, 100, 103, 104,
109-10, 115-18, 121, 123, 125, 148,
217, 224
army, 76
book, *L'Italia nella seconda guerra
mondiale,* 14, *note;* 116, *note;* 118,
note
cabinets, 71, 72, 117
government, 14, 15, 30
named to succeed Mussolini, 5, 11-12
resignation, 124
Balkans, *xv,* 70
Baltic provinces, *vii, viii, xi*
Banca Commerciale, 49-50
Bank of Italy, 153
"Barberigo" battalions, 103, 174
Barbieri, Monsignor, 73, 86
Bari, 226
Congress of CLN, 94, 95, 97
Barracu, Francesco, 168
Barzini, Luigi, *I communisti non hanno
vinto,* 175
Basile, Baron Carlo Emanuele, 221-22
Bastianini, Giuseppe, 6, 10, 11
Battaglia, Riccardo, 79
Storia della resistenza italiana, 79-80
Bauer (of the CLN), 111
Belgion, Montgomery, *Victor's Justice,*
xvii
Bellomo, General Niccoló, 226-27
Belluno, 197
Bencivenga, General Roman, 110, 112
Berle, Adolf A., Jr., 33-34, 50-51
Berlinguer, Mario, 118, 133, 216
Bersaglieri, 103
Bewley, Honorable Charles, 190
Bianchi, Anna, 206
Bianco (author), book, *Venti mesi di
guerra partigiana nel Cuneese,* 143,
note
Bicchierai, Giuseppe, 138
Biggini, (Minister), 162
bitterness toward Italians, 24
"Black Brigades," 142, 145
black market, 128
Black Shirt Legion, 103
Bodrero, Emilio, 249-50
Bogomolov (Soviet statesman), 104
Boldrini, Arrigo, 199
Bolla, Nino, *Dieci mesi del governo
Badoglio,* 36, *note;* 65, *note*
Bologna, 149, 194
Bolsena Conference, 161-63
Bolzano, 209, 232-33

bombing, atomic, *xi*
bombings of cities, 97, 155-56
Bonomi, Ivanoe, 67, *note;* 85, 124, 125,
136, 153, 155, 158, 160, 163, 193
cabinets, 152-165
books on aftermath of World War II,
xvii
Borghese, Daria, 185
Borghese, Valerio, 143, 225-26, 229
books by, 226
Bosnia, 89, 90
See also Herzegovina
Bottai, Giuseppe, 10
Bottari (author), 139, 139, *note;* 144,
note
Bourbon Kingdom of Italy, 77
Bramante, Salvatore, 95
"Brigate Nere," 142, 145
Brindisi, 19-21, 52, 64, 67, 95, 98
"brinkmanship," *xv*
British bitterness toward Italians, 24, 27
concentration camp at Padula, 190,
191
Intelligence Service, *ix-x,* 184
praise and censure of Mussolini, 58
Brosio, Manio, 87
Buckley, Christopher, 30
Buffarini-Guidi, 137
Buozzi, Bruno, 123
Burn, John Horne, book, *In the Gallery,*
132, *note*
Butcher, H. C., book, *Three Years with
Eisenhower,* 19, *note*
Butler, Nicholas Murray, 56

C

CGIL.. *See* Italian General Confederation
of Labor
CLN. *See* Committees for National Lib-
eration
CLNAI. *See* Committees for National
Liberation of Northern Italy
cabinets, Badoglio. *See* Badoglio
cabinets, Bonomi. *See* Bonomi
cabinets, War and post-War, 35, 117,
124
Caccia, Harold, 72
Cadorna, General Luigi, 13
Cadorna, Marshal Raffaele, book, 82,
note; 84, 85, 87; book, 102, *note;*
130, 140, 141, 147, 166-68, 193
Calabria, 15, 159, 234
Calamandrei, Franco, 112, 135
Calworth, Colonel, 186

Cambaruta, Pietro, 20
camp, concentration, British, at Padula, 190, 191
Campo Imperatore, 12
Canali, Pietro ("Captain Neri"), 206
Candamo, 129, note
Candido, 80
Capocaccia, Domenico, 179
Capone, Al, 170
Caporetto; débacle at, 3, 13
Cappellini, Arnaldo, book, Inchiesta sul dispersi in Russia, 188, note
carabinieri, 7
Carandino, Count Niccolo, 155
Carboni, General Pompei, 2
Carnelutti, Francesco, 224, 225, note
Carolis, De (anti-Fascist), 97
Carretta (prison warden), 153
Carso, the, 103, 161
Carter, Barbara Barclay, Italy Speaks, 153, note
Carton de Wiart, General, 2
Caruso (Chief of Police of Rome), 113, 114, 153
Casablanca Conference, 4
Casati, Count Alessandro, 85
Casati, Marquis, 124, 125, 152
Casserta, 174
Cassibile, 17
Cassinelli, Guido, 4; book, Appunti sul 25 luglio, 1943, page 4, note
Cassino. See Monte Cassino
"Cassius." See Foot, Michael
Castagneri, Colonel, 90
Castellano, General Giuseppe, 2, 7, 17, 214
   book, Como firmai l'armistizio de Cassibile, 2, note
Catholics and Catholic Church. See Roman Catholics
Cavallero, General Count Ugo, 1, 2
Cerabona, 124
Cerica, General Angelo, 7
Chamber of Deputies, 232
Chamberlain, Sir Austen, 55
Chamberlain, Neville, 55, 61
Charles V, 116
Charles, Sir Noël, 155, 158
Chiang Kai-shek, vii, 96
Chigi, Palazzo, 157
Child, Richard Washburn, 56
China, xii, xiv
Christian Democrats, 83, 93, 125-27,

138, 140, 157, 176
Christian Socialists, xi
"Christianitatis antemurale," 70
Church. See Roman Catholics
Churchill, Winston S., ix, xiv, 91, note; 94, 97, 98, 125, 154, 158, 165, 171
   Great Contemporaries, 53
   praise and censure of Mussolini, 53-55
Cianca, Alberto, 95, 124
Ciano, Galeazzo, 60
   condemnation and execution, 15
cities, Italian; bombing of, 97
Civil War, American, v
Clark, General Mark, 65, 76
co-belligerence, 27-47, 105
Code, Military Criminal, 211
Cold War, xii, xv, 180-81
Collegni-Signon, I nostri e la guerra clandestine in Piemonte, 45, note
Colletta, Pietro, Storia de reame di Napoli dal 1734 al 1815, 210, note
colonies, and loss of, 154, 241
Comanche Indians, 86, 107
Commercial Bank, 49-50
commissars, political, 82, 90
Commission, High, for Sanctions Against Fascism, 216
Committees for National Liberation (CLN), 48, 51-52, 80, 82, 83, 85, 87, 89, 93-95, 97, 101, 124, 126, 136, 143, 156, 166, 172, 219-20, 233, 251
   Bari Congress, 94, 95, 97
   woman members, 172
Committees for National Liberation of Northern Italy (CLNAI), 136, 138, 145-47, 161-62, 166-67, 178, 193, 195, 197-99, 200, 210
Communism and Communists; and Party; vi-ix, xvii, 28, 30, 33, 49, 52, 65, 69, 71, 73, 77, note; 79, 80-85, 89, 90, 93, 98, 100, 104, 106, 109-11, 112, 117, 119, 120, 125-27, 133, 133, note; 138, 139, note; 140, 142, 145, 163-64, 166, 168, 173, 175-81, 187-89, 245-47, 250, 251, note
   international, 79, 106
   number of Communists, 137
   responsibility of the United States, xx
   Third International, 106
Como, Lake, 169
concentration camp, British, at Padula, 190, 191

Confederation of Labor, General. *See* Italian General Federation of Labor (CGIL)
Congress of Bari (CLN), 94, 95, 97
Conqueror's Peace, by Rooney and Hatton, *xvii*
Conservatives, 83
Constituent Assembly, 118, 126, 231
Constitution of the Kingdom, 10
Coppola, Geoffredo, 168, 207
Corbino, Epicarmo, 71
"Corps of Volunteers of Liberty," 85
Corriere della serra (Milan), 179
Corsica, 17, 31, 103
Cos, 152, 239
Council for Civil Affairs of the (United States) General Staff, 98
Council of State. *See* Grand Council
Court of Cassation, 210, 211, 235
Court of Justice, High, 210, 211
Courten, Admiral Raffaelo de, 28, 72, 124
Courts, Assize, Extraordinary, 210-12
Courts, Fascist, Special Tribunal, 211-13
"courts, people's," 210
Cranborne, Viscount, 36
Crimes Discreetly Veiled, by Veale, 62, *note;* 171, *note;* 206, *note;* 207, *note*
"crimes, war," *xv-xvi*, 37, 242
criminality; growth of, 156-57
Cripps, Sir Stafford, 70, *note*
Croats; *Ustashi*, 90
Croce, Benedetto, 66, 67, 71, 89, 92, 93, 95, 103, 117, 124, 134
  books, *Per la vita della nuova Italia*, 92, *note; Quando l'Italia era tagliata in due*, 71, *note*
Crusades, *viii*
Cucco, Affredo; *Non volevamo perdere*, 5, *note*
Currie, Lauchlin, 180
Cyprus, *x*
Czechoslovakia, *ix, xi*

D

Dagnino, General, 75
Dalmatia, 89, 175
Danzig, 241
Daquanno, Ernesto, 168, 207
Davidson, Captain, 191-92
"Decima Mas," 143, 173, 186, 226
Decima Mas, la, by Borghese, 226
Declaration of Moscow, 68-73

"defascistization," 118
democracies, *vi, vii*
democracy; meaning of, 68
Denmark, *x*
depression, financial, in the United States (1929), 57
Diaz, Armando, 3, 13, 225
diplomats; ill-treatment of, 188-90
dissensions, domestic, 48, 63
Dodecanese, 152, 239
Dodi, General, 123
Dolmann (interpreter), 108, 112
Dombrowski, Roman, 204
  Mussolini: Twilight and Fall, 207, *note*
Domodossola, 144, 145
Dongo, 168, 169, 171, 179, *notes;* 208
"Dongo gold" trial, 205-07
Dresden, *ix*
Duff-Cooper, Alfred, 55, 61
Dulles, Allen W., 87
Dulles, John Foster, *xv*

E

East Africa, 241
  prisoners of war in, 182
Eastern Approaches, by Fitzroy MacLean, 91, *note*
Economist, 25
Eden, Anthony, 68, 70, 94, 154
Eisenhower, Dwight D., 17-19, 27-29, 32, 38, 40, 42, 46, 47, 50, 74, 76, 92, 98
Elena, Queen, 233
Emilia, 146, 168, 194, 198
end of hostilities, 166-75
"epuration," 72
Espinosa, Agostino Degli, 63, *note;* 67, *note*
  Il regno del sud, 52, *note;* 62, *note;* 116, *note*
Esposito, General, 174, 182
Ethiopia, *xiv*, 53, 55, 60, 61, 184, *note*
  Viceroy. *See* Badoglio
  War in, 3
Europe, Central, *xv*
evaluation of Mussolini, by Villari, 60

F

Fabre-Luce, Alfred; book, *Histoire de la Révolution européene*, 201, 201, *note*

Fabretti, *Redivivus*, 188, *note*
Facchini, Eugenio, 102
Fanfanni, Amintore, 181, 249, *note*
Farinacci, Roberto, 10, 125
Farouk, King, 172, *note*
Farran, Roy, *Winged Daggers*, 146, 146, *note*
Fascism and Fascists, *xii*, 33, 36, 37, 44-45, 59, 73, 76, 79, 80, 84, 95, 96, 104, 111, 115, 118, 126, 127, 132, 133, 136, 139, 145, 147, 166, 168, 169, 245, 250
  achievements, 24-25, 99, 126
  and the Church, 127
  and the King, 13
  anti-Fascists, 1, 30, 73, 79, 86, 96, 98, 110, 166, 178; anti-Fascist legislation, 132, 209-20; "defascistization," 118; "epuration," 72; Vigilance Organization Against Anti-Fascist Crimes, 214-15
  condemnation, 68
  dissolution of Party, 15
  fall of, 1, 31
  Grand Council. *See* Grand Council
  history of, 52-54
  murders of Fascists, *xx*, 172-74, 203-05
  organizations, 45
  sanctions against; High Commission for, 216
  seizure of property of Fascists, 216-17
  suppression of, 31
  trials, 152-53
  views of A. A. Berle, 33-34
Fascist Criminal Camp, by Mieville, 186
Fascist Economic Policy, by Welk, 59-60
Fascist Federation, Rome, 111
Fascist Special Tribunal, 211
Federation of Labor. *See* Italian General Federation of Labor
Federzoni, Luigi, 111, 134
Feltre, 5-6
Fenulli, Martelli, 113
Ferrara, 194, 198
"Fiamme Verdi," 83, 152, 197, 239
finances, post-War, 248-49
Finland, *vii*
Finzi, Aldo, 113
Fisher, Thomas R., 177, 177, *note;* 178
Fiume, 161, 175
Flight in Winter, by Thorwald Juergen, *xvii*
Florence, 135, 136, 145

Foggia, 152
"Folgore Division," 123
Foot, Michael ("Cassius"), book, *The Trial of Mussolini*, 54, *note;* 63, *note*
foreign opinion of Italians, 22
Fornaciari, Bruno, 14, 15, *note*
fortifications, frontier, 242
Fortune on Fascism, 59
Fosse Ardeatine. *See* Ardeatine
Four-Power Peace Pact of 1933, *xvii*, 60
Fourteen Points, *xiii*
Fragebogen, by Ernst von Salomon, *xvii*
France, 242
  Maquis; *Résistance* Movement, 77, 201
  Revolution, *v*
France: 1940-1955, by Alexander Werth, 201
France: The Tragic Years, by Sisley Huddleston, *xvii*, 201, *note*
Francis I, 116
Francis Joseph, Emperor, 157
Franco-Prussian War, *v*
Frascati, 18
"Free Italians," 33-34
Freedom, 202
Freemasons, 24
Frignani, Colonel Giovanni, 110, 113

G

GAP. *See* Partisan Action Groups
Gambara, General Gastone, 76, 229
Garda, Lake of, 13
Gargnano, 12, 19
Garibaldi, Giuseppe, 2
"Garibaldi Battalions," 82, 90
"Garibaldi" Communist unit in Yugoslavia, 164
"Garibaldi" partisans, 163-64
Gasperi, Alcide de, 35, *note;* 124, 125, 127, 157, 222
Gaulle, General Charles de, 33, 96
Gayre, G. R., 22-24, *note;* 95, 128
  book, *Italy in Transition*, 22, *note*
General Confederation of Labor. *See* Italian General Federation of Labor
Geneva Conference and Conventions, 63, 187, 219
Gentile, Professor Giovanni, murder of, at British instigation, 119-20
George VI, 35, 184
Gerard, James W., 57
Germany, 14
  Army; capitulation of, 174-75

authorities, military, 2
declaration of war against, 32
expulsions from, xi
relations with, 4-6
Southern, 165
splitting up of, xi
war with, 33, note
  See also Morgenthau Plan
Gianna, 206
Giannini, Alberto, 215
Giglioli, Giulio Quirino, 191
"Giunta," executive, 98
Giustizia e Libertà, 83
Glasgow, George, 22, 93
Gobbati, Ugo, 197
"gold, Dongo." See "Dongo gold"
Gollancz, Victor, ix
  In Darkest Germany, xvii
  Our Threatened Values, xvii
Gorizia, 3, 89, 96, 162, 239
Gorresio (author); book, Un anno di
  libertà, 122, note; 133, note
Gorrieri, Dante, 205, 207
"Gothic Line," 136
Gottardi, Luciano, 15
Government; after Mussolini, 13
  Badoglio. See Badoglio
  choice of, 34
  imposition by foreigners, 191
  occupation, xiv, 29
  three governments (1945), 193
Graf (Austrian State Secretary), 150
Grand Council of State, 8, 10, 11, 15
Grandi, Dino, 7, 8, 10, 15, 51
Gray, Ezio Maria, 2, 133, note; 229
Graziani, Marshal Rodolfo, 3, 74, 76,
  168, 174, 223-25, 229
  book, Io difeso la patrie, 225, note
  book on, 225, note
Grazioli, Giacomo, 197
Great Contemporaries, by Churchill, 53
Greece, 69, 96
"Green Flames," 83, 152, 197, 239
Grenet, de (diplomat), 97, 110, 113
Grey, Sir Edward, xiv
Gronchi, Giovanni, 124, 125, 153
Guareschi (editor of Candido), 80
Gullo (Communist), 117, 124, 176, 180

H

Hague Convention on laws of war, 63,
  102, 113, 219
Halifax, Lord, 55, 59, 61
Hamburg, ix

Harriman, Averell, 105
Hauser, Colonel, 112
Haydon, T. K., 58
Hazon, General, 7
Herzegovina, 89, 90
  See also Bosnia
"Hexarchy," 124, 126, 127
Heydrich, Reinhard, ix
High Cost of Vengeance, by Freda Utley,
  xvii
Himmler, Heinrich, 112
Hiroshima and Nagasaki, xi
Hiss, Alger, 180
"Historicus," 5, note
Hitler, Adolf, xii, xv, xvii, 5-6, 12, 14,
  60, 61, 112, 162, note
Hoare, Sir Samuel, 55
Holborn, Louise and Hajo; book War and
  Peace Aims of the United States, 34,
  note; 158, note
Holt, John Henry, 187
Holdsworth, Colonel, 141
Holy Alliance, 68
hopes for Italy, 251-52
hostages; execution of, 112-13
hostilities; end of, 166-75
Hötzendorff, Field Marshal Conrad von,
  Memoirs, 157, note
Huddleston, Sisley, France: The Tragic
  Years, 1939-1947, xvii, 201, note
  Terreur 1944, xvi
Hull, Cordell, and Memoirs; pages and
  notes, 27, 35, 68-70, 105, 115, 118,
  124
Humbert II (former Prince of Naples),
  1, 8, 12, 14, 19, 51, 65, 95, 124, 127,
  169, 232
  Lord Lieutenant, 115-21, 124
  son, 67
Hyde Park, New York; meeting at, 154

I

Imperatore, Campo, 12
imposition of government by foreigners,
  191
In Darkest Germany, by Victor Gollancz,
  xvii
In the Gallery, by Burn, 132, note
Indians, Comanche, 186, 187
Indochina, x
"International Brigades," 82
International Red Cross, 184
Ionian Islands, 90
Irredentist movement, Trentino, 157

Isonzo river, 162
Israel, *x*
Istria, 89, 96, 161, 164, 175, 239
Italian Foreign Policy Under Mussolini,
  by Villari, 60, 168
Italian Social Republic (RSI), 12, 19,
  30, 52, 74, 79, 87, 101, 102, 108,
  114, 119, 121, 131, 136-38, 140, 142,
  145, 162, 163, 166, 168, 172, 174,
  175, 189, 195, 199, 200, 205, 211,
  217-20, 224, 226, 238
  butchery of ministers, 168
Italy Speaks, by Barbara Barclay Carter,
  153, *note*

J

Jacomini, Ambassador, 229
Japan, *xiv*
  atomic bombing of, *xi*
Jews, *xi*, *xii*, 108, 113
Johnson, Samuel, 247
Joyce, General Kenyon A., 72
Juin, General Alphonse, 122
Jung, Guido, 71
"Justice and Liberty," 83

K

Kahn, Otto H., 56
Kappler (German jailer), 108, 110, 113
Kant, Immanuel, 22
Katyn Forest massacre, *vii*, *xi*, *xiii*
Kennard, Sir Howard, 61
Kenya, *x*
Kesselring, Field Marshal Albrecht, 19,
  76, 108, 112, 123, 136-38, 218
Kingdom. *See* Monarchy
Kingdom in the South, 21-26
Kings of Italy. *See* Humbert II; Victor
  Emmanuel III
Kipling, Rudyard, 172
Kirk, Alexander, 131, 155, 163
Koch (German jailer), 110
Kostilov, Ambassador, 175

L

Labor, Italian General Federation of. *See*
  Italian General Federation of Labor
  (CGLI)
labor unions, 178
Lampredi, "Guido," 170
La Piana and Salvemini, *What to Do
  With Italy*, 54, *note*
Lateran Pacts of 1929, 109
Latian hill districts, 109

Lausanne Conference, 50
laws, anti-Fascist, 209-20
laws of war, 219
  See also Hague Conventions
Leftists, 14, 126
Leghorn, 106
"Legnano Division," 75
Legoli, Julio, 148, 149
Lehmann, General, 138
Leto, Guido, 215; book, *Fascismo e anti-
  fascismo*, 215, *note*
Lett, Major Gordon, *Rossano*, 142, *note*
Liberals, 34-35, 126, 138, 155
"Liberated Provinces," 155
"liberation," *vi-x*
Libya, 241
Lidice, *ix-xi*
Life, 180, 187
Liguria, 137, 142, 144, 234
Lippmann, Walter, 71
Lloyd, Lord, 58
Lodge, Henry Cabot, 245
Lombardi, Garbrio, *Il corpo italiano di
  liberazione*, 76
Lombardi, Riccardo, 137
Lombardy, 137, 177, 195
"Long" and "Short" Armistices. *See*
  Armistices
Longo, Luigi, 79, 79, *note;* 80-82, 82,
  note; 83, 83, *note;* 138, 141, 142,
  166, 170, 173
  Un popolo alla macchia, 79, 82, *note*
Lord Lieutenancy, 115-21
Lordi, 113
Louis XIV, *v*
Luciano, "Lucky," 23, *note*
Lulu, 142
Lupo, Major, 148
"Lupo Battalion," 174
Luxembourg Peace Treaty of 1947, 237

M

MVD, Russian, 83
MacCaffery, George B., 87
MacFarlane, General Frank Mason, 32,
  67, 104, 115, 124, 125
Machiavelli, Niccolo, 81
Mackensen, General von, 112
MacLean, Fitzroy, *Eastern Approaches*,
  91, *note*
MacMillan, Harold, 92, 115, 158
Macrelli, Cino, *La riscossa*, 84, *note*
Maddalena, Island of, 12
Madia, Titta, 213-14

Mafia, xx, 23-24
Malaya, *x*
Malta, 28, 191
Mältzer, General, 108, 110
Manzi, Count, 143
Maquis, French, 77, 143
March on Rome, 53
Marchini, Alfio, 112
Maremma, the, 142
Maria Jose, Princess, 8
Marinelli, Giovanni, 151, 204
market, black, 128
Maroni, Lorenzo, 152
Marshall Plan, 250
Martin, Sergio, 200
Marzabotto affair, 146-51
Mascharelli, Agostino, 200
Masons (Freemasons), 24
massacres by partisans, 193-208
Massigli (French diplomat), 92
Massimo, Prince Vittorio, 192
Mastino del Rio, Giorgio; 224, 225, *note*
Matteoti, Giacomo; murder of, 125, 203-04
"Matteoti Units," 83
Matthews, Herbert L., 71, 73
Mazzini Society of New York, 33
Mazzolini, Count Serafino, 103, *note*
McClellan, Senator John L., 23, *note;* 24, *note*
Meana, Countess Fulvia Ripa di, 110
book, *Roma clandestina,* 87, *note*
Mediterranean Advisory Council, Algiers, 69
Mediterranean Sea, 165
Mellini, Alberto, 103, *note*
Menaggio, 169
Merlo Gallio, il, 215
Merry del Val, Cardinal, 58
Messe, Marshal Giovanni, 74
Mezzasoma, Ferdinando, 168
Miele, Renato, 179
Mieville, Roberto, *Fascist Criminal Camp,* 186
Mihailovich, General, 70
Milan, 136, 169, 170, 172-74, 175, 195, 196
bombing of, 156
military activities, 135-51
Military Criminal Code, 211
Millay, Edna St. Vincent, *x*
Modena, 194, 198
Molotov, Vyacheslav, 68

Monarchists. *See* Royalists
Monarchy, Italian, *xiv,* 66, 126-27
early, 77
end of, 94-97, 231-36
referendum on, 233-34
succession to, 11
Mondragone, 75
Monte Cassino and area, and bombing of, 96, 99, 112, 123, 135
Monte Lungo, 75-76
Montenegro, 81
Montevideo meeting of Italians, 50
Montezomolo, Colonel Giuseppe Cordero di, 85, 87, 97, 110, 113
Montgomery, Field Marshal Viscount, 88
Monti Lepini, the, 99
monuments, historic; destruction by Germans, and Fascists, 135-36
Monza, 13
Moranino, Giuseppe, 180
Mordano, Count of. *See* Grandi, Dino
Moretti, Michaele, 170, 206
Morgagni, Manlio, 6, 6, *note*
Morgan, J. P. and Company, 251, *note*
Morgenthau Plan, *viii, ix, xi-xii*
Moroccans, 122
Morosini, Giuseppe, 119
Moscatelli, Vincenzo, 196
Moscow Conference and Declaration, 68-73, 93
Moscow Congress of Third International, 106
Muller, Hermann J., *xv*
Mundelein, Cardinal, 58
Munich Conference, 61
Murphy, Robert, 27, 92, 115, 118, 124
Mussolini, Benito, 1, 11, 25, 30, 32, 36, 50, 52, 70-71, 95, 102, 103, 106, 110, 113, 114, 120, 124, 125, 134, 137, 138, 162, *note;* 168, 181, 251, *note*
and the Church, 86-87
and the murder of Matteoti, 203-04
arrest, 12
assassins, 170
books in defense, 54, *note*
burial, 171
condemnation in the terms of the "Long Armistice," 44
defects in foreign policy, 60
evaluation of, by Villari, 60
government, 13-14, 19
government in Northern Italy, 30, 75

meeting with Hitler at Feltre, 5-6
mistakes, *xvii*
murder of, *xviii,* 53, 168-71
Northern army, 76
peace efforts, *xvii,* 60
praise by Americans, 56-57
praise by British, 53-55, 61
praise by Pope Pius XII, *xviii*
praise and censure by Churchill, 53-55
removal of, 5
rescue by Germans, 12
works, public, 24-25, 62, 99, 126
"Mussolini Battalion," 75
Mussolini: Twilight and Fall, by Dombrowski, 207, *note*
"Muti Battalions," 195

N

Nagaski and Hiroshima; bombings, *xi*
Naples, 25-26, 71, 73, 77, 129, 210, *note*
Naples, Prince of. *See* Humbert II
Napoleonic era, *v*
National Research Council, 3
Nationalists, 127
Navy, Italian, 69, 72, 104
Nazism, 96, 104
Neghelli, Marquis of. *See* Graziani, Marshal Rodolfo
Nelson, Admiral Horatio, 210, *note*
Nelson, HMS, 28-30
"Nembo Division," 29, 31, 103
Nenni, Pietro, 35, *note;* 110, 110, *note;* 127, *note;* 204, 215
"Neri, Captain," 206
New Republic, 53
Nicola, Enrico de, 94-95
"non-liberated" Italy, 101-03
Northern Italy, 30
   See also Committees for the National Liberation of Northern Italy
nuclear war, *xv*
Nüremberg trials, *viii,* 37, 218, 242

O

OVRA, *See* Vigilance Organization Against Anti-Fascist Crimes
OZNA, Yugoslavia, 83
occupation governments, *xiv,* 25, 118
O'Connell, Cardinal, 58
Odenigo, Armando, 139; book, *Priginni moscovite,* 190, *note*
Omodeo, Adolfo, 65, 117
Onofrio, Edoardo d', 188

Operti, General, 82, 84, 107, 141
Oradour, France, 150
Orizzonte, xviii
Orlando, Vittorio Emanuele, 249
Ortona, 96
Ossola Valley, 144
Our Threatened Values, by Gollancz, *xvii*
Oxilia, General, 90

P

Pacciardi, Randolfo, 240
Pace e Libertà 180
Padoan, Agostino, 234
Padua, 199
Padula; British concentration camp, 190, 191
Padula, by Page, 190, 191
Page, Giorgio Nelson, *Padula,* 190, 191
Pajetta, G. C., 146
Palazzo Chigi, 157
Palazzo Vidona, 3
Palermo, University of, 22
Panslavist Congress, 70
Pantalleri, 15, 243
Paolucci, Caboli de, Marquis, 32
Papal Assistance Commission, 108, 198
Papal States, 78
Pappagallo, Don, 113
Pareschi, Giuseppe, 15
Pariani, General, 229
Parini, Piero, 120
Paris, *xii*
Paris Peace Conference, *xiii*
   See also Versailles Treaty
Parma, 146
Parri, Ferruccio, 49, 80, 80, *note;* 81, 87, 87, *note;* 120, 137-40, 142, 146, 166, 237
parties, political, 48-63, 65
Partisan Action Groups (GAP), 102, 136
partisans, *xii, xix,* 72-78, 82, 85, 102, 110, 111, 119-21, 123, 131, 159, 160-62, 169, 171, 172, 175, 188, 221
   activities, 135-51
   massacres by, 193-208
   numbers of, 140, 167
   political persecution of, 221-30
Partito d'Azione. See Party of Action
Partito Popolare. See Popular Party
Party of Action (*Partito d'Azione*), 49, 65, 72, 80, 83, 113, 117, 120, 127, 135, 137, 140, 145, 187
Pavelich, Ante, 89, 90

Pavia, Battle of, 116
Pavolino, Alessandro, 102, 143, 168, 169
"Peace and Liberty," 180
Peace Conference with Turkey, 50
peace treaties, harsh, v
Peace Treaty of 1933; Four-Power, 60
Peace Treaty of 1947, 31, 36, 125, 175, 209, 237-45
Pearson, Drew, 81
Peirce, Guglielmo; book, Un popolo alla macchia, 79, note; 82, note
Pelagian Islands, 243
Pella, Giuseppe, 249, 249, note
Pellegrini-Giampietro, Domenico, 196
"People's Courts," 210
Perretti, Lieutenant, 140
persecution, political, 221-30
Pertini (of CLN), 111
Pescara, 19
Petacci, Claretta, and murder of, 169-71, 206, 207
  burial, 171-72, note
Peter, King of Yugoslavia, 70
Piana, George La, and Gaetano Salve-mini, What to Do With Italy, 54, note
Pianosa, 243
Picardi, 64, 65
Piccinni, Franco, Sunless Africa, 182
Piedmont, 82, 101, 137, 144, 195, 234
Pignatelli, Prince Valerio, 159, 229
Pilotti, Massimo, 235
Pisenti, Piero, 120, 137, 138; Revisione in cammino, 220, note
Pisino, 89
Pitacco, Giorgio, 163
Pius XII, Pope, 159-60, 163
  praise of Mussolini, xviii
Pizzoni, Alfredo, 141, 146, 178
Poland, vii, viii, xi
Poletti, Charles, 130, 131, note; 132, 134
political parties. See parties
political persecution, 221-30
Pontine, area, 99
Ponza, Island of, 12
Pope, the. See Pius XII
Popular Party (Partito Popolare), 125, 154, 157
prisoners of war, 158-59, 182-92, 219
Procida, 229
property, enemy; return of, 244
property, Fascists'; seizure of, 216-17

Protestant Revolution, v
"Provinces, Liberated," 155
Prunas, Renato, 64, 163
Prunas-Tola, Vittorio, and N. Rodolico, Libro azzurro sul referendum, 236, note
Prunier, André, 202

Q

Quantrill, William Clarke, 84
Quarnero Island, 90
Quebec Conference, ix
Quintieri (banker), 117
Quirinal, the, 11

R

RSI. See Italian Social Republic
Rahn, Ambassador, 138, 173
Rainer (Gauleiter), 162
Rasella, Via. See Via Rasella
Ravello, 98
Ravnich (Istrian), 164
Red Cross, International, 194
Red Star Brigade, 148
Reder, Major Walter, 148-51
referendum on Monarchy, 232-34, 236, note
Regency, 65, 67, 85, 87
  proposed by Sforza, 65
Reggio Emilia. See Emilia
Regina Coeli Prison, 153, 229
Reisoli, General, 99
religious; persecution of, 108-09, 109, note
Repaci (author), Taccuino politico, 129, note
reparations, war, 244
repatriates, 164
Republic; vote on, 232, 233, 236
Republica Socialista Italiana (RSI). See Italian Social Republic
Republican National Guard, 145
Republicans, 14
Research Council, National, 3
Résistance, French, viii, xii, 77, 143
results of "liberation," 248
Reynolds, J. R., 146, note
Rhodes, 152, 239
Ribbentrop, Joachim von, 6
Rieti, 120
Rightists, 83
Ripa di Meana, Fulvia, 87, note
Risorgimento, 10, 109
Roatta, General Mario, 28, 69, 74, 194

Rodolico, Niccolo, and V. Prunas-Tola, *Libro azzurro sul referendum*, 236, note
Roman Catholics; and the Fascists, 127
in the partisan movement, 85
praise of Mussolini, 57-58
Vatican, the, 123, 128
Romano, Ruggiero, 168
Rome, *xix*, 108, 111
Allies in, 122-34
bombing of, 6
evacuation of, 123
fall of, 124
lack of food, etc., 127-28
march on, 53
Rome Fascist Federation, 111
Romita, Giuseppe, 124, 232, 236
Rooney and Hutton, *Conqueror's Peace*, *xvi*
Roosevelt, Franklin D., *xiv*, 4, 5, 27, 28, 35, 69, 94, 97, 98, 104, 118, 125, 154, 158, 161, 163, 250
advisers, 180
book, *Roosevelt and Hopkins*, by Sherwood, 158, note
praise of Mussolini, 57
Roosevelt, Nicholas, 56; *A Front Row Seat*, 57, note
Rossano, by Lett, 142, note
Rosselli (partisan), 143
Rossi, Cesare, 153
Rothermere, Lord, 55
Rovigo, 143
Royalists, 82, 83, 160, 163
See also Monarchy
Rubini, Giuseppe, 207-08
Ruggieri, De, 124
Ruini (cabinet member), 124
Rumania, 189
Russia, Soviet. *See* Union of Soviet Socialist Republics
Russia, Tzarist, 70
Rutelli, M. G., 235

S

SHAEF. *See* Supreme Headquarters Allied Expeditionary Forces
Sabina, the, 99
Sabotino, Marquis of the. *See* Badoglio
Safety, Service of. *See* Sicherheitsdienst
Salerno, 95, 98, 125, 132, 190
Salò, 17, 72
Salò government. *See* Italian Social Republic
Salomon, Ernst von, *Fragebogen*, *xvii*
Salsomaggiore; meeting at, 5
salute, Roman, 182
Salvador, Max, 167
Salvemini, Gaetano, 63, note
Salvemini and LaPiana, *What to Do With Italy*, 54, note
Sandalli, General, 28
San Paolo College, 108
Santin, Monsignor, 163
Saragat, Giuseppe, 111, 124
Sardi, Baron, Alessandro, 229
Sardinia, 243
restoration to Italy, 98
Savoy, House of, 10, 77
Scelba, Mario, 150-51, 194
Schacht, Hjalmar, 57
Schuster, Cardinal, 138, 168, 169
Scoccimarro, Mauro, 155, 179-80
Scorza, Carlo, 5, 11
Scott, Sir Walter, 251
Sea Devils, by Borghese, 226
Security Council, United Nations, 240
Senate, 134, 232
Seravo, Riccardo, 222
Sforza, Count Carlo, 48-51, 65, 67, 71, 87, 96, 97, 117, 118, 125, 133, 134, 152, 153, 212, 216, 228, 232, 240
Sherrill, General Charles H., 14, 57
Sherwood, Robert, *Roosevelt and Hopkins*, 158, note
Sicherheitsdienst, 185, 190
Sicily, 21, 22, 24, 77, 95, 112, 243
Mafia in, 23
occupation by Allies, 15
restoration to Italy, 98
separatist movement, 24, note
Silienti (cabinet member), 124
Silvestri, Carlo, 101, 114, 114, note; 120, 137-41, 203-04
book, *Mussolini, Graziani e gli antifascisti*, 114, note; 138, note
Simiani, Carlos, *I giustiziati fascisti dell' Aprile, 1945*, page 196
Simon, Lord, 55
Simon, General Max, 148
Simoni, General Simone, 110, 113
Skorzeny, Major Otto, 12
Slavs, 198
See also Tito; Yugoslavia
Smith, General Walter Bedell, 17
Social Democrats, 110
Social Republic, Italian. *See* Italian Social Republic

Socialist Party, 101, 106, 110, 126, 138, 215
Sogno, Edgardo, 146, 180
Soleri (cabinet member), 124
Somaliland, 183
Sommavilla, General, 162
Sorice, General Alfonso, 5
Southern Italy; division of, 87
  in servitude, 93-100
  Kingdom in, 21-26
Soviet Union. *See* Union of Soviet Socialist Republics
Spanish Civil War, 82, 106
Spalato, 90
Sprigge, Cecil, 71
Stahel, General, 108
Stalin, Joseph, *vii, viii, xi-xiv,* 63, 68, 69, 94, 104, 106, 158, 161
Stefani Agency, 61, 179, 207
Stevens, Colonel, 146
Stimson, Henry L., book, *Prelude to Invasion,* 36, *note*
Stone, Admiral Ellery Wheeler, 116-17, 155, 158, 163
Strohm, Lieutenant, 187
Sturzo, Luigi, 49
Suardo, Giacomo, 11
Sudetenland, *xi*
"surrender, unconditional," 4
Suvich, Fulvio, 57, 229

T

Tagliamento Legion, 218
Tagliamento river, 162
Tamaro, Attilio; *Venti anne di storia,* 6, *notes,* pages 6, 67, 93, 107, 118, 159, 162, 188, 237
Tarchiani, Alberto, 117, 154
Taylor, General Maxwell, 32, 52
Taylor, Myron C., 57
Tebaldi, Doctor, 145
Teheran Conference, *vii, xiv*
Terreur 1944, by Huddleston, *xvii*
Teruzzi, Attilo, 194, 194, *note*
Terzi, Pietro, 205
Testi, Carlo, 199
thefts of government property, 208
Third International (Communist), 106
Thorwald, Juergen, *Flight in Winter, xvii*
Time, 181, 181, *note*
Tirol, 111
Tito, Marshal, 67, 70, 90, 90, *note;* 91, *note;* 96, 103, 120, 161, 162, 164, 174, 175

ambitions, 162-63
  See also Yugoslavia
Todt organization, 142
Togliatti, Palmiro, *viii, xx,* 35, *note;* 105-06, 115, 117, 124, 163, 170, 173, 176, 178, 179-80, *note;* 181, *note;* 202, 228, 230, 235
Tombolo forest, 156
Toscano, Mario, 69, *note*
Trabucchi, General, 167
  book, *I vinti hanno sempre torto,* 83, 84, 167, *note*
treaties, 17
  Luxembourg, 237
  peace, harsh, *v*
  Peace, of 1947 (1955), 125, 209, 237-45
  Versailles, 60, 237, 241
trials, war-crimes, *viii, xv,* 171
  See also Nuremberg
Treviso, 198
Trieste, 96, 161-63, 165, 174-75, 239-41
Tripoli, 241-42
Trizziono, Commander, book, *Navi e poltrone,* 15, *note*
Trotsky, Leon, 106
Tucker, Colonel, 182-83
Tupini, Umberto, 124
Turati, Augusto, 6, *note*
Turin, 106, 173
Turkey; peace conference with, 50
Tuscany, 81, 102, 234

U

Udine, 144, 162, 164, 200
Umbria, 81
Unamuno, Miguel de, 236
Union of Soviet Socialist Republics, *vi, xi, xiii-xv,* 69, 72-73, 85, 94, 96, 163
  ambitions, 165
  and the Balkans, 70
  intervention by, 104-07
  purge trials, *viii, xiii*
unions, labor, 178
Unità, 1, 71
United Nations, *xvi,* 5, 17, 38, 73, 98, 159, 171, 228
  Security Council, 240
United States; aid from, 251, *note*
  depression (1929), 57
  financial aid for Italy, *xx*
  policy of, 250-51
  responsibility for Communism in Italy, *xx*

University of Palermo, 22
Urbano, Lazzaro, 170
Ustashi, Croatia, 90
Utley, Freda, *The High Cost of Vengeance, xvii*

V

V-J Day, *xi*
"Valerio, Colonel." *See* Audisio, Walter
Valtellina, the, 168, 169, 205, 223
Vatican, the. *See* Roman Catholics
Veale, F. P. J., 62, 63, *note;* 150, 169
  Advance to Barbarism, v, xvii
  Crimes Discreetly Veiled, 62, *note;*
  150, *note;* 171, *note;* 206, *note;* 207,
  207, *note*
venereal diseases, American and British
  soldiers', 23
Venetia, 143, 161, 197, 199
Venezia Giulia, the, 89, 120, 161-65,
  174, 209, 232-33
Venice, 164, 165
Vergani, Pietro, 207
Verona trials, 15
Versailles, Treaty of, *v, xiii, xvii,* 60,
  237, 241
Via Rasella outrage, 108-14, 122, 139
  See also Ardeatine
Victor Emmanuel III, 8, 10-14, 19, 20,
  27, 29, 30, 32, 49, 51, 52, 65-67, 71-
  73, 85, 87, 88, 93-95, 97, 99, 100,
  113, 115, 117, 124, 126, 127, 134,
  231-36
  abdication, 232
  abrogation of powers, 115
  and Fascism, 13
  book by, *Corpus Nummorum Italicorum,* 12, *note*
  grandson, 67
  son. *See* Humbert II
Victor's Justice, by Belgion, *xvii*
Vidoni Palazzo, 3
Vienna Congress, 68, *note*
Vigilance Organization Against Anti-
  Fascist Crimes, 214-15
Villa Savoia, 11
Villari, Luigi, 216, *note*
  evaluation of Mussolini, 60
  imprisonment, 228-30
  Italian Foreign Policy Under Mussolini, 60, 168
  retirement, 216
Vittorio Veneto, Battle of, 3
"Volunteers of Liberty," 85, 147
Vyshinsky, Andrei, 92, 104

W

War, Cold. *See* Cold War
  crimes, *xv-xvi,* 37, 242
  end of, 166-75
  future, *xv-xvi; See also* World War III
  laws of, 219; Hague Convention, 107
  nuclear, *xv*
  with Germany, 33, *note*
    See also Ethiopia; World Wars I,
    II, and III
"War Cabinet," 117
warfare, "civilized," *v*
warfare, modern, *x-xi, xv, xvi*
Wehrmacht, 166
Welk, William G., *Fascist Economic
  Policy,* 50, 60, *note*
Welles, Sumner, 245
West Virginia, 245
Werth, Alexander, *France, 1840-1955,*
  201
White, Harry Dexter, *xii*
Wilson, Sir Arnold, 248
Wilson, General Maitland, 92, 147
Wilson, Woodrow, *xiii, xiv*
Winged Daggers, by Farran, 146, *note*
Wolff, General Karl, 146
woman members of the CLN, 172
World War I, *v,* 54, 157
World War II, *v, xiii, x, xi, xii, xvi, xix,*
  52, 54, 60, 78
  books on, 251, *note*
World War III, *xiv*

Y

Yalta Conference, *xiv,* 158
Young, Owen D., 56
Yugoslavia, 69, 89, 96, 158, 161-63,
  174, 175, 177, 239, 241, 242, 245
  atrocities by, 89-90
  King Peter of, 70
  See also Tito

Z

Zaniboni, Tito, 95, 216
Zara, 175, 239
Zellerbach, James D., 181
Zerbino, Paolo, 168
Zingales, General, 206, 207
Zink, Harold, *American Military Government in Germany, xvii*
Zoli Cabinet, 249, *note*